OUR STUDIES, OURSELVES

EN M. BLEE | **HÉCTOR L. DELGADO** | SUSAN A. OSTRANDER | MARK S.

PHYLLIS MOEN | **ARLENE SKOLNICK** | JANE MANSBRIDGE | CYNTHIA

HT | **CHRISTOPHER WINSHIP** | SHERRYL KLEINMAN | JODY MILLER | JO

DO | SUSAN A. OSTRANDER | **MARK S. MIZRUCHI** | WILLIAM H. FRIEDL

CK | **JANE MANSBRIDGE** | CYNTHIA FUCHS EPSTEIN | DOROTHY E. SMI

SHERRYL KLEINMAN | JODY MILLER | **JOSHUA GAMSON** | SHULAMIT R

ANDER | MARK S. MIZRUCHI | **WILLIAM H. FRIEDLAND** | HOWARD SCH

OUR

DGE | CYNTHIA FUCHS EPSTEIN | **DOROTHY E. SMITH** | BARRIE THORN

MILLER | JOSHUA GAMSON | **SHULAMIT REINHARZ** | VERTA TAYLOR |

H. FRIEDLAND | **HOWARD SCHUMAN** | JOHN WALTON | HERBERT J. GA

THY E. SMITH | **BARRIE THORNE** | ROBERT R. ALFORD | GARY L. ALBRE

MIT REINHARZ | **VERTA TAYLOR** | KATHLEEN M. BLEE | HÉCTOR L. DELG

AN | **JOHN WALTON** | HERBERT J. GANS | PHYLLIS MOEN | ARLENE SK

BERT R. ALFORD | **GARY L. ALBRECHT** | CHRISTOPHER WINSHIP | SHER

DO | **SUSAN A. OSTRANDER** | MARK S. MIZRUCHI | WILLIAM H. FRIE

HIA FUCHS EPSTEIN | **ROBERT R. ALFORD** | GARY L. ALBRECHT | CHRIS

RZ | VERTA TAYLOR | KATHLEEN M. BLEE | HÉCTOR L. DELGADO | SUS

EDITED BY

BARRY GLASSNER and **ROSANNA HERTZ**

STUDIES, Ourselves

SOCIOLOGISTS' LIVES AND WORK

OXFORD
UNIVERSITY PRESS

2003

OXFORD
UNIVERSITY PRESS

Oxford   New York
Auckland   Bangkok   Buenos Aires   Cape Town   Chennai
Dar es Salaam   Delhi   Hong Kong   Istanbul   Karachi   Kolkata
Kuala Lumpur   Madrid   Melbourne   Mexico City   Mumbai   Nairobi
São Paulo   Shanghai   Taipei   Tokyo   Toronto

Copyright © 2003 by Oxford University Press, Inc.

Published by Oxford University Press, Inc.
198 Madison Avenue, New York, New York 10016

www.oup.com

Oxford is a registered trademark of Oxford University Press

Library of Congress Cataloging-in-Publication Data
Our studies, ourselves : sociologists' lives and work /
edited by Barry Glassner and Rosanna Hertz.
    p. cm.
Includes bibliographical references.
ISBN 0-19-514661-1
1. Sociology—Research—North America—Case studies.
2. Sociologists—North America. 3. Sociology—Philosophy.
I. Glassner, Barry. II. Hertz, Rosanna.
HM578.N7 O97 2003
301'.07'207—dc21   2002151655

9 8 7 6 5 4 3 2 1

Printed in the United States of America
on acid-free paper

ACKNOWLEDGMENTS

Without Dedi Felman, our editor at Oxford, this project would not have been completed, and we especially valued her close attention to and comments on every chapter. We are lucky to have worked with such an outstanding editor.

We thank Jennifer Rappaport and our production editor, Robin Miura.

We thank Margaret Centamore for compiling the initial chapters and Cherie Potts and Christina E. H. LaPointe-Nelson, who turned twenty-two separate files into a seamless manuscript.

We thank Aryeh Rothman, who generously agreed to allow us to use his watercolor on the cover.

Thanks also to our colleagues at Wellesley College and the University of Southern California and to our families for their support.

Above all, we thank the authors of these twenty-two chapters for agreeing to participate in this volume and for sharing so many insights into their lives and their work.

CONTENTS

CONTRIBUTORS

I RACE & SOCIAL CLASS

1 KATHLEEN M. BLEE
University of Pittsburgh

2 HÉCTOR L. DELGADO
University of La Verne

3 SUSAN A. OSTRANDER
Tufts University

4 MARK S. MIZRUCHI
University of Michigan

5 WILLIAM H. FRIEDLAND
University of California, Santa Cruz

6 HOWARD SCHUMAN
University of Michigan

7 JOHN WALTON
University of California, Davis

8 HERBERT J. GANS
Columbia University

HÉCTOR L. DELGADO | SUSAN A. OSTRANDER | MARK S. MIZRUCHI |

OEN | ARLENE SKOLNICK | JANE MANSBRIDGE | CYNTHIA FUCHS EPSTE

PHER WINSHIP | SHERRYL KLEINMAN | JODY MILLER | JOSHUA GAMS

A. OSTRANDER | MARK S. MIZRUCHI | WILLIAM H. FRIEDLAND | HOWA

ANSBRIDGE | CYNTHIA FUCHS EPSTEIN | DOROTHY E. SMITH | BARRIE

EINMAN | JODY MILLER | JOSHUA GAMSON | SHULAMIT REINHARZ | VE

OUR STUDIES, OURSELVES

RK S. MIZRUCHI | WILLIAM H. FRIEDLAND | HOWARD SCHUMAN | JOH

IA FUCHS EPSTEIN | DOROTHY E. SMITH | BARRIE THORNE | ROBERT R

SHUA GAMSON | SHULAMIT REINHARZ | VERTA TAYLOR | KATHLEEN M.

ND | HOWARD SCHUMAN | JOHN WALTON | HERBERT J. GANS | PHYLLI

H | BARRIE THORNE | ROBERT R. ALFORD | GARY L. ALBRECHT | CHRIST

Z | VERTA TAYLOR | KATHLEEN M. BLEE | HÉCTOR L. DELGADO | SUSA

WALTON | HERBERT J. GANS | PHYLLIS MOEN | ARLENE SKOLNICK | JA

ORD | GARY L. ALBRECHT | CHRISTOPHER WINSHIP | SHERRYL KLEINM

A. OSTRANDER | MARK S. MIZRUCHI | WILLIAM H. FRIEDLAND | HOV

PSTEIN | ROBERT R. ALFORD | GARY L. ALBRECHT | CHRISTOPHER WIN

TAYLOR | KATHLEEN M. BLEE | HÉCTOR L. DELGADO | SUSAN A. OSTRA

BARRY GLASSNER / ROSANNA HERTZ

INTRODUCTION

How much does personal biography matter in research? How much does a person's research matter to her biography? These are the central questions addressed in the twenty two chapters by prominent American sociologists in this volume. Even as sociologists' research shapes the discipline of sociology and how the social world is understood, their personal and professional lives shape their research. Many of the authors in this book were profoundly affected by tragedies and triumphs in their daily lives and in the workplace. Situations beyond their control, such as illness, reproductive mishaps, or loss of a loved one, became opportunities for learning and new insights that continue to shape and reshape their worldviews. At other times it was a political event or the fate of a social movement that profoundly influenced the course of a person's research.

In these chapters a diverse group of scholars reflect on how events in their own lives and the world variously pushed or pulled them into or out of particular areas of study, political commitments, and identities. For many, the centrality of race, social class, and gender for understanding society and for making sense of their experiences became pivotal for their adult sense of self. As they reflect upon their lives—both personal and professional—the stories they tell are embedded in the recent social history of the United States and the social institutions within which they have lived. As changes occurred in the social world and in their own personal and professional development, they found themselves adjusting both their expectations about society and their research agendas. Many of those expectations originated in their families of origin. They recall ways in which growing up in their particular families and neighborhoods was important in what they saw and, ultimately, in what they studied. They also recall how those early influences shifted from foreground to background as they grew older. The foreground became political commitments and professional orientations, and the authors rethought both their research agendas and who they are. Some of them moved only slightly in their areas of expertise and political commitments from where they began; others moved far; but as we will see, none has stood still.

Much of their discussion, implicitly if not explicitly, is about constraints and how they have carved careers and personal lives despite those restrictions. Faced with academic institutions that did not hire persons of their gender, race, or sexual orientation, they found routes to success within their fields. Faced with physical disability, they found research opportunities that made use of their changing selves and physical capabilities. Faced with disappointments in political organizations to which they were devoted, they found ways to integrate their disillusionment into their research agendas.

When many of these authors were in graduate school, Robert K. Merton's telling distinction between "ascribed" and "achieved" status was in vogue. This distinction is worth resuscitating. Social class, race, and gender were viewed in the Mertonian system as fixed categories into which one was born. Achieved statuses, on the other hand, were acquired by means of degrees, titles, awards, income, and the like. These chapters demonstrate that ascribed statuses continue to have a profound impact on almost anyone's life course, often in unexpected and unpredictable ways. In recognition of both the persistence of ascribed statuses and the surprises and attainments in individual lives, we have divided this volume into three parts: the first two reflect the importance of ascription as a point of biographical departure, and the third focuses on the dynamic of ascription and achievement. In recent decades, sociologists have rightly come to see ascribed statuses in terms of process rather than as fixed variables in equations. Statuses and identities evolve over the course of a person's life, and these chapters reflect that reality.

I. RACE AND SOCIAL CLASS

The authors in the first section of the book reflect upon the entanglement of their lives and their research in the context of a society that is structured along lines of social class and racial distinctions. In diverse ways each author locates his or her research within changing definitions of class and race. Who they are and how their racial and class positions clash with the ideologies or interests of those they study become a central focus of these autobiographies.

As editors of this volume, we have been moved by the authors' willingness to reveal their personal struggles and admit their own limitations and perplexities. Thus, in the first chapter, Kathleen Blee openly discusses her preconceptions and fears about studying the Ku Klux Klan as a white woman. As in many of the chapters that follow, this one sheds light on how sociologists come to terms with their own emotional, intellectual, and even physical vulnerabilities in the course of conducting research. A researcher's ethnic, racial, or class background can be located in larger social structures or in more microsociological ways, such as the researcher's family background. Héctor Delgado dissects the numerous ways in which race structures his life. He recalls the discrimination he experienced as a Puerto Rican in primary, secondary, and university educational institutions and how, from his life experiences, he created a research agenda that counters stereotypes about undocumented workers.

For Susan Ostrander, the issue was class. In her chapter in this volume she has written about her own class background. She considers how observations of members of her immediate childhood family helped give rise to a series of questions about fitting in and not fitting in. Her astute eye for detail about the upper class facilitates her ability to study the behavior of the upper-class women who populate her books. In turn, her ethnographic work in upper-class communities has provided her with new understandings of her own place in U.S. society and a revised perspective on upper-class privilege.

Other authors in this section reflect upon a different sort of insight into social class that their personal and professional biographies have afforded them: theoretical insight. Mark Mizruchi began his studies of elites from a strongly Marxist perspective, and he describes the path that took him away from that orthodoxy. Similarly, William Friedland traces his political and theoretical commitments to working-class revolution. Returning to the university after burning out politically, Friedland worked at creating "praxis" in both his teaching and his research. Now he reflects on the possibilities for—and constraints on—becoming a leader for change while working within the academy.

For several authors in this volume, the Vietnam War is a critical moment in their personal, political, and intellectual development. Howard Schuman addresses these issues most directly. He openly discusses his difficulties in developing an appropriate methodology for analyzing how the war is understood and remembered in American collective memory and Mills's famous "intersection of history and biography" is the theme of the next chapter as well. John Walton shows how it is only in hindsight that we understand how history has shaped our lives, as well as how history need not be simply hegemonic but can be inclusive of the working class. In the final chapter in the first section, Herbert Gans takes a particularly personal approach to issues of social class and inequality. In describing his lifelong investigation into urban poverty, he reflects on his own youth: although his family had little money, he did not feel poor, and he became a pioneer in studying the interlocking relationship between race and class.

II. GENDER

Gender is not simply a variable in an equation but a socially constructed and lived reality that leads to distinct opportunities and life courses for women and men. The authors in this section reflect upon the historical moments that shaped the biographies and research agendas of several generations of women. Each author in her own way learned how to push the structure of the workplace and navigate the constraints imposed upon her because of her sex. Work versus family dilemmas shape every generation of women. The older generations pushed the structure of the academy enough to finally change it, and younger women with doctorates could imagine having careers similar to their male counterparts. Unlike the authors in the previous section, whose pessimism about the likelihood of a leveling of social class is palpable, the authors in this section remain hopeful that all arenas of U.S. society will continue to improve for women.

Phyllis Moen had not expected her professional career to become crucial to her and to her family's financial and emotional well-being. Like several other authors in this section, she expected marriage and children to be her central concerns. But events altered those expectations. An expert on the life course, Moen devotes her chapter to making sense of the events that altered hers. For Arlene Skolnick, as well, deviating from the roles of wife and mother was problematic. Yet she found a place for herself and her research that paralleled male tenure-tracked professorships, a track rarely available to women of her generation. In her chapter here, she describes how she came to be part of a research institute and to collaborate with her husband on text-books while conducting her own research on families.

When Jane Mansbridge arrived at Harvard, women were not even allowed in the faculty club unless they were escorted by men. "So, when the women's movement arrived, I was ready," she writes. Hers was the generation of women who paved the way for subsequent waves of feminist involvement in political, social, and academic life. In this chapter, as in her books and articles, Mansfield wrestles with what equal power might look like and how it might be achieved.

The remaining chapters in this section, although autobiographical in their own right, focus more expressly on gender inequality in U.S. society. The locus of Cynthia Fuchs Epstein's research is a case in point. She takes on the study of a premier male profession—the law—in order to explore how that occupation remains largely male, masculine, and white. In her reflections here, she considers how her sociological studies and political activism have changed the legal profession.

Dorothy Smith's intellectual and political mission is to change her own profession of sociology. She urges sociologists to explore how the self and society exist within texts. Specifically, in the present volume, Smith carries forward her ongoing feminist meditation on how to understand institutional discourse from gendered experiential encounters. This section concludes with Barrie Thorne, an ethnographer of children, whose scholarship is committed to bringing children's perspective to our attention, particularly children who are differentially located because of their immigrant status or disadvantaged class position. She finds her own life energized by highlighting those who challenge subordination. For Thorne, as for many of the authors in this volume, research is a calling, an intellectual, emotional, and political mission.

III. EVOLVING IDENTITIES

Sociologists are paying ever more attention to the fluidity of identity. Whereas few disagree that a person's racial and gender designation is difficult to change or, for that matter, that social class is predominantly fixed at birth, self-identity is considerably more open to reinvention. Sometimes identity change is imposed upon a person from the outside or by bodily changes. At other times, identities shift because individuals voluntarily alter their sense of self or their place in the social world.

In this concluding section, sociologists discuss how external forces and shifting personal commitments have resulted in significant changes in their identities and those of people important to them, including those they study. They also examine how their changing identities have helped to shift their research programs. As the social world has become more accepting of particular identities, individuals with those identities have become more accepted.

This section opens with what is arguably the most powerful disclosure in this volume of revealing essays. Robert Alford, a devoted pianist who has published scholarly work on professional musicians, lets us know about the agony of losing his hearing. He shares excerpts from letters he wrote in the years following his realization that his hearing loss was affecting his ability to hear music. Through these letters, we witness an ongoing transformation in Alford's personal identity as he struggles against being imprisoned by his loss. We are saddened that he did not live to see this collection. The vicissitudes of his life become the theme of his chapter as he writes of the work he hoped to continue.

Gary Albrecht, by contrast, looks at disability from the outside in and makes the connection between physical disability and poverty. He learned early in his research career that, as he puts it, "The poor became disabled and the disabled became more isolated and vulnerable." He calls upon his own experience in academic departments to examine how the change in context alters the meaning and significance of studying this topic.

Our consideration of the relationship between methodological approaches to research and personal and professional identity continues with Christopher Winship's chapter. A quantitative methodologist, Winship argues that some scholars spend their entire careers delving ever deeper into a single field of inquiry, whereas others, including himself, master and move among multiple topics and methods. He raises questions about how some identities are better suited for one approach rather than the other and why disciplines tend to favor depth over breadth. To parse multiple topics, Winship's chapter shows, a scholar reinvents himself in multiple ways.

Sherryl Kleinman, a qualitative scholar, maps out her route to becoming a feminist fieldworker and prominent auto-ethnographer. Her own personal and professional evolution has been concerned with pushing boundaries and dissolving the categories of researcher and research subject, as well as teacher and student. Kleinman offers parallels between fieldwork and memoir writing.

Feminist ethnographic research is the topic of Jody Miller's chapter as well, but her perspective is different than that of nearly all the other authors in this volume. The youngest contributor, Miller represents a generation that grew up in the Reagan era, by which point there was a firm grounding of feminism in universities and the larger society. In this chapter, Miller grapples with her own emotional responses to what she sees in her fieldwork and the extent to which there should—or can—be boundaries between the researcher and those she studies. Whereas some sociologists of an earlier generation would have worried about contaminating the social setting in which they do their research by being too involved, Miller's principal concern is with honest engagement.

Even as the social world had sufficiently shifted so that Jody Miller could openly and proudly proclaim herself a feminist scholar, so had it become possible for another member of this generation, Joshua Gamson, to build a career as an openly gay activist and scholar. Paradoxically, the increasing acceptance of gays and lesbians has allowed Gamson to undertake the reflections he shares in his chapter, which traces his route away from the role of academic rebel. A salient feature of Gamson's research on the influence of popular culture and the media is the interplay between gender and sexuality. His crisis of identity is about a structural shift in the social world and a shift in what qualifies as novel and acceptable approaches to research.

The body and embedded identities as loci of study frame Shulamit Reinharz's discussion as well. She reveals how her own miscarriage was a turning point in her intellectual and self-identity. By exploring deeply the tabooed topic of miscarriage and how it is interrupted and silenced in U.S. culture, she exposes the schism between lived experience and researchable topics. Unable to find herself in the literature, she wrote about her experiences. In turn, this transformative experience allowed her to see other topics that are missing from discussion.

The final chapter in our volume is also about missing pieces. For many years, Verta Taylor felt she needed to hide at work, who she was. Now, however, she proudly declares herself "the lesbian den mother of sociology." In a forthright personal chronology, Taylor traces the historical events and personal circumstances that led her to become a scholar of social movements. She explores how personal setbacks of the very sort she was studying gave her new insight into what she earlier viewed in purely abstract terms.

Taylor joins with the other authors in this volume in closely examining the potential and pitfalls for sociological scholarship to empower the powerless and those outside the dominant culture. At once a reflection upon personal biographies and upon changing social structures, this volume demonstrates how inequalities and injustices can be made into motors for scholarly research, which in turn have the power to change individual life courses and entire societies.

RACE AND SOCIAL CLASS

Part I

EE | HÉCTOR L. DELGADO | SUSAN A. OSTRANDER | MARK S. MIZRUCH

MOEN | ARLENE SKOLNICK | JANE MANSBRIDGE | CYNTHIA FUCHS EPS

STOPHER WINSHIP | SHERRYL KLEINMAN | JODY MILLER | JOSHUA GAI

N A. OSTRANDER | MARK S. MIZRUCHI | WILLIAM H. FRIEDLAND | HO

MANSBRIDGE | CYNTHIA FUCHS EPSTEIN | DOROTHY E. SMITH | BARR

KLEINMAN | JODY MILLER | JOSHUA GAMSON | SHULAMIT REINHARZ

MARK S. MIZRUCHI | WILLIAM H. FRIEDLAND | HOWARD SCHUMAN | J

THIA FUCHS EPSTEIN | DOROTHY E. SMITH | BARRIE THORNE | ROBER

JOSHUA GAMSON | SHULAMIT REINHARZ | VERTA TAYLOR | KATHLEEN

LAND | HOWARD SCHUMAN | JOHN WALTON | HERBERT J. GANS | PHY

ITH | BARRIE THORNE | ROBERT R. ALFORD | GARY L. ALBRECHT | CHR

ARZ | VERTA TAYLOR | KATHLEEN M. BLEE | HÉCTOR L. DELGADO | SU

WALTON | HERBERT J. GANS | PHYLLIS MOEN | ARLENE SKOLNICK |

LFORD | GARY L. ALBRECHT | CHRISTOPHER WINSHIP | SHERRYL KLEI

AN A. OSTRANDER | MARK S. MIZRUCHI | WILLIAM H. FRIEDLAND | H

S EPSTEIN | ROBERT R. ALFORD | GARY L. ALBRECHT | CHRISTOPHER V

A TAYLOR | KATHLEEN M. BLEE | HÉCTOR L. DELGADO | SUSAN A. OS

KATHLEEN M. BLEE

1

STUDYING THE ENEMY

For two decades of studying organized racism, I have been careful to maintain as much anonymity as possible, revealing little about myself to the racist activists I meet. So in writing this chapter I feel particularly exposed, although this is an apt time to reflect on my entanglement in the study of organized racism. After years of emotional gymnastics, I've decided to stop doing this kind of research. Studying the racist right has been intellectually and politically rewarding but personally too difficult. The reasons that this is the case may suggest lessons that are useful to other scholars, even those with less unsavory research interests.

Since the early 1980s, I have studied racist groups in the United States. Concretely, this means I have spent countless hours in disgusting tasks: reading vicious propaganda about African Americans, Jews, gay men and lesbians, non-Caucasian immigrants, and others; transcribing the messages of racist telephone "hate lines," radio programs, cable TV shows, and videos; hanging out at racist rallies and headquarters; and locating and interviewing dozens of people who see the meaning of their life as eliminating or expelling from the United States people like me and those I love. How did I, a white woman from the Midwest, a leftist and feminist academic, find myself in this profoundly unpleasant line of work? And why did I then decide to leave it?

Like many academics of my generation who were influenced by the anti-war and feminist movements of the 1960s and 1970s, I began my professional life with a tighter fit between my personal politics and my intellectual pursuits than was later the case. As a graduate student and new faculty member, I studied working-class heroes and heroines in early twentieth-century labor struggles in the upper Midwest. I found this work deeply satisfying. I believed that restoring ordinary women and men to the canon of American history would contribute to a larger movement for progressive social change.

Things changed unexpectedly. While looking for labor union documents in a New York library, I stumbled across a pamphlet from the mid-1920s that heralded the extension of suffrage to women. At first glance, it was nothing unusual. But across the back was the publisher's name: Women of the Ku Klux Klan. I was shocked and puzzled. This did not fit my sense of the Klan's politics or message. It was appalling to realize that a group like the Klan could embrace an issue like women's rights. Yet it also seemed an intriguing find for an untenured professor. Here was an unknown social movement organization with an ideology rife with messy contradictions that I could untangle. Although I had been studying groups far more compatible with my own politics, I was surprisingly drawn to the challenge of looking across the political divide. It was the 1980s—the era of Ronald Reagan and the new Christian right—and it was increasingly clear that progressive scholars and activists needed to take the political Right more seriously. And if I was concerned about the declining appeal of the Left, I was also frustrated with the growing strength of separatist ideas in my local feminist movement. I found the idea of challenging radical feminist beliefs about the inherent moral and political superiority of women appealing.

Looking back, I see that there are two other factors that may have predisposed me to follow up that pamphlet. My years in Catholic schools—memorizing rote catechism in the 1950s, then watching the most thoughtful and interesting priests and nuns leave the church in the 1960s—left me with a lifelong interest in debunking orthodoxies, especially those close to my own life. In addition, I had several friends in college who joined groups that advocated radical measures, even violence, to stop the war in Vietnam, end other imperialist ventures, and create greater racial and social class equality in the United States. My flirtation with the far Left (negatively labeled the ultra Left) was confusing but exhilarating. I felt the anger of other progressive and Left activists whose political work was undermined by the exclusive, elitist networks and foolhardy acts of the far Left. But I also got a glimpse of the seductiveness of self-righteousness and violence in politics.

In retrospect, it is distressing to realize the many levels of my naiveté at the time. Resurrecting heroic stories of past working-class struggles did challenge dominant characterizations of the prominent and wealthy as the only historical actors. But work like mine neglected the racial, gender, national, and sexual inequalities that made these struggles possible and sometimes successful.

It was also naive, but more productively so, to think that I had "discovered" the women's Klan of the 1920s, as a chemist might regard herself as detecting a new element. In fact, several (male) historians of the Klan had written about women's Klan groups as an aside to the story of the real (male) Klan. But if the presence of Klan women was noted, their significance was dismissed. Women's groups appeared in Klan histories as auxiliaries to the men. Klan women were seen, but not seen, much as the way in which women appeared, but were overlooked, in accounts of leftist groups I studied or to which I belonged. It took feminism to see how gender shaped the old and new Left. Through a "lens of gender" it was possible to take seriously a women's Klan that enlisted more than half a million women in the mid-1920s and to see its terrible effects.

In the 1920s, Klan women rarely took part in the terroristic night riding of Klan men. Their actions were different but no less destructive. Klan women created networks of women ("poison squads") through which they could spread gossip to destroy the reputations and livelihoods of Jewish merchants. They used their positions as mothers to drive Catholic schoolteachers from their jobs. They stepped out of the traditional boundaries of middle-class, white domesticity, traveling without husbands and fathers to women's Klan meetings and rallies, to ensure that African Americans would be confronted with the fearsome power of white supremacy at every turn. And they fought to safeguard and extend the rights of women like themselves, crusading for protection against sexual harassment, greater legal rights for married women, and an eight-hour workday for white, Protestant, native-born women. Their mixture of women's rights rhetoric with vicious racism, anti-Semitism, anti-Catholicism, and xenophobia reflected the constraints and opportunities of these women's lives. The political actions of these women created a female tradition of bigotry that is dangerously obscured if they are regarded as simply an auxiliary to a male Klan world.

After publishing a book about the 1920s Klan,[1] I received many invitations to speak to academic and community groups. Although some audiences were interested in exploring the antecedents of contemporary organized racism, most were more concerned with extrapolating to the present. Public attention to the contemporary racist Right had increased in those years as David Duke, a former Klan and Nazi member and founder of the National Association for the Advancement of White People (NAAWP), made inroads into Louisiana electoral politics. I was now tenured and felt an obligation to create a research agenda on organized racism that would be directly useful to antiracist efforts, that would benefit more than my career. No one was studying women in the far Right. Indeed, few scholars were researching racist groups at all except by analyzing their propaganda. Thus it seemed that a project on the modern Klan and other racist groups was feasible. I had some contacts with Klan groups from my interviews with former (and then quite elderly) members of the 1920s Klan. Although these interviews left me uneasy, I felt confident that I could maneuver in the racist world with some measure of safety—a third measure of my naiveté. It seemed a fairly unproblematic extension of my former work to begin to study modern racist groups. My goal was a politically useful study, one that would indicate how to counter recruitment efforts by racist groups.

I began with David Duke, who was attracting a large number of women supporters to his race for the Louisiana governorship. With some trepidation, I took a tape recorder to Duke's campaign headquarters, in a carport adjacent to his house, down a small street and up a driveway flanked by angry-looking men with weapons. The setting was more unnerving than I expected. I circled the area several times before I ventured up the driveway, but the interview was anticlimactic and I emerged with a full tape. The interview seemed flat, however, as Duke spoke to me just as he did before media microphones, reeling off well-practiced statements and sound-bites of racist rhetoric. I was struck by how similar his cautious, measured talk was in form, although certainly not in content, to the wary, yet self-aggrandizing tone I had heard in leftist groups when (male) leaders confronted unsympathetic outsiders. This pattern was repeated over and over in my encounters with other Klan and neo-Nazi leaders, many of whom were far less accommodating to interviewers than the aspiring governor Duke. One racist leader would only be interviewed through written questions brought by an intermediary. Another angrily denied me an interview at the last moment and declared that I was an "academic race traitor," a designation whose implications worried me greatly. Overall, interviewing racist leaders was full of intrigue and generated inflammatory quotations, but it resulted in little material that I regarded as genuine or informative. Like mainstream politicians, these leaders only parroted rehearsed slogans in response to my questions.

To avoid this problem, as well as to understand how and why fairly ordinary people were attracted to organized racism, I decided to study the members rather than leaders of racist groups. To do so, I spent time with racist, activist women in neo-Nazi, Klan, white supremacist, and white power skinhead groups across the country. The women ranged in age from young teens to women in their eighties. Some led relatively normal lives and kept their racist group affiliation secret from all but their closest family members and friends. Others more fully embraced racism as a lifestyle, socializing only with other racist activists and working in racist enterprises. In addition to observation and informal conversations, I conducted lengthy life history interviews with 34 women from a variety of racist groups. After selecting a sample of racist groups with female members, I spent years developing contacts and persuading a woman member from each group to agree to be interviewed.[2]

It is impossible to convey fully the emotional, intellectual, and political complexities of a decade spent tracking down and studying racist group members. But it is instructive to consider how some aspects of my life and experiences in the field affected my interpretations of these groups and how studying the enemy in turn changed me.

EFFECTS ON INTERPRETATION

One way in which my life and research became enmeshed was through the issue of race. Like other whites in this white-dominated society, for most of my life I was fairly oblivious to my own whiteness. Despite my academic study of race, I had the luxury of rarely needing to be conscious of myself as a raced person in daily life.[3] I soon learned, however, that members of organized racist groups are highly conscious of being white. For them, whiteness is a central aspect of identity, shaping how they see the world and how they act politically. Although everyone I contacted for interviews assumed I had white skin, many were less sure about my racial loyalty and less ready to believe that I was "really white." Many racist activists who are arrested have been betrayed by other whites, even other members of their groups. Thus "true whites" are revealed only by their commitment to white power politics, or at least by their failure to betray the "white cause." It was not possible to assume that these respondents would continue to view me as white and as a nonenemy. I could not count on racial immunity from violence. Although personally unnerving, my fear of violence at the hands of racist activists proved helpful not only for understanding how racist groups use fear to terrorize enemies and intimidate members but also for seeing how whiteness, when wielded for strategic ends, can become a highly differentiated racial category.

Similarly, my experiences of becoming numb at times to the horrors of racist groups, although immensely distressful, was useful for understanding organized racism. Reflecting on his convalescence from a leg injury, the neurologist and author Oliver Sacks writes of his discovery that his visual depth perception had become foreshortened during his confinement to a hospital room: "Not the least part of the terror was that I experienced no terror. I had no sense, no realization, of how contracted I was, how insensibly I had become contracted to the locus of my sickbed and sickroom."[4] Over the decade of my research on organized racism, I followed a similar path of unconscious perceptual attenuation. At times my insight was sharp and my emotions wrenched. At other times my vision and emotions were numb, worn down by the emotional confinement of studying racism from within. This suggests something about what it must feel like to be inside a racist group—how the bizarre begins to feel normal, taken for granted, both unquestioned and unquestionable. It suggests how Jews or African Americans or gay men and lesbians might come to seem so demonic and so personally threatening that you could be moved to actions that seem incomprehensible to those on the outside. It is a perceptual contraction that is all but imperceptible to the actor.

A more nebulous issue is that of serendipity. I began to study the modern far Right, hoping to find a general explanation for its appeal. I wanted to know *why* women joined organized racism. Since I came of age academically when positivism was hegemonic, I was (and continue to be) highly susceptible to what the geographer Derek Gregory terms the "seductive" nature of generalizations.[5] In this pursuit, the study of organized racism has been frustrating. After two decades of study, I can explain *how* people become racists. Most join racist groups through contacts with previous group members, not by seeking out these groups. They learn hard-core racism and anti-Semitism by being in and around racist groups; few hold intense, activist, and conspiratorial racist beliefs before coming into contact with racist groups. But I cannot explain very well *why* people join racist groups. Many people are exposed to racist group members, but few join. Even fewer stay in racist groups longer than a single visit. So why do some join when most do not? Psychological explanations are not particularly satisfactory since racist activists do not seem to differ significantly from the general population in personality traits or social circumstances before they come into contact with racist groups. I can only conclude that there is a puzzling serendipity in why people affiliate with organized racism. The women I interviewed relate drifting into a racist group after fairly casual encounters with racist activists at parties, in grocery stores, or in public libraries. Few seemed to have considered the consequences of becoming a racist activist. Most had only the faintest notion of racist ideologies or goals before joining. It is disturbing to think that becoming a racist may be even partly a matter of accident, of social drift. Yet the myriad of chance occurrences that shape all lives, like those that transformed me from a chronicler of the Left to a scholar of the Right, is evident in the life stories of racist activists in which simple happenstance is a remarkably important element in racist affiliation.

EFFECTS ON LIFE

If personal experiences have molded my studies, it is also the case that researching the racist Right has shaped my life, sometimes in unexpected ways. Certainly, collecting life histories has made me more skeptical about how I tell the story of my own life, in conversation and in this chapter. In my life history interviews with racist activists, I asked them to tell me how they ended up in racist groups. Each responded with an elaborate story, detailing the experiences in their backgrounds that predisposed them toward racist ideas and propelled them to join a racist group. This is how narratives work, by linking events and selves of the past to those of the present, by integrating and making coherent the various threads of life. Narratives assemble incidents of the past to explain the self of the present; they are retrospectively "sense making."[6]

Reflecting back on an earlier, nonpolitical life, many racist women described their current political commitments as the result of a decisive awakening in which the essential difference between good and evil was revealed and explained. It was at that moment that they became acutely aware that Jews, African Americans, or federal agents controlled the economy, politics, or even the minutia of daily life. Yet such narratives conceal, as well as reveal, the dynamics of these women's lives. When they string together incidents of their past, these women signal the significance of each event in shaping their current self. Yet current racist commitments retrospectively influence heavily the incidents from the past that appear in life history narratives. Some are accorded great importance, even when they may have been minor at the time. Clashes with children from other races on school buses or playgrounds, for example, are often evoked as pivotal events in narratives, although the triviality of most of these incidents suggest that they may have assumed greater significance or have become racialized only in retrospect. I worry that I have adopted a similar although less dramatic selectivity to shape the explanation of my life and work in this chapter and in other venues of self-presentation.

I have also been transformed and humbled by the successes and failures of my effort to do research that would enhance antiracist activism. On a positive note, researching the racist Right has given me the opportunity to talk to many community groups across the country. It is immensely satisfying to be in a position to provide information that can help protect communities from racist hate groups, inhibit new members from joining, and lure existing members away.

More worrisome are lingering, seemingly insolvable ethical and political problems that plague this kind of work. For example, literary theory suggests that people make sense of events of their lives and the historical past by placing these in narratives, in story lines. If this is so, is it not possible that studies of racial, national, or religious intolerance might help racist activists construct a narrative that "makes sense" of their participation in racist groups?[7] Is such research potentially empowering to its subjects by indicating their importance in making history? What does it mean to promise confidentiality and thereby safeguard the identities of people who are mobilizing for abhorrent political ends?[8] And is it possible to fully reconcile a scholarly approach to understanding racist groups and their members with a politically progressive interest in seeing these groups as the enemy?

The emotional work of studying organized racism is raw and on the surface. It is not easily ignored nor readily amenable to traditional norms of scholarly detachment. Earlier feminist dictums to respect the truth of individual experiences, preserve the integrity of ordinary people's lives, and seek what Judith Stacey calls "an egalitarian research process characterized by authenticity, reciprocity, and intersubjectivity between the researcher and her subjects"[9] work well for studies of union organizers, feminist activists, civil rights workers, and others with whom we find some common experience and whose life stories and worldviews are laudatory. However, as more recent discussions of feminist reflexivity make clear, these principles provide little guidance for studying those we loath or fear.[10] Would it even be possible, to say nothing of desirable, for example, to strive for an empathic connection with members of the Klan? It is one thing to try to understand the world through the eyes of someone for whom you have even a little sympathy, but it is a very different matter to develop an emotional tie to a racist activist who is trying to annihilate you or others like you.

I found it impossible to maintain emotional balance in this research. Often, I was afraid, yet fear can easily slip into voyeurism. It is embarrassing but true that the search for underground racists can be exciting, as well as horrible. Walking down David Duke's driveway, sitting on death row with a shackled white supremacist murderer, driving to secret Nazi encampments, being ushered into white supremacist publishing dens, and venturing into Klan cross burnings in which alcohol, kerosene, and hatred make a volatile mix are scholarship-as-adventure. Barrie Thorne captures perfectly this aspect of fieldwork as "venturing into exciting, taboo, dangerous, perhaps enticing social circumstances; getting the flavor of participation, living out moments of high drama; but in some ultimate way having a cop-out, a built-in escape, a point of outside leverage that full participants lack."[11]

I was never able to find a comfortable and usable personal stance in this research. Ultimately, I became emotionally exhausted and needed to stop. One day, back from a Ku Klux Klan rally, I met with a graduate student. She had just returned from a meeting with activists who were fighting abuse by psychiatrists and psychiatric institutions. She was exhilarated, brimming with the feelings of empowerment that she had felt, and eager to give voice to the stories and sentiments she had encountered. In sharp contrast, I felt, at best, numb. What I really wanted to do was to forget, to avoid confronting what I had seen rather than proclaim it. It was a year before I could bring myself to open my notes on the rally, sheets of paper to which faint scents of smoke and kerosene still seemed to cling. If my student wanted to gather people together to hear her research stories, I found myself dodging occasions to speak about my study, worried that I would be sullied by the political stigma attached to the racist groups with which I was spending time.

The emotions invoked in sociological fieldwork, a staple of informal talk among researchers, are rarely discussed in print.[12] Pondering one's emotional state can seem an unseemly departure into narcissistic self-reflection. Yet the hidden substructure of research is the emotional and personal life of the researcher. I did not begin to study organized racism solely because of my intellectual interest in the topic. Clearly, events and issues in my life were significant factors in why I chose this topic. And, conversely, I did not leave this area of study because there were no more questions to ask. In fact, there is a critical need for research on racist networks; international ties among racist groups; the extent to which people remain in racist groups over time; whether young, racist skinheads eventually move into adult racist groups; whether children raised in racist, activist families retain that allegiance over time; and a host of other issues. I have the contacts among racist groups to investigate most of these topics. But I do not have the will to continue.

I have never talked to another researcher of the racist movement in which the issue of emotional burnout does not come up.[13] But the trajectory of my work also has implications for scholars in less problematic areas of study. It suggests that researchers, especially those using qualitative methods, need to consider and discuss with colleagues, students, and friends the anger, resentment, fatigue, indignation, annoyance, aggravation, outrage, and irritation that are evoked by entanglement with their subjects, whether alive or long dead, whether anonymous or known personally. We are more honest as scholars when we acknowledge the myriad ways in which our personal lives and emotions are intertwined with who, what, and how we study.

NOTES

1. Kathleen M. Blee, *Women of the Klan: Racism and Gender in the 1920s* (Berkeley: University of California Press, 1991).

2. Details of the methodology of this study are found in Kathleen M. Blee, *Inside Organized Racism: Women in the Hate Movement* (Berkeley: University of California Press, 2002).

3. See Ruth Frankenberg, *White Women, Race Matters: The Social Construction of Whiteness* (Minneapolis: University of Minnesota Press, 1993).

4. Oliver Sacks, *A Leg to Stand On* (New York: Simon & Schuster, 1984), 156–57. I am grateful to Sharon Betcher for pointing me to this example.

5. Derek Gregory, *Geographical Imaginations* (Cambridge, Mass.: Blackwell, 1990), 203.

6. On narrative, see Jerome Bruner, "The Narrative Construction of Reality," *Critical Inquiry* 18 (1991):1–21; Patricia Ewing and Susan S. Silbey, "Subversive Stories and Hegemonic Tales: Toward a Sociology of Narrative," *Law and Society Review* 29 (1995):197–226; and Margaret Somers, "The Narrative Constitution of Identity: A Relational and Network Approach," *Theory and Society* 23 (1994): 605–49.

7. Kathleen M. Blee, "Evidence, Empathy and Ethics: Lessons from Oral Histories of the Klan," *Journal of American History* 80 (1993): 596–606.

8. Kathleen M. Blee, "From the Field to the Courthouse: The Perils of Privilege," *Law and Social Inquiry* 24 (1999): 401–5.

9. Judith Stacey, "Can There Be a Feminist Ethnography?" in *Women's Words: The Feminist Practice of Oral History*, ed. Sherna Berger Gluck and Daphne Patai (New York: Routledge, 1991), 112.

10. For excellent examples of such work, see Tamar El-Or, "Do You Really Know How They Make Love? The Limits on Intimacy with Ethnographic Informants"; Faye Ginsburg, "The Case of Mistaken Identity: Problems in Representing Women on the Right"; and Rahel R. Wasserfall, "Reflexivity, Feminism and Difference," all in *Reflexivity & Voice*, ed. Rosanna Hertz (Thousand Oaks, Cal.: Sage, 1997), 169–89; 283–99; 150–68. My thanks to Rosanna Hertz for drawing my attention to this volume.

11. Barrie Thorne, "Political Activist as Participant Observer: Conflicts of Commitment in a Study of the Draft Resistance Movement of the 1960s," in *Contemporary Field Research: A Collection of Readings*, ed. Robert M. Emerson (Prospect Heights, Ill.: Waveland Press, 1983), 216–34, 225.

12. This is less true in anthropology, in which expressions of scholarly reflexivity are more normative, but sociology's traditional emphasis on distancing researcher and subject has made such discussions much more exceptional.

13. A tighter community of scholars of the racist Right would be helpful, although collaboration is difficult in research that depends on secrecy and individual contacts.

HÉCTOR L. DELGADO

2

REFLECTIONS ON THE

INTERSECTION OF RESEARCH

AND POLITICS IN ACADEMIA

Immigrants from Mexico and Central America have been blamed for further crowding already crowded cities, creating daily gridlock on Los Angeles freeways, and depleting the country's genetic pool. More serious are the accusations that they depress wages and take jobs from native workers. The stereotypic image of the lazy Mexican persists despite their hard work and low employment rates. It is an image projected onto their children in a society that rewards virtually everything they are not. The hardships and injustices Central American and Mexican immigrants endure in their own countries, which are further compounded in this country, and their persistence in the face of extraordinary obstacles attract me intellectually but also—and not accidentally—personally and politically.

In *The Fire Next Time*, a book that immeasurably influenced my thinking and feelings about race and ethnicity, James Baldwin reminded his nephew that as an African American he came from "sturdy, peasant stock, men who picked cotton and dammed rivers and built railroads, and, in the teeth of the most terrifying odds achieved an unassailable and monumental dignity."[1] His brother's failure to recognize this had defeated him. He had a "terrible life" and was "defeated long before he died because, at the bottom of his heart, he really believed what white people said about him."[2] Whereas the experience of African Americans is certainly unique in several important respects, other groups have suffered and continue to suffer untold indignities in a country fond of reminding itself of its goodness (resoundingly, in the aftermath of the World Trade Center attacks) and commitment to social justice. But as Baldwin wrote elsewhere, white people are flattered by their history—and well they should be since they wrote it. In my own work on immigrant workers and unionization, I try to tell a story that gives visibility and due respect to actors on the margins of the white man's history. What I hope emerges from my research is a clearer understanding of the lives of human beings who have overcome seemingly insurmountable obstacles and endured untold insults to achieve "an unassailable and monumental dignity."[3]

My initial study of immigrant workers, which culminated in a book titled *New Immigrants, Old Unions*,[4] was a deviant case analysis of a plant in Los Angeles in which a work force of approximately 160 Mexican and Central American immigrant workers, overwhelmingly undocumented, voted for union representation and negotiated a collective bargaining agreement with an employer who vigorously resisted unionization. I spent many months in the field over a two-year period, talking with union and community organizers, immigrant workers, the owner of and supervisors from the plant, owners of other plants who rely principally on undocumented workers, INS (Immigration and Naturalization Service) officials, and Border Patrol agents. By organizing, these workers helped to belie the stereotypic image of passive and frightened Latin American immigrants hiding in the shadows. As I wrote in my book, "cheap labor is not necessarily docile labor."[5] And this was not the first time Mexican and other Latin American immigrant workers had demonstrated this resolve. The twentieth century is replete with examples—ranging from the fields to manufacturing and service sectors in urban areas—of immigrant workers organizing to demand fair treatment by their employers.

This subject was a natural one for me. The research included issues of race and ethnicity and the dirty jobs people of color perform for marginal wages, often under inhumane conditions. As a political activist myself, attempts by undocumented workers to unionize intrigued me. Going into the project, I had mixed feelings about organized labor, partly because of a bad experience I had with my mother's union following her death but also because of organized labor's long history of excluding immigrants, women, and workers of color. But I also believed that a strong social justice movement required the participation of workers and that there were signs of change within the labor movement. Some unions were already attempting to organize immigrant workers. I wanted to examine the conditions under which undocumented workers could be organized.

Many, but not all, organizers believed that undocumented workers could not be organized by labor unions. They advanced the following: undocumented workers undermined organizing efforts in firms in which they constituted the majority of the work force because of their fear of apprehension and deportation by the INS. On its face, the proposition seemed reasonable enough when I entered the field in 1986. It had become, in Robert Merton's words, a "pseudo-fact."[6] But because I knew (from experience and study) that people can and often do act in their own interest even under the most oppressive conditions, I chose to examine the deviant case or anomaly; that is, I decided to study a campaign in which undocumented workers organized despite strong employer resistance.

The fact that I was Puerto Rican, spoke Spanish, and was culturally proximate to the workers I interviewed facilitated access and accelerated the process of establishing the necessary trust to do the research. But simply being Puerto Rican, of working-class origins, and an immigrant does not guarantee that one will care deeply about or develop an intellectual interest in social inequality (although I suspect it helps). The terrain was not entirely unfamiliar since my own biography was that of an immigrant who had traveled to the United States as a child (although under more congenial circumstances than the immigrants I studied). And despite living most of my life in the United States, speaking English fluently, and obtaining an advanced degree, I remain in some measure on the margins.

I was born in Puerto Rico in 1949. My father and mother, born and raised in rural Puerto Rico, were not well educated. My father joined the army, fought in World War II and the Korean War, and in 1954 was transferred to an army base in Virginia. As children of a soldier in the U.S. army, my older brother and I attended school with the children of officers and lived in military housing. This provided us with an education and living conditions far superior to those of Puerto Rican children who were going to school and living in the slums of New York City and other depressed urban areas in the United States. But these advantages did not insulate us completely from racial and ethnic bigotry—certainly not in the Virginia of 1954.

In 1955 I entered first grade, frightened, unable to speak much English in a place that reminded me very little of Puerto Rico. I was different—an outsider, an immigrant—and on the first day of school my first-grade teacher reminded me of all of these things. She gave the class some instructions close to the noon hour, which, because of my limited English, I did not understand. When I finally deciphered what she was saying, with the help of a classmate, it was too late, and she punished me by not allowing me to eat lunch. Later that day she rapped my knuckles (with a pencil or ruler) because I was unable to draw an "O" between two lines. Predictably, my father was unfazed by the knuckle rap, but both he and my mother were upset that I was not allowed to eat lunch. My parents and I went in the next day to see the principal. The teacher wasted little time in lecturing my parents to stop speaking Spanish at home. My mother, visibly nervous, told the teacher (in her badly broken English) that it was her (the teacher's) job to teach me English. We were Puerto Rican, she said, and Spanish was what we spoke in our home. The principal, to his credit, transferred me to another class. The new teacher shepherded me and another Puerto Rican boy through our first year. We both excelled as students. I still recall the day the teacher put his arm around my shoulders and told someone that I was his best student.

I have wondered in the past (and now once more) if my interest in teaching is perhaps partially rooted in my experience with this teacher. But it was my mother's intervention that had the most enduring effect, in part, no doubt, because we were extremely close. The most immediate effect was that I enjoyed going to school and for the rest of my life continued to love it. When I was much older, and especially after I began to study sociology, I realized how frightened my mother must have been. She was a poorly educated woman, raised in a culture where a woman's place was very well defined and at a time when professionals, especially teachers, were revered and certainly not questioned. Yet, in this instance, as she would do again in the future, she questioned authority. It took me many years to also realize that the teacher was years, if not decades, ahead of his time in his commitment to his pupils, even, to quote former president George H. W. Bush, "the little brown ones."

In 1957 my father was transferred to France, where we lived in a housing project for four years. The experience of living in a French neighborhood during a period of relatively high anti-American sentiment provided important life lessons. In retrospect, there is a certain irony about being disliked for being something I was not fully accepted as in the United States: an American. I began thinking much more about who and *what* I was. My high school years were important in this respect as well, but it was my last 2 years as an undergraduate (1969–71) that were especially critical for me politically and intellectually.

I attended Temple University on a baseball scholarship. There was an infectious energy on campus and in the country, but sports immunized me. The war in Vietnam was escalating, as was the level of militancy in the civil rights movement, but I was, as were most athletes, relatively oblivious to these and other events. Ironically, it was an incident with my baseball coach that broke this protective bubble. During a pregame warmup, the coach hit a ball to me in the outfield, but my vision was blocked accidentally by a teammate and this caused me to react slowly to the ball. From the coach's vantage point it appeared that I was not hustling. A teammate told me when this occurred that the coach had referred to me as a "fucking Puerto Rican bastard." After the game I confronted the coach and quit the team. Prior to this, Puerto Rican was simply a cultural or ethnic category in my mind, but the incident awakened me to the reality that in the United States Puerto Rican was a powerful, negative racial category as well. The incident forced me to rethink earlier events in my life, including the episode with the first-grade teacher.

Leaving the team created an enormous vacuum, which I filled by taking more stock of the world around me, devoting more time to my studies, and cultivating new friendships. These changes in my life, a stint as a writer for the alternative campus newspaper, and the war in Vietnam all helped to politicize me. In my senior year I applied for and was granted conscientious objector status, and I started to think seriously about going to Canada or to jail because the possibility existed that I could be drafted and sent to Vietnam in a noncombatant role. I did not want to be a cog in the machine (in the parlance of the day). Although I had a low number in the lottery, I was never called.

In my first job out of college, as an admissions officer at Rutgers University, I coordinated the recruitment of Latino students to the university's New Brunswick campus. I worked under a man named Willie Hamm, who influenced me tremendously. Hamm had devoted a major portion of his life to increasing the number of and improving conditions for minority students on campus. He waged his own civil rights struggle within the university system, and he nurtured me along the way. During this time I recruited minority students to Rutgers and served as an unofficial advisor to many of them once they were on campus. The experiences of visiting high schools; speaking with students, counselors, and principals; and battling with university officials to admit and then to retain larger numbers of minority students made me more aware of social inequality and prompted me to pursue graduate work in education and to become more active in a number of nonprofit organizations at the local and state levels. I received a master's degree in social and philosophical foundations of education and completed my coursework for a doctorate in the sociology of education at Rutgers University, but I left the program before completing my dissertation because of too little mentoring and too much political activism—a familiar story for many minority graduate students at the time.

My activism revolved principally around issues of education and educational access and the political status of Puerto Rico. At Temple University I became interested in the political status of Puerto Rico and its independence movement. My interest in U.S. imperialism and colonialism in Puerto Rico broadened to include U.S. intervention in other parts of the world and the relationship between foreign intervention and immigration. My work reflects my belief that the issue of immigration cannot be divorced from the intervention of the United States in the political and economic affairs of other countries and the economic penetration of markets worldwide by U.S.-based corporations. Simple push-pull theories of immigration are antiquated. The conditions that initially drove and continue to drive immigration to and settlement in the United States by Mexican and Central American immigrants were created in substantial measure by U.S. foreign policy and the practices of multinationals in the country's "backyard." Clearly, my research interests have been fueled by political concerns and reflect a portion of my biography that began to take shape in the late 1960s and early 1970s, a defining time for many of us in the discipline.

My social activism included working with community-based service organizations, proindependence organizations, and groups trying to stop the U.S. military from using Vieques, an island municipality of Puerto Rico, for target practice and as an ammunition depot. The matter is still unresolved, but the movement to stop the bombings is much larger and stronger today. In thinking both about the relationship between Puerto Rico and the United States and the lack of access by Puerto Ricans in New Jersey to high-quality education, a sociological perspective was the most useful. In my doctoral program in education, half of the coursework was in sociology.

In 1980 I accepted a position at Princeton University as an assistant dean of students. The time I spent at Princeton played a critical part in my decision to return to graduate school three years later. Princeton is an institution with a long history of exclusion, now trying to be more inclusive but never fully understanding how institutional racism made the task so difficult. I read voraciously on the subject of institutional racism and occasionally even shared some of my insights in the student newspaper, including an opinion piece in which I recommended the formation of a blue ribbon committee to study institutional racism at Princeton University. The recommendations were not received in the spirit in which they were offered. I became a target of an ultra-conservative newsletter on campus, and Princeton's provost invited me for a "friendly" lunch to discuss some of the points contained in the piece. The provost asked me if I believed he or Princeton was racist. I replied that if an institution has policies or engages in practices that have a particularly adverse effect on certain racial or ethnic minority groups, the institution is then behaving in a racist manner, however unintentionally. The only thing I really cared about was changing the policies and practices in question. Intent is important but not nearly as important as actions and their consequences, both intended and unintended. The debate energized me and helped me realize that what I wanted to do was explore these issues in greater depth and in a different environment.

I applied to graduate programs in sociology and chose the University of Michigan. The school's reputation was an important consideration, but it was the fellowship that finally brokered the deal because it demonstrated a commitment to minority recruitment by the university and the program. On campus I continued my activism, forming, with a graduate student in history, an antiapartheid organization—the Free South Africa Coordinating Committee (FSACC). I was active in a Puerto Rican student organization and supported actions by other organizations, including engaging in protests and acts of civil disobedience against the *contras* in Nicaragua and death squads in El Salvador and Guatemala. I was a member of the committee that created a Latino Studies Program at Michigan and taught some of its first courses. A course on action research taught by Mark Chesler helped me to think more clearly about the relationship between the things we study and the things we do. Chesler encouraged me to study issues about which I cared a great deal personally and politically. This was refreshing, even liberating, since I had heard all too often about the *dangers* of doing precisely this. And it is what I did when I decided to study the unionization of immigrant workers.

The research was cutting-edge work since it challenged a commonly held assumption about these workers and shed new light on what it means to be undocumented. The research helped to spawn more work in sociology and other disciplines on the unionization of immigrant workers, and I continue to work in the area. I conducted research on the Los Angeles Manufacturing Action Project (LAMAP), an ambitious attempt in Los Angeles in the mid-1990s to organize the largest concentration of manufacturing workers in the country. The architects of this multiunion, community-based campaign targeted the largely Latino, immigrant work force in the area between Los Angeles and the San Pedro and Long Beach ports. The campaign failed ultimately to secure the support of the AFL-CIO (American Federation of Labor and Congress of Industrial Organizations) and all but one of the unions that expressed interest and invested in the campaign initially. But in the process, the campaign raised important questions about tactics and strategies that organized labor was willing or able to employ.

The demise of the campaign torpedoed, at least for the time being, my research agenda, but I eventually studied multiunion campaigns in three cities: Stamford, Connecticut; Seattle; and Los Angeles. The campaigns differed from one another in numerous ways but shared a commitment to orchestrate coordinated campaigns by two or more unions.

Despite important successes, a preliminary analysis of these campaigns and the experience of LAMAP raises serious questions about the ability of unions to organize collectively, as well as organized labor's capacity to build or participate in a broad-based social movement. The obstacles are both external and internal. Employer resistance and complicity by the government in attempts to weaken unions is well documented, and the political climate is not the most conducive for union organizing, despite attempts in the last five years by the AFL-CIO to make organizing the cornerstone of the federation's mission. Within organized labor, union activists, organizers of color, and women historically have encountered and continue to encounter countless obstacles as they attempt to move up within the union hierarchy, despite a renewed openness and commitment to change by the AFL-CIO leadership. Racial, ethnic, and gender divisions continue to plague organized labor, and it is an issue that drives much of my interest in this subject and forces me to recognize the difficulty of organizing across these and other divides.

Without question, sociology has helped to shape my life both personally and politically. In the broadest sense, it has made me more pessimistic about the future of racial and ethnic relations and oppressed people worldwide. Derrick Bell captures my own feelings about racism: "Racism is an integral, permanent, and indestructible component of this society."[7] There is a certain comfort in thinking of racial discrimination purely in its individual or intentional forms. These forms seem much easier to change than the institutional variety introduced to me by sociology—one much more difficult to decipher, let alone to eliminate or reduce. The events of September 11 and thereafter make the task all the more difficult.

Even before September 11, one of the most interesting questions for sociologists was posed as a paradox by Larry Bobo: "Although there is continuing improvement in whites' beliefs about blacks and support for the general principles of racial equality and integration . . . there is pronounced opposition to specific policies aimed at improving the social and economic positions of blacks, as well as to participation in social settings where blacks are a substantial majority."[8] The civil rights gains of the 1960s and 1970s have been eroding steadily, and the erosion may even accelerate. Yet I am attracted in my work and as an activist to struggles my own sociological imagination tells me are ultimately likely to fail, or at least to fail in my lifetime (even if I live a long life).

In the preface to the 1992 paperback edition of *Faces at the Bottom of the Well*, Bell responds to the question "Why struggle?" with the following: "The obligation to try and improve the lot of blacks and other victims of injustice (including whites) does not end because final victory over racism is unlikely, even impossible. The essence of a life fulfilled—a succession of actions undertaken in righteous causes—is a victory in itself.[9] I agree, but I also believe that the victory is more than just fighting the good fight. The perseverance of immigrant workers and the ability of racial and ethnic minorities to improve the quality of their lives, even if only in relatively small increments, are victories nonetheless—and perhaps set the stage for more meaningful victories and fundamental change in the future. But fighting the good fight also means the possibility of changing people's lives in positive ways, as my own life was changed in positive ways by people close to me, as well as by political activists whom I never met. The work I do and the activism in which I engage (and have engaged in the past) are motivated in substantial measure by an *obligation* I feel to people who sacrificed so much even in "the teeth of the most terrifying odds." As teachers, our potential for this type of impact on people's lives is enormous.

Although sociology provides me with a vehicle to see the world in a way that makes sense to me, becoming an academic, a husband, and a father reduced my political activism. It is difficult to gauge the importance of one's work in social justice debates and struggles, and if one feels a certain amount of guilt for not participating more directly, it is easy to convince oneself that one's work is enormously important. I try not to do either, that is, feel guilty or exaggerate the importance of my work. There is no substitute for direct action. But I chose to get married and we chose to have children, and both meant reapportioning my time. While I remain active politically, the time I devote to social issues has decreased and the risks I am willing to take have changed (since the consequences are no longer mine alone to bear.) Yet being an academic allows me to care for my family and to be political. The academy is a place where I can address important social issues intellectually and urge students and pressure the institutions they attend to behave in a more socially responsible manner. Playing the role of critic within and outside of the academy and studying what I study and in the way that I do come with a price, although a relatively small one in the larger scheme of things. Studying the lives of immigrant workers certainly puts all of my troubles in proper perspective. One of the best measures of how effective you are as an agent of change is the price you pay for your activism. If you are not terribly inconvenienced, you are probably not doing enough. At this time in my life I fear I am not doing enough.

On a personal level, sociology has given me invaluable insights into my everyday actions that have made me, I trust, a better citizen, friend, partner, and father. An example of this occurred some 15 years ago. As a graduate student in Ann Arbor, Michigan, I was returning to my car late one evening without an umbrella in a heavy downpour. I was running, failing to see a woman on the other side of a fairly wide street. As I ran diagonally across the street, a fair distance from her, she stopped abruptly and gasped. We were the only two people on the street, late at night, and I, six feet tall, with an old Army jacket that made me look a few inches taller and several pounds heavier, had terrified her. I never understood male privilege better. I moved away from her quickly and apologized. I tell this incident to students and ask them to think of other examples of privilege and to consider both the intended *and* *unintended* consequences of our actions.

I am perhaps as much a historian as I am a sociologist. As scholars we can give both voice and visibility to people silenced or rendered invisible by neglect or ignorance. On a good day the work can be used in even more constructive ways by other activists, but ultimately political struggles are more about power than they are about a good argument. This limits the impact of our work. I study oppression and resistance at various levels, including at the ground level, where people make important decisions to improve their lives and the lives of fellow workers, family members, and even strangers. I happen to focus on the lives of immigrant workers who organize to improve their conditions of work and in the process contribute to a larger social justice movement. But as an immigrant, a Puerto Rican, and the son of working-class parents, I believe that this research agenda is not pure happenstance and not solely an academic enterprise.

NOTES

1. James Baldwin, *The Fire Next Time* (New York: Vintage International, 1991), 10.
2. Ibid., 4.
3. Ibid.
4. Héctor L. Delgado, *New Immigrants, Old Unions: Organizing Undocumented Workers in Los Angeles* (Philadelphia: Temple University Press, 1993).
5. Ibid., 58.

6. Robert K. Merton, "Notes on Problem-Finding in Sociology," in *Sociology Today: Problems and Prospects*, ed. Robert K. Merton, Leonard Broom, and Leonard S. Cottrell, Jr. (New York: Basic Books, 1959), ix–xxxiv, xiv–xvi.

7. Derrick Bell, *Faces at the Bottom of the Well: The Permanence of Racism* (New York: Basic Books, 1992), xiii.

8. Lawrence Bobo, "Group Conflict, Prejudice, and the Paradox of Contemporary Racial Attitudes," in *Eliminating Racism: Profiles in Controversy*, ed. Phyllis A. Katz and Dalmas A. Taylor (New York: Plenum, 1988), 85–114, 88.

9. Bell, *Faces at the Bottom*, xi.

SUSAN A. OSTRANDER

WORKING OUT CLASS WHILE

STUDYING ELITES

3

Sociologists rarely "study up." The names of those who have examined upper-class elites are too few and come too easily to mind. Elites are boundary keepers who create and actively maintain social barriers between themselves and nonelites. Somewhat to my surprise, I have found it less difficult to cross these barriers than I first expected and other social scientists seem to imagine.[1] Even more surprising, despite—or because of—my (more or less) working-class background, I sometimes feel a deep affinity with upper-class elites, even when I disagree with their worldviews. How could this be? Why do I feel this connection to some members of the upper class?

I began to study the upper class at a time when class was still measured and defined largely by men's occupational status, income, and education. Women's class was determined mostly by husbands' and fathers' positions. Women of the upper class received only passing attention because the study of elites focused on the power, authority, and social backgrounds of men who were elite decision makers. I published *Women of the Upper Class*[2] in 1984 as feminist scholars were making visible the important ways in which women's unpaid work in families and elsewhere in society creates and maintains the social fabric. My research explained how the upper-class women I interviewed, through their work at home and in their elite clubs and local communities, reproduced the social fabric of the upper class and, thus, the larger class structure. They accomplished this within a set of complex and contradictory relationships. Simultaneously, they were subordinate to the men of their class and dominant over women and men of other classes. Since that initial research, I have continued to choose research topics and sites that focus on people from the upper class. I have conducted a study of three old-established social welfare agencies whose boards included significant numbers of upper-class members,[3] and an ethnography of a now thirty-year-old progressive philanthropic foundation founded by and still supported by people of inherited wealth.[4]

Until now, I have not written about my own class background and how people and early events probably influenced my decision to study the upper class. Nor have I considered before how my research continues to reshape my experience of upper-class people, including my unexpected feeling of connection, which comes (I now believe) because elites typically "get it" about class. In the language of social science, upper-class people—like a number of people from my own working-class background—know that class position matters to their lives and the lives of others. This shared affinity across class boundaries has made me wonder about when and how I acquired my own class consciousness.

Although I had had other experiences of being set apart from middle- and upper-class people, a country club dance in high school brought into bold relief my understanding of my family's location in the class structure. A boy I had been dating had taken me to the club dance in the summer. Months later it was time for the Holiday Ball. This time he said he couldn't invite me because the dance was for club members only. By then, I had decided he wasn't all that special, so it didn't break my heart. What the experience did instead was give me a glimpse into an exclusive and elite class world that I hardly knew existed. This led to lots of questions: what did people have to do to get into this club? How much did it cost? Why, besides going to dances, did people join? Who belonged, and how were they different from me and my family?

We (my mother, my younger brother, and I) lived with my maternal grandparents in upstate New York from the time I was six or seven (after my father left, never to return, which is another story). We lived in the country in a house built next to what had been the family dairy farm, owned initially by my second-generation, Irish-Catholic great-grandparents, near one of those rural colleges on a hill. Years before we moved there and after the farm was sold, my grandfather had worked as a postal deliverer, carrying mail throughout the area. (Coming from a background of landowners complicates my class background since working-class people typically don't own land.) My mother told me that when she was growing up, during the Depression years, the family had been grateful for my grandfather's job with the post office when so many others had no work.

My grandfather was a quiet man. When he did speak, it was usually the last word, whatever the subject. Nearly every day, from my years in grammar school through high school, he drove the half-mile down the road to meet my younger brother and me in the afternoons where the school bus dropped us off. He didn't like me walking home across the fields, saying it wasn't safe for a girl.

My grandfather read a lot and listened to the news on the radio several times a day and, later, on television (especially during the 1950s McCarthy hearings). He was smart and a bit mysterious. I wanted to be like him—but I also wanted the education I knew he had not had. His sister, my great-aunt, who was a teacher and another important role model for me, had acquired the education. Years later, when the Vietnam War came and my brother, cousins, and (by then) my young husband were threatened with the draft, my grandfather told them, "You do whatever you have to to stay out of it." His critical view on Vietnam came earlier than most, and I saw it later as a reflection of his knowledge and intelligence about what was going on in the world, as well as his own experience. He had been briefly in a war (Cuba), and his sons had fought in World War II. They had all come home safe, but he knew what war did to people and he was against it.

While I was growing up, my grandmother was employed a few days a week doing housework for some of the local faculty wives. (It was a men's college. To my knowledge, there were no women on the faculty.) My grandmother had raised four children on a family farm, cooked big dinners for hired hands at midday, done the family laundry by hand (with her husband's help, my mother tells me). What my grandmother called "helping out" the women she worked for probably seemed relatively easy in comparison. We never named it so, but now I say she worked as a domestic. As with most domestics (I later learned), her employers sent used clothes and other second-hand items home with her. We didn't need them and gave them away. I wondered why she accepted them. She said she didn't want to hurt "the ladies'" feelings.

We were a liberal Democrat family, unusual in rural, upstate New York, and we talked politics a lot at home. I loved the excitement when voices were raised and debates ensued. One frequent topic was union politics, especially when one of my uncles was laid off or on strike and money was getting tight but crossing a picket line was out of the question (another class lesson). One uncle was a sheet metal worker, one a typesetter (and union officer), the third a mechanic at a local airbase. They kept telling my aunt, who was a nurse, that nurses had to unionize or she would never get the pay and respect she deserved; turns out they were right about that.

My mother worked as a secretary at the nearby college. (I don't remember hearing talk at home about the benefits of a union for secretaries.) She could take shorthand really fast while her boss dictated letters, and her fingers flew over the typewriter. I think she liked her job. To this day, she has only good to say about the men she worked for. It seemed to me that over the some 30 years of her employment, she trained more than one new boss for a job she could by then have done herself for a lot more pay than she earned as a secretary. (She disagrees and says she wouldn't have wanted a different job.) As a teenager, I benefited from the respect she had earned at the office by being given part-time and summer jobs. I knew I couldn't be careless because it would reflect badly on her. I was a good envelope stuffer and switchboard operator.

By my senior year in high school, I was attending fraternity parties— partly because the children my age whose fathers taught at the college didn't invite me to their parties (a first cut on class and one that hurt), and I vowed not to care. Who needed boring high school parties anyway? (It's not accidental that my first husband was a member of one of those fraternities.)

When I graduated from high school, I went to nursing school in Rochester, New York. I didn't know then that many working-class girls from Irish and Roman Catholic families went to nursing school. I didn't know that what I thought was my individual career choice was part of a class and ethnic (and certainly gender) pattern. I was the first person in my family to live away from home to attend school. I wanted to go away to a big city, and I had a New York State scholarship that meant I could go where I wanted. I knew that my move was about beginning a different life—urban and faster paced— and I wasn't sure what else but I knew, but I wanted to find out.

Based on vocational tests taken in high school, my teachers told me I would be a good nurse. They were wrong. Still, I finished nursing school and learned a lot—especially about people different from me. The big-city hospital I had chosen for nursing school was a class- and race-mixed environment, ·and my work there taught me something about how class intersected with race in sometimes complicated ways. African-American (then called Negro) coworkers and fellow students took me to inner-city jazz clubs on Sunday afternoons. A Jewish boyfriend (whom my grandpa favored, so any family objections were silenced) took me to a country club dance, where a black doctor I knew sat at the bar and ordered a mint julep served by a white bartender who called him "sir." It was the 1960s, and class and race barriers were being challenged.

Growing up, I had known only one class of blacks, although I knew of a black intellectual, Alex Haley, who had spent a year in residence at the nearby college, where my mother worked. People I knew were proud that he had chosen to come to where we lived to write what became the acclaimed book *Roots*.[5] But most of the blacks in the area were hard-scrabble migrant workers who stayed from late spring to early fall to pick whatever was growing in the fields and orchards around home. They lived in camps just a half-mile from where I lived. Often in the summers, adults and children from the camps walked on the road past our house on their way back and forth to town, three or four miles away. I sold lemonade (or its less tasteful, less nutritious counterpart, Kool-Aid) on the road sometimes and exchanged pleasantries with the walkers when they stopped to buy. Once in a while, children from the camps were in my class at school for a few weeks. They worked in the fields alongside their parents, except for the very youngest, some of whom were cared for at a local church in the village, where I volunteered occasionally.

A few people from town, including one of our country neighbors whom I knew well, went to the camps in the evenings to teach the migrant workers how to read. I remember thinking that if I had spent all day doing exhausting work in the hot summer fields, I might not have the will or the energy to take classes at night. I remember admiring the migrant workers, and I knew their choice came from a life I knew nothing about.

After graduating from nursing school, I chose to work on the psychiatric ward of the city hospital to earn money for more schooling, which led eventually to the liberal arts degree that took me into sociology. From the start, I was a small thorn in the doctors' sides since I often raised issues I later learned came from a sociological view of mental illness. I remember one factory worker who was hospitalized for depression. He had been ostracized by his coworkers for rate breaking (working too fast), and they blamed him for subsequent speed ups. I took the view that he wasn't mentally ill but rather struggling to cope with a difficult situation. My view, though I didn't know it then, was a sociological one since it explains individual behavior as shaped by social conditions and circumstances. But the doctors and the other nurses I worked with didn't see it that way, so I lost that argument and several subsequent ones. It went on like that until I discovered sociology in one of my night courses, got myself out of nursing, and found my professional and intellectual home.

Some of the questions about class that I had wondered about in high school when I wasn't invited to faculty children's parties and when I was shut out from that first country club dance finally were answered when I did the research for my doctoral dissertation, which became the book *Women of the Upper Class*.[6] Although I didn't have those experiences in mind when I selected the topic, my study went a long way toward helping me understand the role of exclusive clubs in creating and maintaining class boundaries, as well as other exclusive aspects of upper-class life. It also explained how some of the women I interviewed made sense of class and gender. They recognized their own subordination to the men of their class—accommodating their daily lives to what their husbands wanted and adjusting to circumscribed roles considered acceptable for women in the community philanthropic organizations in which they volunteered—and mostly they resented it. At the same time, they were not about to seriously challenge the power of those men who provided the advantages of upper-class life, which the women were not about to give up. So they traded a certain measure of gender subordination at home and elsewhere in an unstated bargain necessary to hold on to the privileges of a male-dominated class. As I've since heard Bill Domhoff summarize my work, for these women, class trumped gender.

After my 1984 book was published and I received tenure at Tufts University, I set out to practice my progressive politics, born in political discussions at home, nurtured in sociology classes in the late 1960s and 1970s, and sharpened by my analysis of traditional, inherited-wealth women. Around this time, the head of the Boston Women's Fund (having seen my 1984 book, which included a critical discussion of traditional philanthropy) asked me to join a fund committee (and later the board). This fund was known for supporting local grassroots community organizing by women for social and economic justice, and so I entered the world of progressive philanthropy—a vivid contrast to the kind of class-conserving, upper-class philanthropy I had learned about for my first book and an opportunity to meet an unfamiliar kind of upper-class person.

I soon heard about what other researchers who study philanthropy have called "the prototype of the alternative funds,"[7] and "a democratically representative alternative that is close to the kind of philanthropy that might truly be for the public good"[8]: Haymarket People's Fund in Boston. In early 1990, I began the ethnographic research for what became *Money for Change*.[9]

The Haymarket Fund brought me into contact with inherited-wealth donors who came from such families as the "club people" (who had kept me from the dance when I was in high school) and those I had studied for my early research on upper-class women. The big difference was that the upper-class people I met at Haymarket were calling into question and actively *chal-*

lenging the class structure that offered them privilege and power, not reinforcing it through class-exclusive clubs and other ways. They were engaged in
what they called "committing class suicide," by which they meant that if they
accomplished their political goals, their own class would be eliminated and
the class structure seriously undermined.[10] They understood the conflicts inherent in being both upper class and politically Left, calling it "living the
contradiction." One donor said that giving away his fortune to low-income
and working-class activist groups was like finding a wallet full of money on
the sidewalk and returning it to its rightful owner. This idea is expressed in
the mantra Haymarket uses to describe its philanthropy: "Change, Not Charity," meaning "Giving to others what belongs to you is charity. Giving to others what belongs to them is social justice."[11]

At Haymarket, I met wealthy elites who share my own progressive politics. I also began to figure out the vaguely felt kinship I had experienced before with people from this class, even those whose thinking was diametrically
opposed to mine. I came to understand how people from old-wealth families—similar to many working-class people—often understand the importance of class and where they stand in relation to it. Middle-class people, in
contrast, are more inclined to minimize class (and race) by claiming, in well-
meaning liberal ways, that people are really all the same. In the middle class,
it's education and income that matter, along with the status and material
comforts they bring. Power and privilege are often erased or denied. Upper-
class people, whatever their politics, know about power and privilege.

I had seen this clarity about class (and class interest) both in my interviews with upper-class women and in the interviews I did for a study in the
early 1980s (before my Haymarket project), which looked at how child and
family welfare agencies were coping with federal budget cuts. Once I talked
with a member of one agency's board of directors, a top business executive
from an old-money family, at his luxuriously appointed office. I asked for his
thoughts about that day's local news concerning the increasing number of
children in the city who were becoming homeless as a result of the cuts. I
knew from hearing his opinions at board meetings that he opposed others in
the agency who wanted to increase their advocacy with state legislators to restore the monies that had reduced their programs. He looked me straight in
the eye and said, "You have to understand; I'd have to change my whole way
of life to really solve the problem [of those children], and I'm just not willing
to do that."

What he said both repelled and thrilled me. I was horrified, yet I respected his sharp candor. He knew he *could* make a positive difference in poor

children's lives—he had the power and the resources—but he wasn't going to do so because it would mean giving up his own privileged lifestyle.

I saw this sharp understanding once before, in the mid-1970s, while gathering data for what later became *Women of the Upper Class*. I asked one upper-class woman what she saw as her personal responsibility as a board member of several social service agencies. She answered without a second's hesitation: "My job is to keep things from going too far to the Left." Just to be sure I had understood her correctly, I asked, "You mean to the political Left?" "Yes, of course," she said. So she knew that it takes active engagement and work—what sociologists call agency—to maintain the class structure in America.

While I was doing research at the Haymarket Fund in the early 1990s, the members organized an evening forum about understanding class in one's own life and in society. The author of a new book on class was invited to speak. He argued that Americans were confused about class. They couldn't make sense, he said, of how class works and what it means to their lives. I'd been asked to join him on the podium to respond to his comments and spark discussion. I said that I thought only middle-class people were confused about class and that working-class people and people from upper-class, inherited-wealth families understood class very well. The audience clapped and nodded in agreement. They were mostly either Haymarket donors from the upper class or Haymarket grantees from the working class. I knew I was referring partly to myself and my own feelings of connection to some members of the upper class across the barriers of my own class upbringing.

So what have I learned about class through my research, especially insights that have influenced my personal thoughts and feelings, as well as my scholarly and political views? Certainly one lesson from my earliest research, especially stark in the two examples above, is (as I tell my students) that the class structure and the power and privilege inherent in it didn't just drop from the sky. People created it and maintain it and could choose to change it. Most will probably not make that choice. But a few people from the elite classes, like those I met at Haymarket (and at the Boston Women's Fund and elsewhere in my own activist work), really do work for Left causes that challenge class and will mean altering their own privileged lifestyle. Upper-class people in these settings bring to the table a variety of additional resources along with their money. For example, they tend to think big about what can be accomplished to change the current system. In the progressive funding organizations where I volunteer and do research, when the time comes to set annual goals for how much money to raise, it is often the people of wealth in the room who set the bar high. Others not from wealthy backgrounds are more cautious. To those raised in monied families, it doesn't seem so much, and they know who the others are who have surplus wealth to contribute. They can access money and power in ways that make them important allies in social movement organizations.

My Haymarket Fund research also reinforced a lesson I had learned from my earlier study of upper-class women, a lesson that enhances my feeling of affinity with elites over a shared sense of how much class matters in negative, as well as positive, ways. As my aunt who still works as a nurse put it after she read my 1984 book, "So I guess being rich isn't all that great. The women you write about don't seem all that happy with their lives." Although upper-class people surely do receive many benefits from class privilege—freedom, independence, and economic security among them—there are also cracks and strains in what may look to people of other classes as the most ideal life.

This argument ought not to be confused with self-serving common images of the "rich white man's burden" or the "poor little rich girl." People of wealth certainly do not experience the same kinds of hidden injuries of class that poor or working-class people do, but neither is a life of privilege devoid of its own special difficulties and dilemmas. If you really can do whatever you want, what is that exactly? Once you have all that anyone could want and more in the way of material comforts and intellectual and cultural experiences, what do you do with all that money and on what basis do you decide and who do you trust to advise you? What if you and your family, from whom you have inherited (or will inherit) all this money, have profound differences about what ought to be done with it?[12]

I came to understand once and for all during my two-and-a-half years of doing research at the Haymarket Fund that the hierarchy inherent in a class structure wounds even those who benefit from it most. It seems profoundly important to recognize the radical potential of this idea since it means—as the wealthy people who choose to work in progressive organizations like the Haymarket Fund know well—that everyone has something to gain from class equality (even those who also have much to lose). This understanding can (and does) create allies from this most privileged and powerful class, admittedly few and far between, who can be counted on to act in collective social movements across class—just as there are a few whites who work for racial justice and a few men who are active profeminists. As one wealthy donor told me, "Our society's been built on the notion that people who *have* keep the people who don't from having. To make a link between those people is pretty wild. It would be a pretty powerful movement to have those people come together."[13]

NOTES

1. Susan A. Ostrander, "'Surely You're Not in This Just to Be Helpful': Access, Rapport, and Interviews in Three Studies of Elites," *Journal of Contemporary Ethnography* 22, 1 (1993): 7–27. Reprinted in *Studying Elites Using Qualitative Methods*, ed. R. Hertz and J. B. Imber (Thousand Oaks, Calif.: Sage, 1995).

2. Susan A. Ostrander, *Women of the Upper Class* (Philadelphia: Temple University Press, 1984).

3. Susan A. Ostrander, "Elite Dominance in Private Social Service Agencies: How It Happens and How It Is Challenged," in *Power Elites and Organizations*, ed. G. W. Domhoff and T. R. Dye (Newbury Park, Calif.: Sage, 1987).

4. Susan A. Ostrander, *Money for Change: Social Movement Philanthropy at Haymarket People's Fund* (Philadelphia: Temple University Press, 1995); Susan A. Ostrander, "When Grantees Become Grantors: Accountability, Democracy, and Social Movement Philanthropy," in *Philanthropic Foundations: New Scholarship, New Possibilities*, ed. Ellen Condliffe Lagemann (Indianapolis: Indiana University Press, 1999).

5. Alex Haley, *Roots: The Saga of an American Family* (New York: Random House, 1976).

6. Ostrander, *Women of the Upper Class*.

7. Michael O'Neil, *The Third American: The Emergence of the Nonprofit Sector in the United States* (San Francisco: Jossey-Bass, 1989), 148.

8. Teresa Odendahl, *Charity Begins at Home: Generosity and Self-Interest Among the Philanthropic Elite* (New York: Basic Books, 1990), 184.

9. Ostrander, *Money for change*.

10. Ibid., 64.

11. Ibid., 62, 63.

12. For further examples and discussion, see Nelson W. Aldrich, Jr., *Old Money: The Mythology of America's Upper Class* (New York: Vintage Books, 1988); Amy Domini, *Challenges of Wealth: Mastering the Personal and Financial Conflicts* (Homewood, Ill.: Jones-Irwin, 1988); Christopher Mogil and Anne Slepian, *We Gave Away a Fortune* (Philadelphia: New Society Publishers, 1992).

13. Ostrander, *Money for Change*, 103.

MARK S. MIZRUCHI

4

WORLD EVENTS AND

CAREER EXPERIENCES

A PERSONAL PERSPECTIVE

started college as a math major, but I was also interested in world events. It was the early 1970s; the student movement was in decline; a progressive presidential candidate, George McGovern, had just been soundly defeated; and I wanted to know why. Like many students of that generation, my quest for understanding eventually led me to Marxism. Elements of a crude, unconscious Marxism were already present in my worldview, but I now began to read Marx and Marxist literature, trying to figure out why American workers had not revolted against capitalism. I gradually reached the conclusion that they were victims of "false consciousness." Their hostility toward students and the poor rather than big business reflected their inability to see the "true" sources of their malaise. The cause of this malady, I reasoned, must be big business itself, that is, the capitalist class. The capitalist class, through its control of all major societal institutions, must inculcate the working class with a set of beliefs that run counter to the workers' own interests. Simplistic though it was, I thought that I had uncovered the key to understanding the lack of socialist sentiment among the American working class.

Somewhere during this period I abandoned math (something I now regret) and took up sociology (which I do not regret, but there's no reason I could not have done both). The primary theoretical debates in American sociology in the early 1970s were between Parsons-influenced structural functionalists and Marx- and Mills-influenced conflict theorists. Given my views, I quickly sided with Marx and Mills. Societies might possess generally shared value systems, I figured, but these values were imposed on the masses by the powerful, through their control of the school system, the media, cultural institutions, and the political system. The remainder of my undergraduate years was spent in reading and thinking about these debates.

In my second year of graduate school at the State University of New York (SUNY) at Stony Brook, I discovered a project, directed by Michael Schwartz, that examined links among large U.S. corporations. Schwartz's goal was to identify the locus of power in the corporate world as a means of locating the center of power in society. Schwartz argued that business played a dominant role in the American system and that the key actors in the corporate world were large commercial banks, which were able to transcend the narrow interests that characterized specific industries and instead focus on doing what was best for the business community as a whole. To demonstrate the dominance of financial institutions, Schwartz and his students examined the ties created by overlapping board memberships among corporations, known as interlocking directorates. Using an emerging approach known as network analysis, they developed a set of mathematical models to identify the most central nodes in the system of interfirm relations. These central units tended overwhelmingly to be the large, primarily New York-based commercial banks and insurance companies, just as Schwartz's theory had predicted.

My exposure to this project was quite fortuitous. Numbers were always my first love. When I left math and took up sociology, however, I fancied myself a theorist and decided that quantitative sociology violated every principle for which I stood. It had never occurred to me that one could address an important theoretical and substantive issue by using quantitative methods. Yet here was a project that used mathematical models to test Marxist theory. I quickly joined Schwartz's project, read the appropriate Marxist theory, dusted off my by then rusty mathematical skills, and began to learn about this new approach called network analysis. It was the beginning of a career venture that, nearly twenty-five years later, still forms the basis of most of my work.

THE PROJECT AND ITS EVOLUTION

As I've indicated, the primary goal of Schwartz's project was to understand the structure of the capitalist class. The most prominent debate of the period was between pluralists, who believed that the United States was essentially democratic and that the inherent conflicts within the business world provided the preconditions for this democracy, and elite theorists and Marxists, who believed that the United States was democratic in name only because the overarching unity of the corporate elite allowed this relatively small group to dominate the state. Both groups conceded that the degree of business unity was the key variable in determining whether the United States was a democracy. Even pluralists admitted that without such internal conflict, business would use its enormous resources to advance a unified, classwide interest. The question, then, was how unified the business community actually was.

In the early twentieth century, muckraking journalists, progressive and populist activists, congressional committees, and even Supreme Court Justice Louis Brandeis viewed interlocking directorates as indicative of the concentration of power among large corporations. "The practice of interlocking directorates is the root of many evils," wrote Brandeis in his classic book about the power of banks, *Other Peoples' Money*.[1] The social scientists who resuscitated the study of interlocks beginning in the late 1960s similarly viewed them in terms of their potential for restricting both economic and political competition. The more tightly interlocked the largest firms were, these scholars argued, the more cohesive was the capitalist class. A prominent pluralist sociologist, Arnold Rose, conceded that "interlocking directorates, where they occur in the larger corporations, give them a high degree of cohesiveness."[2] Of course, Rose also insisted that "interlocking directorates are the exception rather than the rule."[3] Sentiments such as these suggest that if interlocks were in fact widespread, the largest corporations were indeed politically cohesive.

Schwartz and his students, especially Beth Mintz, were focused not primarily on the overall cohesiveness of the interlock network but on the centers of power within that network, which they hypothesized to be the leading banks and insurance companies. Still, the findings from their studies (based on data from the 1960s) indicated that more than 90% of the corporations in the *Fortune* 800 were within four or fewer steps of one another as traceable through interlocks.[4] This seemed to indicate that the largest firms were highly cohesive. Because the Schwartz studies were largely cross-sectional, however, there was little basis for comparison. How dense would an interlock network have to be to be considered cohesive? How sparse would it have to be to be considered divided?

One way to address this issue would be to examine interlock networks over a period of time. This approach would have the added benefit of allowing researchers to test an argument raised by several scholars, including Daniel Bell, Ralf Dahrendorf, David Riesman, and Talcott Parsons, that there had actually been something resembling a cohesive capitalist class in the early 1900s but that this class had decomposed over time. Schwartz had told me about an economist, David Bunting, who had a data set of interlocks at several different points between 1900 and 1975. After insisting on some perfectly reasonable conditions, Professor Bunting generously allowed me to use his data. My dissertation was to be a panel study of the development of the American corporate interlock network at seven different points between 1904 and 1974. My initial interest in why the white working class in the United States was so conservative had evolved into a study of whether, and the extent to which, the American corporate elite was a unified force. In other words, was there a cohesive capitalist class in the United States? If so, I argued, this had ominous implications for the status of American democracy.

Did I actually believe the Marxism I was professing at the time? The answer is partly yes and mostly, I suspect, no. When I discovered Marxism as an undergraduate, I accepted it wholeheartedly for a brief period (probably about a year), but some of my acceptance was more wishful thinking than anything else. I suppose that some people in the 1970s seriously believed that the American working class would overthrow the U.S. government. Even in my most radical phase I doubted that this would ever happen. I recall reading glowing accounts of life in revolutionary Cuba and similar praise of China during the Cultural Revolution. A part of me wanted to believe these stories, but I was always suspicious. At Stony Brook there was a large contingent of Marxist graduate students, and I quickly fell in with them. Whatever Marxism I professed during that period was primarily of the academic variety, however.

As I became immersed in my research, I began to understand the need to concern myself with my career. There was a strong anticareerist bias among the most radical of my fellow students, so it was necessary to detach myself from them, at least in part. I recall being among the leaders of a university-wide graduate student strike that took place two weeks before I was scheduled to defend my dissertation in May 1980. Outwardly I was exhorting my fellow students to close the place down. Inwardly I was hoping that we would quickly lose so I could complete my degree.

These tensions were reflected in my dissertation. On the one hand, I had a vision that my work could be a force, however small, for social change. Helping us understand the nature of the capitalist class and the possibility that the United States was not really a democracy, as I aimed to do, seemed like a virtuous goal. On the other hand, even then I was slowly on the way to becoming a "respectable" sociologist. That is, I wanted to do a careful work of scholarship, and I therefore made a special effort to avoid making claims that my data could not support. I deduced a series of hypotheses about historical trends in the structure of the interlock network; for example, if Bell, Dahrendorf, and Riesman were correct, we would expect to see a decline in network density over time. I found that the density of the network did decline sharply between 1912 and 1935 but that it stabilized and even increased slightly between 1935 and 1970. This suggested that the "decomposition of the capitalist class" theorists were partly, but not completely, correct. I found that the proportion of firms that were within three steps of the most central firm did not change at all. Virtually every member of the network could reach the most central firm through no more than three directors in 1970, as well as in 1900. I also found, however, that the number of individuals who sat on six or more boards declined sharply, from twenty-seven in 1912, to fourteen in 1919, to only three in 1935, and to none in the 1960s and 1970s.

From these findings I argued that there had been an "institutionalization of intercorporate relations." The small number of powerful individual capitalists who dominated the business world at the turn of the twentieth century had been replaced by networks of large bureaucratic organizations. Even when the leading firms in these networks were directed by the offspring of Morgan, Rockefeller, Baker, and others, the sons' power did not approach that of their fathers. Still, the interfirm directors' ties that the elders had established largely remained. There was a generally cohesive capitalist class, I argued, but it was based on connections among those at the head of large organizations, regardless of background, rather than on individual power or family ties. I concluded with the warning that these findings still had serious implications for American democracy. But it was a carefully worded statement, tempered by my attempt at scholarly detachment. I still considered myself a radical, but my professional socialization had begun to chip away at my political commitments.

After completing graduate school in 1980, I took a position as a statistical consultant in the computing center of the Albert Einstein College of Medicine, in the Bronx. Although this was a full-time job that provided neither opportunities nor the expectation that I would publish, I slowly discovered that I could do my work at night and on weekends. I had no library and had to use the small local college libraries in my area, but I was a staff member of a computing center and therefore had access to state-of-the-art computing facilities. I also had a supportive boss who, although the job did not provide any opportunity for my own work, was willing to look the other way when I used our facilities, as long as it did not detract from my job performance. I decided to forge ahead, so I continued to write. I was able to publish several articles, as well as a book[5] based on my dissertation.

A number of things affected the trajectory of this project over the next three years. First, on a purely intellectual level, as network analyses of interorganizational relations emerged in the late 1970s, it was considered sufficient simply to document the existence and structures of corporate interlocks. As we moved into the mid-1980s, however, critics began to raise what I termed the "so what?" question.[6] It was one thing to document the existence and prevalence of interlocks. It was another to demonstrate that these ties actually affected the behavior of corporations. With a small number of exceptions, this had not been done. Second, as I learned network analytic techniques for my dissertation research, I discovered that they were intrinsically interesting, independent of my substantive topic. I also learned that an increasing number of prominent sociologists were involved in the study of social networks. I found that people in this area were interested in my work, regardless of its political implications, simply because it used network models. Network analysis became, like the regression models used by Erik Wright and others, a way of making the Marxism I espoused intellectually respectable in the discipline. Third, these developments took place during the early years of Ronald Reagan's presidency. Although I strongly opposed virtually every one of his policies, Reagan had the paradoxical effect of taming my radicalism. I had been extremely critical of Jimmy Carter, and the Marxism I learned in graduate school suggested that whether Carter or Reagan was president made virtually no difference since both Democrats and Republicans were controlled by the capitalist class. I recall defiantly sitting out the 1980 election, confident that it did not matter who won. Over the next few years I decided that I had been seriously mistaken. The idea that elections mattered did not have an immediate impact on my work, but it did, in retrospect, signal a key point in what became a conservative drift over the next decade.

DEALING WITH THE "SO WHAT?" QUESTION

My initial reaction to the "so what?" question was denial: it did not matter if we could not demonstrate behavioral consequences of networks because, as critical political sociologists had argued, the most significant forms of power were unobservable. I even wrote an article to that effect, in which I argued that although boards of directors rarely engage in day-to-day decision making, their ability to step in during times of crisis was enough to demonstrate their ultimate control of the firm. Ironically, the article[7] became a favorite of management scholars who were working within an economic approach called agency theory. I suspect that few of these people had any idea why I wrote it. Still, the "so what?" question would not go away, and I began to realize the need to demonstrate that corporate interlocks had behavioral consequences.

The solution I came up with—in discussion with a colleague, Tom Koenig, who had pioneered the study of the topic among sociologists—was to examine the effects of interlocks on corporate political contributions. Here was a newly available form of data that were behavioral, systematic, and easily obtainable. The idea would be to see if there was a link between interlocks and campaign contributions. After considerable thought, I determined that what I was interested in was not the behavior of firms per se but the level of cohesion and common activity between and among firms. It was therefore necessary to operate at the interfirm, rather than the firm, level of analysis. My units had to be groups of firms. I decided to focus on dyads, or pairs of firms. The proposition was that certain kinds of interfirm ties increased the probability that the firms would exhibit similar contribution patterns. In other words, if interlocks were evidence of cohesion within the capitalist class, this would be manifested in part by interlocked firms that were contributing to the same political candidates.

During this time I had developed an alternative conception of social-class and capitalist-class cohesion. Based in part on my dissertation, I had decided that the American capitalist class was based not in kinship and friendship ties among social elites but in economic interdependence among the dominant actors in the business community: large corporations. Elite theorists and Marxists who studied the structure of the capitalist class had viewed interlocks as indicative of social ties in the corporate elite. An alternative view of interlocks had arisen within organizational theory, however:

here interlocks were seen as responses to firms' dependence on the resources held by other firms. One way to coopt organizations that held these crucial resources, several scholars argued, was to interlock with them.[8] Interlocks could thus be seen as reflections of interfirm resource dependence. I was sympathetic to the resource dependence model. For one thing, this approach did much to legitimize the study of interlocks at a time when such work was viewed by critics as the province of conspiracy theorists. I also found the resource dependence argument compelling. Organizations did exist in turbulent environments, and they spent considerable effort trying to gain control over those environments.

My synthetic model of class cohesion was a simple three-variable path model. Consistent with the resource dependence model, interlocks were viewed as flowing from economic interdependence between firms. Consistent with the elite and class models, interlocks were viewed as independently facilitating political cohesion within the capitalist class. And, in my own argument, the economic interdependence between firms was hypothesized to have a direct effect on corporate political cohesion. Interdependence was thus viewed as having both a direct effect on cohesion and an indirect effect, through its effect on interlocking. To test my argument, I conducted network analyses of interfirm dyads, showing that pairs of firms that operated in interdependent industries and were tied to the same banks were likely to exhibit similar political behavior.[9]

Although my original intended audience for this work was my fellow power structure researchers, as well as Marxist state theorists, my analyses attracted more attention from organizational and network theorists than from political sociologists. I began to care less what power structure and Marxist state theorists thought of what I was doing and concerned myself more with the views of mainstream sociologists.

In 1987, after seven years at Albert Einstein, I accepted a teaching position in the sociology department at Columbia University, which under the direction of Ron Burt was developing into a center for social network research. During my four years at Columbia, and subsequently at the University of Michigan, I continued my network analysis of corporate political behavior, which culminated in my 1992 book, *The Structure of Corporate Political Action*.[10] In rereading the book, the tensions I was experiencing in defining my identity are clearly evident. The first two chapters speak primarily to a political sociology audience, with a focus on Marxist theories of the state. As I move into the study itself, however, the intended audience becomes less clear. By the middle of the book I am focusing on network methods, and the remainder of the volume is filled with detailed (some might say tedious) quantitative analyses of network and nonnetwork effects on corporate behavior.

I recall a conversation with Ron Burt after he had read the manuscript, asking who was the intended audience for the book. "The people who are interested in the substantive questions are not likely to care about the technical stuff," I remember him saying, "while those who are interested in the technical material are not likely to care about the substantive issues." He was right. What this dilemma reflected, though, was a tension in my own intellectual identity. I had moved some distance from my earlier ideal of the scholar as agent for progressive social change, but I had not completely left this view behind. I still cared about making a better world and hoped that my work, in however small a way, might contribute to that end. I was even more adamant in the view that only serious, detached scholarship would provide a means of furthering this goal. The goal was still there, but by that point it was more a glimmer than a flame.

THE EFFECTS OF CHANGING SCHOLARSHIP ON POLITICAL VIEWS AND VICE VERSA

Meanwhile, my political views continued to evolve during the late 1980s. In addition to Reagan's presidency, my years as a tenants' rights activist in the early 1980s had further confirmed my view that there really was a difference between Democrats and Republicans. In my work I no longer even attempted to argue that business *was* unified (which would have called American democracy into question). Instead, I argued that business unity was a variable, high in some situations and low in others. The key issue, I suggested, was to understand the conditions under which business unity occurred. One of my graduate students at Columbia even accused me of being a pluralist. It is interesting that although I protested, I was not fazed by this accusation.

Without realizing it, I was becoming more conservative. I felt comfortable and well integrated at Columbia. Meanwhile, as a new parent, I found myself concerned primarily with protecting my family, something that was of immediate salience because of living in Morningside Heights during the late 1980s and early 1990s, when crime and the crack epidemic in New York were at their peak. Two world events were especially significant for me, though. The first was the 1989 fall of Soviet control over Eastern Europe and the subsequent dissolution of the Soviet Union itself. The second was the Gulf War of 1991. Of the two, the former had a more significant effect on my scholarship. I had never had much regard for the Soviet Union, even in my most radical days as an undergraduate. The collapse of this bankrupt system did not have to be an embarrassment for the Western Left. One could even argue that the failure of communism supported Marx's claim that socialism had to emerge in the most advanced capitalist countries. To this day I think that Marx was right—that socialism as he envisioned it could only have succeeded in the most developed capitalist countries—and that Leninism was a complete distortion of Marxism. The fact is, however, that socialism in the Soviet Union failed not only because it was imposed from above on an underdeveloped country but also because the planned economy had basic, irremediable flaws. The socialist dream, which had motivated my research from my undergraduate days through my ascension to a tenured position in a leading sociology department, was dead. What was I going to do now?

What I did was to continue my work but shift my focus away from politics toward the economy. I was no longer motivated by political questions, and the discipline of sociology seemed to have lost interest in studying corporate power in any case. Virtually all research on inequality was now focused on the issues of race and gender, areas in which the debates contained more ambiguity for me than did the earlier debates on class. Although I certainly consider myself sympathetic to the rights of historically excluded groups, I have significant differences with many radical sociologists and activists in these areas in terms of the means by which these problems should be rectified. I often find myself on what is deemed as the conservative side, despite the fact that within the larger society my views would probably be considered liberal. This sense of dissonance has hastened my retreat from politics.

THE EFFECT OF MY RESEARCH ON MYSELF

To this point I have focused primarily on how my political views and life experiences affected my research. At the same time, my scholarship had significant effects on my worldview, including my politics. Although as I argued earlier, I had tried to be careful in my work even in my earlier, more political days, my work was becoming increasingly less political. In speaking more to the mainstream of the discipline, I was having growing success. This increasing success may have influenced my growing conservatism. A number of scholars who had become eminent academics in the post–World War II period had been radicals during the 1930s but became significantly more conservative in later years. One prominent explanation for these scholars' increasing conservatism was that it was a function of their career success, which allowed them to live comfortable existences and gave them a stake in preserving the system from which they benefited.[11] Is it possible that the same thing was happening to me? This was not a thought I relished.

I should note that when I say I became increasingly conservative, I do not mean that I became *a* conservative. What it meant instead was that I had become less of a radical and more of a liberal. I was also more willing to entertain and consider the tenability of conservative ideas. In fact, perhaps my biggest change was that I no longer felt committed to a particular political perspective. Rather, my concern now was with trying to understand the world from as detached a perspective as possible. I am not so naive as to believe that it is possible for a social scientist to be entirely objective. I do believe, however, that the less committed one is to a particular political perspective, the more credible are one's accounts of various social phenomena, other things being equal.

But back to my question: had I become more conservative because I was now benefiting from the system I had previously criticized? I will not deny that this is at least part of the explanation. The center does look different from the inside. It is more complex, less monolithic, and people are far more sensitive and thoughtful than we were led to believe as radical graduate students. I certainly felt little reason to criticize either the discipline of sociology or my universities, first Columbia and later Michigan, from which I was not only benefiting but also had come to love. I will not go so far as to say that the world of sociology is a pure meritocracy, but I discovered that the field is far more meritocratic than I had originally thought. I came to the view that much of the critical work that is rejected from the leading journals is rejected not because of political bias but for two other reasons: first, most work of all types is rejected at the top journals; and second, much of this critical work does not meet the standards of logic and evidence that good social science requires. I have become a strong defender of evaluation criteria that would probably be described as conventional or traditional. And I have become a fierce critic of postmodernism, which I unfortunately must concede has clear roots in certain tenets of the Marxism I so admired.

There is much more to my increasing conservatism than simple economic and positional self-interest, however. I suspect that, as for many others, world events and political experiences have also played an important role. There are events, for example, that affected me on a social-psychological level. There was the disillusionment and sense of betrayal I began to feel as one myth after another crumbled. The workers weren't going to revolt; that became evident quite early. Revolutionary Cuba, China, and Vietnam were horribly repressive societies in which I would not have wanted to spend five minutes. This realization was also evident to me before I entered graduate school. Other realizations came later. Communism was not a legitimate economic system that just happened to be saddled with a repressive political apparatus. It was an unworkable system even in economic terms, rife with corruption and incapable of satisfying even the most basic human needs. I became skeptical of the views of committed activists of any stripe, concerned that they tended to ignore or suppress evidence that failed to confirm their assumptions. My increasing desire to examine issues in their fullest complexity, which flowed directly from my experiences in doing research, may have been the single most important factor in my growing conservatism.

HOW HAS THIS AFFECTED MY WORK AND MY CURRENT VIEWS?

Most sociologists I have known work on projects for which they have great passion. Even those who are able to suspend their views to examine issues in a detached fashion, that is, those I respect the most, tend to care deeply about the topics they study. Some scholars are driven by a single overriding question throughout their careers. As long as their projects continue to yield unresolved problems, they can continue on these studies in perpetuity. The project I have described here—my attempt to understand the structure and behavior of the American capitalist class—provided a continuing stream of research questions from my early days of graduate school in the late 1970s through my ascendance to a full professorship in the early 1990s. The concerns that motivated me in this quest are simply not salient any more. The relative conservatism of the American working class is irrelevant: socialism is dead. In fact, it is not clear to me whether the working class is even a meaningful category at this point in history. Large corporations do have disproportionate influence in American politics, and this continues to raise concerns about the character of American democracy. I would certainly support efforts to curb their power, but I have little faith that such efforts would be successful. Economic globalization has become a focal point of protest against American capital, but although I share many of the protestors' goals, I have concerns about some of them as well.

The heartfelt political concerns that motivated my long-term project are therefore confined to my personal dustbin of history. I continue to study American business, but my goals are much more of this world. I examine the effects of inter-and intrafirm social networks on firms' and individuals' economic behavior.[12] I have studied the ways in which organizational scholars have ignored issues of power and coercion in their work (a study that retains at least a modicum of my earlier critical perspective.[13] And I am also examining the globalization of American banking, although not to criticize its political implications but to try to understand it as an organizational strategy. I make no apologies for the political commitments that informed my earlier work. Although some parts of those works now make me cringe, in general I am proud of the scholarship they contain. The quality of my current work I see as far beyond that of the earlier material, however, even if (or perhaps because) the political passion that motivated my early work is no longer there.

As for my political views, in my radical days I often felt that the weight of the world was on my shoulders. If there were problems in the world, it was important that I was strongly engaged, even if that engagement was only on an emotional level. As I developed more sober, and subtle, political views, I felt liberated. I no longer had to judge every political event in terms of whether it furthered the revolution. That has made it much easier to analyze and understand political issues. I sometimes miss the feeling of commitment that drove my earlier research. I do not miss the baggage that went with it. I prefer my current situation, in which pure intellectual curiosity plays the primary role in motivating my work.

NOTES

1. Louis D. Brandeis, *Other People's Money* (Washington, D.C.: National Home Library Foundation, 1933), 33.

2. Arnold M. Rose, *The Power Structure* (New York: Oxford University Press, 1967), 33.

3. Ibid., 92.

4. Beth Mintz and Michael Schwartz, *The Power Structure of American Business* (Chicago: University of Chicago Press, 1985).

5. Mark S. Mizruchi, *The American Corporate Network, 1904–1974* (Beverly Hills, Calif.: Sage, 1982).

6. Howard Becker refers to the "so what?" question in his book *Writing for Social Scientists: How to Start and Finish Your Thesis, Book, or Article* (Chicago: University of Chicago Press, 1986. I had begun using the term before the publication of Becker's book, but others undoubtedly had used the term long before I had.

7. Mark S. Mizruchi, "Who Controls Whom? An Examination of the Relation Between Management and Boards of Directors in Large American Corporations," *Academy of Management Review* 8 (1983): 426–35.

8. Jeffrey Pfeffer and Gerald R. Salancik, *The External Control of Organizations* (New York: Harper & Row, 1978).

9. See, for example, Mark S. Mizruchi, "Similarity of Political Behavior Among Large American Corporations," *American Journal of Sociology* 95 (1989): 401–24.

10. Mark S. Mizruchi, *The Structure of Corporate Political Action* (Cambridge, Mass.: Harvard University Press, 1992).

11. See, for example, Alvin W. Gouldner, *The Coming Crisis of Western Sociology* (New York: Avon, 1970).

12. See, for example, Mark S. Mizruchi and Linda Brewster Stearns, "Getting Deals Done: The Use of Social Networks in Bank Decision-Making," *American Sociological Review* 66 (2001): 647–71.

13. Mark S. Mizruchi and Lisa C. Fein, "The Social Construction of Organizational Knowledge: A Study of the Uses of Coercive, Mimetic, and Normative Isomorphism," *Administrative Science Quarterly* 44 (1999): 653–83.

WILLIAM H. FRIEDLAND

5

SEARCHING FOR ACTION

RESEARCH AND TEACHING

Although I came from a background of social consciousness, I missed the Great Depression (being too young) but grew up in its wake, an experience augmented by the rise of Nazism and fascism, the civil war in Spain, and the drama of the Roosevelt years. In high school I had an orientation toward social change, but my political consciousness was still unformed. At the same time, an inherent caution, as well as the geographical isolation of growing up in Staten Island (the most rural borough of New York City), precluded being captured by any of the radical political organizations and movements of the 1930s.

Upon graduation from high school in January 1940, I was little interested in academic life, instead choosing to enter a small Lutheran college on Staten Island, where another new student, himself recently recruited to Trotskyism, brought me into his political orbit. World War II had recently begun, and I found myself recruited to a wing of Trotskyism, led by Max Shachtman, which rejected Trotsky's unshakable commitment to the defense of the Soviet Union. I thus entered one of the splits in Marxism that required me and my comrades to become proletarianized (learn how to operate a lathe) and colonized (abandon Staten Island for Detroit). Detroit (and similar industrial centers), our leadership was convinced (and convinced me), would become the Petrograd of America when the contradictions of capitalism and the war came to full fruition.

Between 1940 and 1953, I witnessed and participated in war production, union activism, and the postwar offensive of American labor. I saw United Automobile Worker (UAW) militancy diverted from our revolutionary expectations to mundane wages and benefits. The speedup in the auto shops was relentless as the UAW leadership abandoned the shop floor for expanded benefits. In addition, McCarthyism had been invented and penetrated not only my Trotskyist party but also everyday life on the shop floor. Disappointed and burned out, I left the party, the UAW, and the United States for Europe, originally intending never to return.

This was not an easy decision. I had been, by then, an experienced shop worker, a shop steward and union activist. I had worked as the assistant education director of the Michigan CIO (Congress of Industrial Organizations) Council and as an engineering representative of the UAW. During the war, along with thousands of UAW members, my comrades and I had been participants in the struggle against the wartime no-strike pledge and, in the postwar, had participated in the capture of the UAW by Walter Reuther and his social-democratic and Catholic faction.

Europe only continued my disenchantment; for a leftist, one was forced to choose between the nightmare of Stalinism or the weak leftism of social democracy.[1] By 1954, I was completely burned out, deciding that the United States might be a pot of shit, but it was *my* pot of shit. I returned with the intention of getting a doctorate and hiding in some academic nook. I returned to university studies, got my degree, and took my first faculty appointment in the School of Industrial and Labor Relations (ILR) at Cornell, where for the first several years I avoided all activism. Avoidance ended with the onset of the student rebellion in 1964. With the demands of radical students for "relevance," I had to reconcile a reviving interest in social action with the demands of academic life. This led to a search for clarity about action research and teaching: how could I integrate teaching responsibilities with the research and publication demands of the university while, at the same time, undertaking activity with a social action trajectory?

After writing several papers for myself and the ILR faculty, I found my format: I would recruit undergraduates to a seminar on field study in the spring, feed them into migrant labor camps as agricultural workers during the summer, and engage them in an analysis seminar in the fall where they would digest their experiences academically. Thus was born the Cornell Migrant Labor Project (CMLP).

The arrival of a wandering United Farm Workers (UFW) organizer interested in organizing the migrant workers at Cornell's demonstration Cohn Farm, operated by the College of Agriculture, panicked Cornell's personnel director. Invited by him to formulate a proposal to deal with "the problem," Dorothy Nelkin, my research associate, and I proposed using the farm as an experimental site for dealing with agricultural labor issues. Although this seemed a useful approach to some Cornell administrators, the dean of the College of Agriculture trumped our proposal by bulldozing the migrant housing on the farm. The lesson was that there was little interest within the agricultural science establishment in exploring human and social relations in the agricultural industries.

I had gone on sabbatical leave in 1967–68 at Stanford University where I had researched agricultural labor in California.[2] This included several back-breaking days while working with a short-handled hoe (*el cortito*) as a stoop laborer, planting celery seedlings and weeding lettuce. It taught me that my instincts in using undergraduates as field researchers were accurate—I was too old and unused to such labor for personal participant observation. My seven years in the automobile shops had not prepared me for agricultural labor. The California experience, nevertheless, gave me an entirely new perspective on agriculture.

I had hitherto been focused exclusively on the use and exploitation of agricultural labor. In California, Cesar Chavez was successfully building the United Farm Workers (UFW) union, and workers' organization had to be understood. But California agriculture was very different from eastern agriculture; if one wanted to understand California agricultural workers, it was necessary to understand the different production systems with which workers were involved. Table grape workers, for example, didn't harvest lettuce, and although some lettuce workers might gain upward mobility by moving to strawberries, production systems were discrete and largely self-contained in production techniques, technical specialization, labor, and growers' organization. My experience in industry and with industrial sociology now became very relevant.

While on sabbatical I met Arlie Hochschild, who had just been recruited to the University of California, Santa Cruz (UCSC). My wife and I had earlier visited UCSC and departed without even getting out of our car. We felt that Cornell was centrally isolated; it was equally distant from any place you wanted to be, but Santa Cruz was even more remote. Arlie disabused me of that notion and a link was made to sociologists at UCSC, where I was invited to talk about the Cornell project.

At that time, UCSC was in its first years of operation. It had opened to students when the Berkeley uprising began. Santa Cruz students were the pick of the crop of California's high schools—brilliant, capable of incredible bursts of energy, kooky, and in some cases positively weird. Many, enthralled by the idea of relevance and the world beyond the university, were going off campus and getting academic credit for field studies, some of which beggared the imagination of their professors. The UCSC faculty was reluctant to suppress these undisciplined ventures but wanted some way to ensure academic legitimacy. The Cornell Migrant Labor Project provided suggestions for building a field study program that would have strong academic qualities and engage student interests in the real world.

I was recruited to UCSC to initiate a new department, Community Studies. The department would have its own faculty and supervise a field-oriented program for undergraduates. Building on anthropological models, I developed a curriculum in which students would take a preparation course to introduce them to participant observation, keeping field notes, and identifying intellectual issues to be pursued in the field. The field period would be focused on social change, with students doing six-month, full-time, *attached* field study with organizations and community groups that had been underserved by the university, such as agricultural workers' organizations, health clinics aimed at poverty constituencies, War on Poverty organizations, and alternative education programs. At the end of the field period, students would take classes in analyzing field materials and writing a senior thesis. The thesis could take any form but had to be a tangible manifestation of the student's learning: for example, a standard social science analysis, a work of fiction or a collection of short stories, a training manual for the organization with which the student had done the field study, or some applied research for that organization. Students would conclude the program with an oral examination that included a person from the organization with which the student had worked.[3]

Community Studies provided a highly satisfying environment for teaching. Because of its field study orientation and focus on social change, it attracted dedicated students who wanted to do something in the real world. Teaching field research methods and how to define and work with intellectual ideas in action-oriented contexts proved exceptionally rewarding. Community Studies provided an opportunity to expose students to a host of social change ideas and approaches, from Marx to Mao, from Saul Alinsky to

Paolo Freire, as well as contrasting social change theorists, ranging from the Right to Left.[4]

Teaching in Community Studies was strongly associated with social change, but what about research? Here the situation was more difficult. Although our faculty members were dedicated to pursuing social change through our teaching and thereby shared a common mission, each of us had our own research areas. My interests in U.S. and California agriculture found little resonance with other faculty members, who were concerned with health problems of women in prisons or the spread of AIDS (autoimmune deficiency syndrome) in the United States and Mexico. Community Studies, while encouraging our individual action research, provided no substantive intellectual community.

In an attempt to overcome this separation of teaching and research, we developed a Second Curriculum in Community Studies. This consisted of offering a seminar on a focused research topic out of which a small group of students continued to work with the faculty member over the next year or so in researching that topic. Research involved work in the field, libraries, interviews, and so on and culminated in individual senior theses. I ran a succession of Second Curriculum projects on agriculture and one on organizing.

I experienced considerable frustration in finding a community of researchers interested in agricultural studies. Coming to Santa Cruz from an interdisciplinary setting in Cornell's ILR, I still identified strongly as a sociologist but found little interest in agriculture in American sociological circles. My agricultural research in California began to focus on two main topics: the social consequences of mechanized processing of tomatoes in California and some broader implications: how do agricultural scientists define their research agendas?

The mechanization of harvesting tomatoes had been the most rapid transition to complete mechanization of any agricultural commodity in U.S. agriculture and had been greeted in the literature as an amazingly successful transition that was yielding universal benefits. Given the relatively modest investment in research, the returns-to-research yields had been phenomenal. My industrial experience had taught me that when technology (capital) substituted for labor, workers usually bore the brunt of the transition. Only a single article by two agricultural economists hinted at the cost to workers of the transition, but aside from this the literature positively glowed with approval.

The tomato research was done in collaboration with Amy Barton, now a graduate student in sociology. Our study came to a very different conclusion from that of the literature,[5] showing not only that harvest workers had been decimated but also that a similar process had occurred with tomato growers.

These findings were later to become the basis for a suit against the University of California, which will be detailed below since it bears on the search for venues for action research.

By placing several students into field study with agricultural scientists at the University of California, Davis, I gained insights into the individual and social forces that produced research agendas of the scientists. Institutional connections based on long-established legislation provided the vital links between scientists and commodity organizations, in which large-scale growers provided not only the questions but also the material resources to conduct research. The institutional basis for agricultural research thus emerged as my social change problematic: how can institutions be restructured so that scientists would be less focused on increasing agricultural output and more focused on the social consequences of their research?

This led to several publications that grappled with new institutional arrangements: *Social Sleepwalkers* proposed the establishment of social impact assessment procedures in the University of California's agricultural division; *Production or Perish*, written with Tim Kappel, one of my undergraduate students, was a response to the state legislature's concerns with the failure of agricultural researchers to consider environmental and consumer issues.[6] It was shaped as a legislative intervention to redirect research goals toward social and environmental outcomes.

When the tomato-harvesting study was completed but before publication, Amy Barton and I followed agricultural research procedures by meeting with several Davis researchers, who had been principals in the harvesting research, to critique the manuscript. Our analysis held up under their scrutiny, but the agriculturists did not find it useful since it was a postfactum study. What, they asked, was its use as far as understanding what might occur in future technological transitions?

Lettuce workers were then organizing themselves into the United Farm Workers union, and two research projects were underway—at Davis and at a U.S. Department of Agriculture research station in Salinas—on resolving the technology for mechanized lettuce harvesting. We felt challenged to produce projections about the social consequences of such a transition.

Joined by Robert Thomas, another UCSC undergraduate, we began the research that culminated in *Manufacturing Green Gold*.[7] This monograph considered the *conditions* under which a transition to harvest mechanization might take place and the *consequences* that could be anticipated socially, economically, and politically.

Neither the University of California nor the state legislature paid much attention to our publications, but California Rural Legal Assistance (CRLA), a public-interest, war-on-poverty law firm, did. The firm, whose mission was to provide legal services to rural people, including agricultural workers, sought to formulate class-action suits that would have a wider impact on farmworkers' lives. For example, CRLA had ended the use of *el cortito*, the short-handled hoe that had destroyed the backs of countless farmworkers, thereby eliminating most stoop labor in California agriculture.[8]

Ralph Abascal, the genial but fierce general counsel of CRLA, had studied agricultural economics before committing himself to law. He was a widely read intellectual who had come across our tomato study and other publications by agricultural social scientists critical of existing social relations in agriculture. Abascal explored how CRLA might develop a class-action suit directed at the University of California's intimate relations with large-scale corporate agriculture in California.

During this period, as I searched for an intellectual community within which my agricultural interests might fit, I learned in 1978 about a meeting to be held one day prior to the annual meeting of the Rural Sociological Society (RSS). A cluster of young rural sociologists, many of whom had been formed intellectually during the turmoil of the 1960s and 1970s, were disturbed by the then-most-recent crisis in agriculture with its usual flushout of thousands of small family-based farms. They had organized a session at the University of California, Davis, to discuss the crisis.

This was my introduction to rural sociology, an area that I, like many mainstream sociologists, had avoided because I saw no value in focusing on the rural. Meeting with several dozen (mainly) rural sociologists in Davis, all interested in agriculture, I finally found a community of interest: social scientists focused on agriculture and concerned to understand the socioeconomic forces in agriculture and seeking to change them. But, if there was interest by some rural sociologists in agriculture, the RSS as a collectivity manifested little interest in agriculture itself. I found this an intellectual conundrum: how was it that rural sociology, formed originally as a result of the changes taking place in agriculture since the turn of the century, no longer manifested interest in agriculture? And what might be done about that?

This led to research in the sociology of knowledge: what had been the forces that had made agriculture an almost forbidden topic since the 1940s and led to several essays presented at professional meetings.[9] The organizational question became this: how can one encourage research by rural sociologists about agriculture? The organizational question came to the fore after the Davis meeting. Several of us, a few years later, organized an underground set of panels at the Guelph meeting of the RSS that were focused on the agricultural crisis.

Developments in the United States were accelerated by the organization of a working group on agriculture of the International Sociological Association (ISA). At its 1978 World Congress in Uppsala, we Americans met social scientists from a number of European countries with similar research and social action interests. The ISA and RSS aggregations were subsequently formalized as an ISA research committee and an RSS section, and they have provided continuing venues to report on agricultural research.

These networks proved valuable as CRLA explored ways to bring a class action that could have institutional consequences for the way in which publicly funded agricultural research got done. The University of California was sued by CRLA because its research produced concentration in agriculture and thus violated the intent of federal legislation that generated publicly funded agricultural research.

Because CRLA consciously integrated agricultural social scientists into their legal activity, we researchers were periodically called into meetings with Ralph Abascal and other CRLA attorneys and community workers to buttress the legal arguments with social science data. Relationships between researchers and the CRLA personnel were stimulating, positive, and encouraging. We had all had experiences with Cesar Chavez and the United Farm Workers. We were all sympathetic to the UFW but found it almost impossible to work with it on any continuing basis because of its inconsistencies.

In my first encounter with Chavez at Cornell, I had arranged for him to meet the migrant labor research group. Chavez's talk was impressive, but his follow-up left a bad taste. When he learned that I was researching migrant labor, he insisted that I leave Cornell and begin working full time for the UFW. Having freed myself from the discipline of the UAW and my Trotskyist party and now building an academic career and a family, I was hardly inclined to accept his suggestion.

This was typical of Chavez, who had little respect for research except as he defined some immediate problem that had to be resolved. At Santa Cruz, Chavistas would occasionally descend upon me with a request for some specific applied research that they needed instantly. I had formed the habit of mobilizing myself and my students to fulfill their requests. Inevitably, I found that research done earlier had been "lost" by the UFW and that there was no cumulative buildup of a research base. I could ignore the guilt trip about Chavez's current emergency, but I could not ignore the burnout and disappointment of students I sent into field study with the UFW.

Working with CRLA, focused on a concrete problem of social change, was far more rewarding. We academics came to respect the acumen of the lawyers and the CRLA community activists just as they respected our research. The suit against the university occupied most of a decade. The first trial, in which I sat for five days as an expert witness for the plaintiffs, went into mistrial. In the second trial, the judge, after having dismissed several of CRLA's charges, found for the plaintiffs and we researchers were again called into consultation by the attorneys to help formulate a remedy. Part of the remedy was reformulated from the proposal I had made years before in *Social Sleepwalkers*—that the university establish a procedure to require social impact statements for all publicly funded research and the creation of a university unit to evaluate the social impact statements at time intervals after the research was completed to develop the methodology of social impact assessment.[10] The university appealed the judge's ruling, and with the majority of the California Supreme Court appointed by a Republican governor and a Reagan U.S. Supreme Court, once the case was reversed in the first appeal CRLA abandoned additional appeals.

As an application of research to applied social change, the CRLA suit was rewarding. I found intellectual companionship and support from researchers and attorneys for my research. It was clear that making the long march through the institutions would be filled with disappointments, but struggling for change was rewarding in itself. At least it was better than supinely accepting what was happening in agriculture throughout the world. I also learned that research that I considered to be important, even if I had little idea of how it might be used practically, should be pursued. Despite a conscious attempt to generate action-research problematics, I recognized that it was the CRLA attorneys who had seen the action potential of the tomato research.

As a result of the tomato and lettuce research and participation in the Rural Sociological Society and International Sociological Association meetings, it became clear to me that modern capitalist agriculture was very different from the *gemeinschaftlich*, family-based agriculture that had once existed. Particularly because of the specialization in commodity production in California, modern capitalist agriculture consists of clusters of discrete production systems, each with its own patterns of organization, labor processes, labor forces, and organizations of growers and processors. Agriculture consists of sets of commodity systems, an approach based on earlier work by Ray Goldberg, an economist at the Harvard Business School.[11] Goldberg paid little attention to labor, an important aspect of my work. Building and elaborating on his work, I produced several publications on the methodology of commodity systems research.[12] The point was to get rural sociologists to start thinking about industrial systems rather than *gemeinschaftlich* social relations. Commodity chains, similar to my systems, were later elaborated theoretically and empirically by the Political Economy of the World System (PEWS).[13] French social scientists had also developed a similar approach, referring to *filières* (channels or networks), thus fitting together three similar approaches to commodity analyses.

Searching for and finding ways to live with academic mores and engaging in teaching and research related to egalitarian social change have not been simple, although finding a solution in teaching turned out to be relatively easy. However, this was the consequence of the program that was built at Santa Cruz, something that would have been impossible at Cornell, which was too institutionalized and reluctant to change whereas Santa Cruz was new and eager for experimentation.

Research was much more problematic. I don't believe I ever resolved the issue of how to make my research consciously relevant to social change activity. It was clear that a relationship to an external, socially active constituency was necessary, but I never was able to develop that relationship except with CRLA. This could, of course, be a personality defect or a product of my shying away from organizational attachments and organizational discipline as a result of my Shachtmanite and UAW experiences.

Perhaps more important, even though my research was useful in the CRLA suit against the University of California, I am aware that its practicality was realized by an attorney for CRLA rather than by me. My various attempts—to get the university to initiate social impact assessment procedures or to have the state legislature require the university to set social goals for its agricultural research—had no impact on their intended audiences.

Despite this, I feel little disappointment. The struggle goes on, and it will take many forms and experiments. Few will succeed, but occasionally some will, and from those successes we have to get our satisfaction. *The struggle is the message.*

NOTES

1. Perry Anderson captured the frustrations of leftists in Europe in this period in *Considerations on Western Marxism* (London: Verso, 1979).

2. On sabbatical at Stanford, I met Irving Louis Horowitz, who was also visiting. One day, standing in a crowded meeting of student rebels who were deciding what to do next, Horowitz and I caught each other's eyes and with a few hand signals agreed to write something about the student rebellion. This later emerged as Irving L. Horowitz and William H. Friedland, *The Knowledge Factory: Student Power and Academic Politics in America* (Chicago: Aldine, 1971).

3. For details on the Community Studies program, see William Friedland and Michael Rotkin, "Academic Activists: Community Studies at the University of California, Santa Cruz," in *Community and the World: Community Development, Education, and Global to Local Transformations*, ed. Torry Dickinson (forthcoming).

4. The early years at Santa Cruz also provided an opportunity to come to grips intellectually with my Trotskyist experiences. While still at Cornell, David Rindos, one of the students working in the migrant labor project, expressed his puzzlement at the obscurities of classical writers such as Marx, Lenin, and others about revolutionary activity. I explained that all revolutionary theory (in contrast to sociological theories of revolution) consisted of four major problematics: theories of the driving force (revolutions are also made by people who are experiencing exploitation, not just by revolutionaries), organization, mobilization, and future arrangements. Later, at Santa Cruz, I worked with Amy Barton, Bruce Dancis, Michael Spiro, and Michael Rotkin (the first three undergraduates and the last a graduate student) to flesh out the discussion with Rindos. We spent an intense and intensive summer, reading, debating, and writing what became William Friedland et al., *Revolutionary Theory* (Totowa, N.J.: Allanheld Osmun, 1982). This was a teaching-learning experience for all of us; we exhaustively explored the four areas to systematize what revolutionaries had to say about the process of making revolutions.

5. William H. Friedland and Amy E. Barton, *Destalking the Wily Tomato: A Case Study in Social Consequences in California Agricultural Research*, Research Monograph No. 15 (Davis: University of California, Department of Applied Behavior Sciences, 1975).

6. William H. Friedland, *Social Sleepwalkers: Scientific and Technological Research in California Agriculture*, Research Monograph No. 13 (Davis: University of California, Department of Applied Behavioral Sciences, 1975); William Friedland and Tim Kappel, *Production or Perish: Changing the Inequities of Agricultural Research Priorities* (Santa Cruz: University of California, Project on Social Impact Assessment and Values, 1979).

7. William H. Friedland, Amy E. Barton, and Robert J. Thomas, *Manufacturing Green Gold: Capital, Labor, and Technology in the Lettuce Industry* (New York: Cambridge University Press, 1981). Bob Thomas went on to the doctoral program at Northwestern, where he continued to pursue lettuce research, culminating in his book *Citizenship, Gender, and Work: Social Organization of Industrial Agriculture* (Berkeley: University of California Press, 1985).

8. Douglas L. Murray, "The Abolition of *El Cortito*, the Short-Handled Hoe: A Case Study in Social Conflict and State Policy in California Agriculture," *Social Problems* 30, 1 (October 1982): 26–39.

9. William H. Friedland, "Who Killed Rural Sociology? A Case Study in the Political Economy of Knowledge Production," paper read at the 1979 annual meeting of the Rural Sociological Society, William H. Friedland, "The End of Rural Society and the Future of Rural Sociology," *Rural Sociology* 47, 4 (1982): 589–608. The first paper remains unpublished, but parts were incorporated into the second.

10. I describe the process in "'Engineering' Social Change in Agriculture," *University of Dayton Review* 21, 1 (1991): 25–42.

11. Ray Goldberg, *Agribusiness Coordination: A Systems Approach to Wheat, Soybean, and Florida Orange Economies* (Cambridge, Mass.: Harvard University, Graduate School of Business Administration, 1968).

12. William H. Friedland, "Commodity Systems Analysis: An Approach to the Sociology of Agriculture," in *Research in Rural Sociology and Development: A Research Annual,* ed. Harry K. Schwarzweller, (Greenwich, Conn.: JAI Press, 1984) 221–35; William H. Friedland, "Reprise on Commodity Systems Analysis," *International Journal of Sociology of Agriculture and Food* 9, 1 (2001): 82–103.

13. For the PEWS theoretical formulation, see Terence Hopkins and Immanuel Wallerstein, "Commodity Chains in the World-Economy Prior to 1800," *Review* 10, 1 (1986): 157–70. For empirical treatments, see Gary Gereffi and Miguel Korzeniewicz, eds., *Commodity Chains and Global Capitalism* (Westport, Conn.: Praeger, 1994).

HOWARD SCHUMAN

6

FROM VIETNAM TILL TODAY

In November 1969, my wife and fourteen-year-old son set out on an overnight bus trip to Washington to join what turned out to be the largest protest ever held against the Vietnam War. Many of my friends and colleagues were also traveling to the capital for the same purpose. I shared their opposition to the war and felt the pull to participate, but at the same time I had vague doubts about the effects of such a mass demonstration. The doubts were not then based on any systematic look at data. But I had a sense that the demonstrators might be overestimating the extent to which the larger public would be positively influenced by such a protest.

For one thing, in a study done after the urban riots of 1967, it became evident that much of the public did not distinguish clearly between nonviolent civil rights protests and outright violence, so that even large demonstrations could backfire unless carefully carried out and carefully portrayed.[1] The media focus made a difference for the Southern civil rights movement only because the crude violence of segregationist officials and mobs contrasted so sharply with the peaceful demonstrations led by Martin Luther King Jr., and others. More generally, a decade of experience in survey research had convinced me that one should be very cautious about assuming that actions perceived in a certain light by one's own community would be seen in the same way by others coming from different backgrounds and with different preconceptions.[2] This is exactly the problem faced today by the United States in a world of huge differences in wealth, ethnicity, religion, and culture.

The upshot of these considerations—plus the practical need for someone to take care of our two younger children—was that I stayed home. I wished my wife success and promised to spend the time by trying to cast some light on how effective mass protests were against the war. So I spent the period of the Washington demonstration watching children, looking at TV coverage of the protest, and rummaging through old files for survey data on war-related attitudes. In retrospect, that politically motivated search provided the initial basis for a substantial article that appeared some three years later, "Two Sources of Antiwar Sentiment in America."[3] It also affected more indirectly the approaches to both content and method in much of my subsequent research.

My first step that November was to review Gallup polls and a few other scattered sources of opinion on the war. These immediately revealed some important facts about public opposition to the war, such as the unexpected finding that opposition to continued American involvement was strongest among the oldest and least educated citizens—those furthest in social background and lifestyle from campus protestors. In addition, the Gallup data had the advantage of offering answers to a variety of questions asked over a period of time, but they were also frustrating because it was not possible to do more detailed analysis—for example, to make sure that the age relation was not indirectly due to the well-known association of older age with less education. Since age and education are negatively correlated in the American and many other populations, their effects are easily confused. Any relationship involving one is more fully understood if the other can be held constant or controlled statistically.

I recalled that the Institute for Social Research had asked questions on Vietnam in its 1968 election study, and I began in my spare time to analyze these national data. The results of this analysis, plus the earlier review, led to a brown-bag talk on public attitudes toward the war. I traced the history of public opinion on the war and spelled out some unexpected correlations between attitudes and such social background factors as age, education, gender, and interest in news. Only indirectly did I attempt any general interpretation. At that point I learned that Philip Converse, one of the primary investigators in the 1968 election study, had separately developed somewhat similar results, and we talked about preparing a piece for broader distribution. Our idea was partly scholarly but equally practical—the two were not in any conflict. We felt that those who actively opposed the war and wanted to do something about it would gain from knowing more about the nature of mass opinion on the main issues.

Together Converse and I prepared an article and sent it to the magazine *Scientific American*, which seemed a good location for a serious but nontechnical discussion of public opinion on the war. The piece was accepted, revised, and published in June 1970, some eight months after the Washington demonstration—quite rapid as scholarly publications go.[4] It stresses the history and demographic correlates of Gallup-type questions about the war, but the last paragraphs adumbrate a more general emphasis that had begun to appear to me more significant than any of the specific findings. We began to see that public opposition to the war was largely pragmatic in nature, in contradistinction to the moral indignation so visible among my friends and colleagues.

Later that summer, on vacation in Maine, I tried to set down this conclusion in a straightforward way, writing what turned out to be the basis for the first several pages of "Two Sources of Antiwar Sentiment." My goal was now even more clearly practical—to communicate to antiwar leaders a fact not then much realized: if they hoped to lead larger public opposition to the war, they had to appeal to the public in its own terms. In particular, broader sentiment against the war was not coupled, as it was on campus, with criticism of the United States, its goals, or its actions in Vietnam, and such criticism tended to arouse defensive support of the president and his policies toward Vietnam. On the contrary, the main concerns of the public seemed to be that the loss of a great many American soldiers was not leading to victory in the war—in other words, a practical view of military action and its costs. I sent this popular summary to several magazines that reach the educated public, but none evinced any great enthusiasm for publishing it. Sadly, I filed the short paper away and turned to other matters.

But the basic idea stayed with me, and I occasionally talked about it to others. As I did, I realized that the evidence for the moral versus pragmatic distinction was too indirect and that additional data were needed. By now it was the spring of 1971, and I was involved in the planning for a large survey of the metropolitan Detroit population. At almost the last minute it became possible to include an open question on Vietnam, asking people for their reasons for opposition to the war—to let them speak in their own words. As useful as closed questions can be for survey analysis, at times it is important to capture more directly and with less preconception the thinking of the general public. To anchor this inquiry to some national standard, I made it a "why" follow-up to a Gallup closed question that had been repeated a number of times over the course of the war: "In view of the developments since we entered the fighting, do you think the United States made a mistake in sending troops to fight in Vietnam?" Those who said "Yes, it had been a mistake" were then asked, "Why would you say it was a mistake?" Thus the issue became the meaning of the word "mistake" and how it might differ in different parts of the population. (The Gallup closed question also had the advantage of allowing comparison of our Detroit data with findings for the general U.S. population, which fortunately showed national and Detroit responses to be quite similar.)

Over that summer we gathered the data that form the basis for much of "Two Sources of Antiwar Sentiment." However, coding the open-ended responses proved to be difficult. On the one hand, I and students working with me wished to include all possible reasons that could exemplify moral or pragmatic objection to the war, if only to test the hypothesis that the moral categories would turn out to be nearly empty. On the other hand, we did not wish to impose this framework arbitrarily on the data. We therefore read a large sample of responses to make certain that categories natural to the respondents were created, whether or not they fit the moral-pragmatic distinction. The standard overall code that resulted from these combined goals proved much too long, and we soon despaired of being able to categorize responses with the necessary reliability. Moreover, use of nondirective probes in the original "why" question had added to the common problem of open inquiries: the occurrence of more than one codable response in the same answer, usually with no clear order of importance. For a time it looked as though there was no way to reduce this rich mass of verbal material to a set of categories that could be summarized and analyzed quantitatively.

At that point I abandoned the attempt to create a single set of exhaustive and mutually exclusive categories into which each answer (or the first or most important response in each answer) could be coded. It seemed better, and certainly more feasible, to allow each total answer to be coded for all the relevant points it contained, without trying to decide which was more important to the respondent or whether one point was consistent with another. This led to a set of ten thematic codes, reported in "Two Sources of Antiwar Sentiment." Each total answer was examined in terms of each theme and coded for the absence or presence of that theme. If the theme was judged to be present, we allowed further subcoding into several mutually exclusive categories, but the ten overall themes themselves were not treated as mutually exclusive. For example, one thematic code concerned "people killed or injured by the war," and we coded respondents who mentioned anyone killed or injured in Vietnam as to whether (1) only Americans were mentioned, (2) only Vietnamese were mentioned, (3) both nationalities were mentioned, or (4) neither nationality was identified. If the theme itself was not mentioned at all (nothing said about people being killed or injured), the response was coded zero. This theme was entirely independent of coding in terms of other themes. The plan not only simplified considerably the task of the coders but also had the advantage of not forcing our own version of consistency on the respondents.

Near the end of the coding operation, I realized that the general population responses could be evaluated more clearly if they could be contrasted with antiwar student responses. Unfortunately, time and other resources did not allow for proper sampling in this case, so we used sociology classroom samples on the assumption that such students had by then been greatly influenced by the faculty-led protest activities and the campus newspaper columns that were strongly critical of the war. (My earlier study of the faculty had shown that antiwar attitudes were especially concentrated in the social sciences, with sociology one of the strongest centers of opposition.) But the more general point here is worth noting: a set of survey data (and other kinds of data as well) can often be illuminated as much by contrast with an external reference as by detailed internal analysis.

Without trying to summarize the entire article here, the moral-pragmatic difference did come through fairly clearly, though some modifications were called for. For example, three-quarters of the general public mentioned only American soldiers as casualties of the war, whereas three-quarters of the students mentioned both American soldiers and Vietnamese as casualties. Other themes also showed marked differences between the two samples, with the general public emphasizing that the war was a mistake because of the practical problems preventing victory; the students, however, though they also showed considerable concern about pragmatic difficulties, were much more likely to define "mistake" in moral terms, to oppose the goals of the war, and to regard U.S. actions as intervention in an internal civil conflict. Of course, there were exceptions on both sides—some in the general public spoke of "mistake" in moral terms, and some of the sociology students cited only practical difficulties—but overall the evidence pointed to the moral-pragmatic distinction as throwing a great deal of light on the basis of public doubts about the war and its distinction from the more visible protests centered on campuses and in antiwar demonstrations.

The article was completed in the early months of 1972, with some sense of time pressure because I still saw it as having some small practical effect on efforts to end the war. In fact, it probably had none at all and must be justified on the same intellectual grounds as most other sociological work. In that sense, its main contribution was probably methodological: emphasis on and analytic use of free responses to a broad, open-ended question. The fair success in working with such data certainly reinforced my own commitment to this approach to the measurement of attitudes and beliefs, as against the more common reliance on sets of simple, closed, attitude items. It also seemed to me to show that a survey could obtain some of the richness of a qualitative study while preserving the advantages of rigorous generalization to a larger population and the use of statistical analysis to clarify the effects of particular social background factors.

Furthermore, having the spontaneous answers of respondents allowed a later insight when I noticed that some respondents who thought the war a mistake referred to the United States as "we" ("we made a mistake getting into the war") and others as "they" ("they made a mistake getting into the war"). Stimulated by an earlier article by Brown and Gilman on the importance of apparently minor differences in grammatical form,[5] I decided to go back and code the "we"-"they" difference in pronoun usage as it appeared in the responses. Subsequent analysis showed that the difference correlated significantly with social background, especially the fact that blacks were more likely to use "they" than did whites. This was consistent with other data, as well as with commonsense observation, that blacks on average felt more alienation from the U.S. government than did whites.[6] Thus, having the open-ended responses allowed the development and testing of new hypotheses not thought of ahead of time.

Much of my own later research has drawn on this experience with thematic coding. For example, my article "Generations and Collective Memory" obtained the national and world events from the last half century that Americans believe to have been especially important, then followed this by asking respondents to explain their choice of events.[7] It turned out to be useful again to develop thematic codes, allowing more than one coding of a response and not insisting on consistency or mutual exclusiveness among the codes. Generally, the success with the Vietnam research supported my personal preference for letting respondents speak for themselves as far as possible, rather than relying on a set of forced-choice or other closed questions ahead of time. It is particularly useful to combine closed and open questions by asking "why" follow-up inquiries in order to encourage people to explain the thinking behind responses to a closed question.[8]

Beyond its concern with question and coding methodology, the analysis raised issues about the nature of recent American attitudes toward war in general, and I remain persuaded of the soundness of the basic argument, though perhaps not of every part. Although the antiwar movement of the 1960s and early 1970s had a strong moral emphasis, the larger public opposition to war grew mainly because of a concern over U.S. casualties and increasing doubts about the possibility of quick and relatively painless victory. It was not the moral protest against the war that turned American opinion and forced first Lyndon Johnson and then Richard Nixon to reduce and eventually end American military involvement. It was the resilience and success of the Viet Cong and the North Vietnamese that made the difference in convincing the public to turn against the war. It is even possible that the focus of some demonstrations and spokespersons on the evils of the United States prolonged the war by rallying support to the administration. Certainly the antiwar moral emphasis of the Democrats in the 1972 election did not gain many votes—Nixon won in a landslide.

Beyond Vietnam, attempts by critics of American policies to marshal public opinion against intervention in Central America were notably unsuccessful. It is most telling that at the time of the 1991 Gulf War, there was a strong attempt to warn the public about the danger of another Vietnam, and the warning aroused some support on the part of cohorts that had been especially marked by the Vietnam experience. Nevertheless, once it appeared that the United States would be successful—and, moreover, successful with almost no casualties—support for the war became overwhelming.[9] For the larger public, the key factors are victory and its cost, at least when the military actions are not seen as absolutely vital to national security.

Of course, consideration of the effects of antiwar demonstrations should take into account more than their immediate effects on mass attitudes. The consequences for both participants and onlookers are many and varied, manifest and latent, and these deserve a more rounded treatment than they received in "Two Sources of Antiwar Sentiment." Although I like to think that my decision to stay home in November 1969 was a useful one, the decision of my wife and others to journey to Washington had, I imagine, positive effects as well.

One final general point can be made about the relation between personal values and scientific method. As John Dewey liked to stress, it is appropriate, often useful, and perhaps inevitable that one's personal values play an important role in defining problems for investigation. At the same time, the scientific method offers guidelines for carrying out an investigation objectively; it provides tools for performance and analysis and, most of all, a framework that permits disconfirmation, as well as confirmation, of one's assumptions and preferred hypotheses. The actual connection between values and methods, however, is not always so simple as this conceptualization suggests. Thus "Two Sources of Antiwar Sentiments in America" provides one example of an attempt to balance the two in a way that is complementary and fruitful rather than antagonistic or subverting. Whether it was a successful attempt is for others to judge.

NOTES

1. Angus Campbell and Howard Schuman, "Racial Attitudes in Fifteen American Cities," *Supplemental Studies for the National Advisory Commission on Civil Disorders* (Washington, D.C.: U.S. Government Printing Office, 1968).

2. I had also been involved at an earlier point in a study of attitudes toward the war by the faculty of my own university, the University of Michigan. Despite its reputation as a site of protest against the war, to our surprise a careful survey found that a majority of the faculty supported continued bombing of North Vietnam at a point when that was the major issue facing the country. See Howard Schuman and Edward O. Laumann, "Do Most Professors Support the War?" *Trans-Action*, (November 1967, 32–35.

3. Howard Schuman, "Two Sources of Antiwar Sentiment in America," *American Journal of Sociology* 78 (1978): 513–36.

4. Philip E. Converse and Howard Schuman, "Silent Majorities and the Vietnam War," *Scientific American*, June 1970, 17–25.

5. See R. Brown R and A. Gilman, "The Pronouns of Power and Solidarity," in *Language and Social Context*, ed. P. P. Giglioi (Harmondsworth, England: Penguin, 1972), 252–82.

6. M. Richard Cramer and Howard Schuman, "We and They: Pronouns as Measures of Political Identification and Estrangement," *Social Science Research* 4 (1975): 231–40. For a more recent recognition of the importance of the "we"-"they" distinction, see Roy Rosenzweig and David Thelen, *The Presence of the Past: Popular Uses of History in American Life* (New York: Columbia University Press, 1998).

7. Howard Schuman and Jacqueline Scott, "Generations and Collective Memories," *American Sociological Review* 54 (1989): 351–81.

8. I did something like this at the beginning of my career as part of research in Bangladesh (then East Pakistan). See "The Random Probe: A Technique for Evaluating the Validity of Closed Questions," *American Sociological Review* 21 (1966): 218–22. One need not take respondent explanations entirely at face value, as Richard Nisbett and Timothy Wilson have argued in "Telling More Than We Can Know: Verbal Reports on Mental Processes," *Psychological Review* 84 (1977): 231–59. But such responses show how questions are interpreted by respondents and indicate the frame of reference within which answers are given.

9. Howard Schuman and Cheryl Rieger, "Historical Analogies, Generational Effects, and Attitudes Toward War," *American Sociological Review* 57 (1992): 315–26. This research is presently being replicated.

JOHN WALTON

_7_

MAKING PROBLEMS

REFLECTIONS ON EXPERIENCE

AND RESEARCH

The writer who is to be anything more than an echo of his predecessors must always find expression for something which has never yet been expressed, must master a new set of phenomena which has never yet been mastered. With each such victory of the human intellect, whether in history, in philosophy or in poetry, we experience a deep satisfaction: we have been cured of some ache of disorder, relieved of some oppressive burden of uncomprehended events.

—Edmund Wilson, "The Historical Interpretation of Literature"

Edmund Wilson's[1] observation about writing history, philosophy, or poetry applies as well to social science. The great critic and author of _To The Finland Station_[2] captures something fundamental about sociological practice as a creative act—or so, at least, it seems to me when I reflect on why we do this kind of work, what deep-down urge drives our activity, and what we hope to accomplish when the work is done. This is not to deny the importance of other perfectly good motives for doing social science, particularly at the university, including decent wages, hours, working conditions, and more deference than we really deserve. We are social scientists because it is a good job. But we, or let me just say I, derive something more from the work, some deeper "ache of disorder" and satisfaction with its cure. Wilson's metaphor might be translated as an awareness of disquieting but tractable questions about society and the rewarding challenge of their solution. That, for me, is how the personal and the professional interact.

It was not always so. The ache of disorder and satisfaction of comprehension are ways of experiencing sociological work that came to me slowly as the result of a series of projects and successive reflections on the accomplishments and limitations of each. I had to learn how to formulate sociological problems as a condition of appreciating their satisfactory solution when it appeared. And I am still learning, still vexed in each new project by "what is the problem?"

Yet one's evolving problem sense begins somewhere. For me, it began in the late 1950s when I entered college and soon exited, at UCLA. I came to the university with little sense of purpose, floundered in youthful debauchery and an ill-conceived course of study, and after a year found myself menially employed in the southern California aircraft industry. So began my search for what we used to call a "rewarding career." What *did* I want to study? How was I to get out of the defense plant and into some fulfilling line of work?

Los Angeles in the late 1950s was a lively place, a new kind of city, prototype of suburban sprawl, capital of a popular culture industry with global reach, and for all the ridicule of its goofy lifestyles, a notably rich and accessible public culture. It was a place in which people of modest means could participate in a democratic cultural life without intimidation or restriction of privilege. Public educational facilities from junior (now community) colleges to the state university were abundant and open. Listener-sponsored radio featured programs in the arts and lectures by public intellectuals. An unremarkable week in the life of an aircraft mechanic might include night school at Valley J.C., a lecture on sane nuclear policy by Linus Pauling, a Van Gogh exhibit at the county museum, and a coffee-house appearance by Joan Baez. The popular novelist Leon Uris opened a book store in my San Fernando Valley neighborhood and schmoozed with regular customers, particularly when he approved their selection of titles such as C. Wright Mills's *The Power Elite*.[3] Uris loved Mills, calling him "such a trenchant writer."

I returned to university gradually, via the tolerant community and state college systems, on the strength of a nascent interest in social science. To be more precise, I returned in the hope of finding an engaging career line that involved the social issues raised in a burgeoning (slick, inexpensive paperback) literature that examined the social world in a new way. Erich Fromm's *Escape from Freedom*,[4] for example, which described how people could abandon their individuality to enthralling mass movements in times of social dislocation, seemed to me powerful, cogent, and most important, an altogether new way of comprehending the world—through social science, new to me but also new to the popular repertoire of work for which one could train. I felt the same fascination for contemporary works like William H. Whyte's *The Organization Man*[5] and Gordon Allport's *The Nature of Prejudice*.[6] They described the world in ways I recognized, and they did it as a craft, a research method that was actually taught at the university. Indeed, at UCLA the sociologist Melville Dalton had written *Men Who Manage*,[7] a book about the organizational life of a chemical firm, which impressed me mightily as a perfect description of the aircraft plant where I had worked. Soon I would discover the same verisimilitude in an article by Joseph Bensman and Israel Gerver on "Crime and Punishment in the Factory," in Erving Goffman's *Asylums*, and in Gresham Sykes's *Society of Captives*,[8] as compared those studies with places where I had worked during graduate school. Social science was hip—hip to the commodification of suburbia, the inner workings of corporations, and the underlife of institutions. These academic writers knew how people cheat on the assembly line or revenge the indignities of institutional discipline. Today, forty years later, I still recall how vividly all this impressed me, how intrigued I became with this kind of work and the possibility that I might be able to do it.

The work fascinated me for its craft and cogency, but equally for its edge. Sociology challenged conventional wisdom and its ways of knowing. It was "debunking," in Peter Berger's phrase.[9] From the vantage of the public university in populist Los Angeles, sociology seemed the perfect antidote to elite pretension, a demonstrable claim to knowledge as a public good. Social science was "radical" in the literal sense of getting to the root of things. It was democratic in practice and result. In the iconic figures of Mills or Veblen, it also smacked of rebellion. I liked everything about it.

For the next six years, I learned sociology in peripatetic fashion, moving from the California state college system (Northridge) back to UCLA and then on to Berkeley and Santa Barbara, looking for an encouraging program and discovering in the process the many varieties of "standard" sociology. Garfinkel's theory at UCLA bore no resemblance to the theory of Bendix or Smelser at Berkeley, which was not too surprising, but even statistics and methods were worlds apart on the same coastline—a useful early lesson in canonicity. With the encouragement of David Gold and a generous NIMH (National Institute of Mental Health) fellowship at Santa Barbara, I took up a dissertation topic that mirrored the interests that attracted me to the field.

Floyd Hunter's *Community Power Structure*[10] was another sociological classic that combined insight and method, a radical way of examining American politics at the tractable local level and a challenge to notions of bourgeois piety. Hunter had devised a way of identifying the big shots who ran "Regional City" (Atlanta), often behind the scenes and in the narrow interests of business. Hunter's (reputational) method inspired legions of imitators and critics. Indeed, as my dissertation proved, the community power controversy came to center more on the ideologies and associated research methods of social scientists than it did on the nature of local democracy. Lost in the academic controversy was Hunter's argument that Alinsky-style community organizing was naive and ineffective in contrast to a scientifically informed strategy of social change that identified and targeted the levers of power. In a series of works that followed, I wrestled with questions about power—how to identify its many forms, what difference they made, and whether democracy worked. The dissertation landed me some journal publications and a good job at Northwestern University. Suddenly I *was* a sociologist rather than a mere admirer.

All this took place at a unique historical moment, although few of us understood fully at the time just how history was shaping our careers. We were on the crest of a wave of university expansion and democratization in higher education. Louis Menand notes:

> In the Golden Age, between 1945 and 1975, the number of American undergraduates increased by almost 500 percent and the number of graduate students increased by nearly 900 percent. In the 1960s alone enrollments more than doubled, from 3.5 million to just under 8 million; the number of doctorates awarded annually tripled; and more faculty were hired than had been hired in the entire 325-year history of American higher education to that point.[11]

Social science was a leading sector in the expansion measured by growing student enrollments, faculty, doctorate programs, and published research. Research became the key quality standard and income source of universities. Social science in its contemporary, largely university-based form, was created in this period by those broader historical changes that defined the period: post–World War II recovery, welfare state expansion, social mobility and professionalization, and the equality revolution. This was not only the history that created modern sociology; it was also, for those of us who entered the university at the time, an instance of what Mills called the "intersection of history and biography,"[12] the proper subject matter of sociology itself and the essence of the sociological imagination. Our careers were shaped by the same historical processes we made a career of researching. Mills, and later Alvin Gouldner,[13] recognized the reflexive nature of sociology as a uniquely human activity in which we examine the social world through a lens that can, and should, be turned on ourselves. The objective is not primarily to understand ourselves in this fashion also but to understand society and our relationship to it as actors and observers.

The point, then, is that my sociological work and its satisfactions depend on making tractable problems—formulating consequential questions and generating new knowledge bearing on their solution. I think this is true for other practitioners and describes our method of operation. This is what distinguishes sociology from journalism, history, or poetry. This is what Karl Marx did when he asked, "Where does value come from?"[14] and turned to human labor in the production of commodities for an answer. This is how Max Weber began *The Protestant Ethic and the Spirit of Capitalism*, in a section entitled "The Problem":

> A glance at the occupational statistics of any country of mixed religious composition brings to light with remarkable frequency a situation . . . namely, the fact that business leaders and owners of capital, as well as the higher grades of skilled labor, and even more the higher technically and commercially trained personnel of modern enterprises, are overwhelmingly Protestant.[15]

It is what Ralf Dahrendorf had in mind when he urged that sociological work begin with a "sense of puzzlement, [a] problem-conscious"[16] attitude.

For years, I have tried to develop this problem sense in my own research and to pass it along to students by describing my experience with various research projects. Let me illustrate with a study begun in 1992 and recently published as *Storied Land: Community and Memory in Monterey*.[17] The inquiry started with a general question about history and its social representation: how history is publicly understood and portrayed in texts, monuments, museums, art, and commemorative practices. My interest was concerned not so much with formal or academic history as with what Carl Becker calls "the history that common people carry around in their heads."[18] It is well known that history is often represented selectively, that it propagates myths and revisionist versions of events. How and to what extent does that happen? The question puzzling me involved not only the social construction of history but also the effects of that process—how society is shaped by beliefs about the past.

I came across this problem in an earlier study of an environmental movement in which groups invented a particular version of their history in the process of mobilizing a struggle to preserve their community.[19] The past was socially constructed in the present to achieve group goals in the future. Perhaps I had uncovered a specific instance of a general phenomenon. How did this thing work in other times and places? I wanted to answer that question in a study tailored to the purpose. Where was I to start?

As it turns out, explanations are available for the selective representation of history in popular culture. The most vivid example I recall occurs in the strife-torn communities of Belfast in northern Ireland. Throughout Ireland, particularly in the North and dramatically between 1969–94, conflicts stemming from British colonial occupation, religious differences, and social inequality have generated a violent struggle over civil rights and sovereignty. The Falls Road community of West Belfast is home to many of the Catholic and republican victims of this struggle. The Falls is also a center of resistance and, lately, of a peace process initiated in 1994. Like nearby Protestant areas, the neighborhood streets of the Falls are adorned with large murals that celebrate the struggle and its martyrs. One of the more artful of these murals proclaims, "History Is Written by the Winners." The message seems unambiguous. British colonialism dominates the area, oppresses its people, and silences their struggle by controlling the historical record. Yet if we step back from the literal message and consider the social milieu, a more nuanced meaning appears. The mural is protest art—colorful, striking, and politically engaged. It is a vital part of the record. It says, "Our history has been silenced, we protest, and we intend to do something about it." The sociological version of this idea is that powerful interests in society typically control the representation of history, but they are not dominant or immune to challenges from below.

In fact, sociologists have raised this general question previously with the concept of collective memory.[20] The term derives from Maurice Halbwachs,[21] a follower of Émile Durkheim and an early exponent of the notion that societies have memories embedded in their language and thought that predate and shape individual memories. Since Halbwachs's original work in the 1930s, a number of subsequent writers have expanded the idea of historical memory: how the past is selectively remembered and, indeed, why history itself is less an objective record of events than a collection of stories, narratives, about the past.[22] Yet, this literature takes us only part of the way. Repeated studies by sociologists, historians, and anthropologists tell us that history is socially constructed but they do not explain why it is. To be more precise, social scientists have advanced theories of how collective memory operates, but they have not subjected those theories to critical evaluation.

All sorts of speculative answers have been offered but not evaluated against their alternatives. In short, we are no better off than the Belfast muralist, who knows that powerful interests generally control but never monopolize history and that challengers can change it under certain circumstances.

Social theorists have developed explanations of this process that may be usefully grouped under two headings. One school of thought maintains that collective memory is a tool of social control, that the state and powerful interests ensure their political and economic control through insidious means of *cultural domination*.[23] The function of collective memory is to maintain order and legitimacy. Lloyd Warner develops the argument in his classic study of "Yankee City," a New England community dominated by a ruling group of business interests that revealed its cultural vision in the town's tercentennial celebration and parade. The historical event was an exercise in legitimization of the local elite who sponsored the production. "If they were to retain their own legitimacy it was mandatory for them to trace their ancestry to the very beginnings . . . for the maintenance of their position it was necessary to invent new myths and new expressive rituals to hold the power of the ancestors."[24]

Alternatively, a theory of *social memory* centers on the idea that groups form distinct memories through the agency of formative class, ethnic, gender, educational, occupational, spatial, and generational experiences.[25] Collective memory is less a matter of instrumental myths and ruling ideas than a plurality of mental worlds that may exist in conflict with or insularity from competing ideas.

Cultural domination and social memory represent two well-developed yet sharply contrasting explanations of how the past is represented. Although I benefited from reading this literature on collective memory, I was not much closer to an answer to my original question. Thinking about my own experience and earlier research, the theory of cultural domination did not work (people challenged power) and the theory of social memory seemed descriptive and overly general. The rich literature did prove useful, however, in helping me to reformulate my research question, which now became "How is public history constructed by contending groups and how does it change over time?"

The case study I selected to develop my own account of collective memory was the social construction of California history from the times of Spanish colonization to the present. As the result of previous work and early problem formulations, this case had been part of my thinking all along. Analytical questions and research methods move back and forth. The California case required more than mere selection. It needed refinement in light of the theoretical question. First, I needed detail, local knowledge that would reveal precisely how history is produced, by whom, under what conditions, and with what effects. Second, I needed to follow this process over a time span sufficient to identify the principal historical narratives and their evolution. Third, of course, I needed a place and a set of events that were well documented in the archival record and built environment. These methodological requirements indicated one solution: in California, only the Monterey area has a continuous, well-documented history, beginning with its settlement as the capital of Spanish California and evolving through Mexican sovereignty, American conquest, western settlement, industrialization, and the advent of a modern service economy—from stories of Father Junipero Serra's mission to John Steinbeck's Cannery Row. That is all true, but it is not the full story. In fact, when I began this study I was living on the Monterey Peninsula, engaged by its history and natural beauty and convinced that there was a sociological brief for combining the collective memory problem with the historical place.

The result of all this is available in *Storied Land*. I discovered, first, that I had to reconstruct the 230-year history of Monterey as accurately as possible before I would be able to explain why certain narratives had been developed in previous works and other voices silenced. If, as Michel-Rolfph Trouillot argues, history is a record of both what happened (events) and what is said to have happened (narratives),[26] then I needed to master materials on both levels. Next, I identified five periods in the historiography of Monterey: Spanish colony (1769–1821), Mexican territory (1821–46), American frontier (1846–1905), industrial town (1905–50), and modern city (1950–present). Each period displayed a distinct configuration of events and pattern of historical representation. The Spanish period, for example, witnessed the failure of a viable colony but also the creation of a hagiographic missionary narrative that portrayed Franciscan priests as a civilizing force among Native-American barbarians. The missionary narrative had its critics among English and French commercial voyagers and doubtless among the Indians themselves, whose voice was silenced but whose resistance crops out of the missionary and archaeological records. Following U.S. conquest in 1846, one dominant narrative of American progress repudiated the colonial past in self-congratulatory accounts of settlement that papered over extermination of the Indian population and growing class inequalities. For a time, the theory of cultural domination worked. At the turn of the twentieth century, however, a prosperous fishing and canning industry developed in Monterey, supporting new historical narratives that represented, on the one hand, propertied interests in a story of the romantic Spanish past and, on the other hand, a new working-class narrative typified in Steinbeck's popular novel *Tortilla Flat*.[27] Today the region has been transformed from industry to a service economy of higher education, marine research, and tourism. New histories revolve around environmentalism and ethnic heritage, reflecting both national trends and local enterprise.

Theoretically, these results suggest that both the theory of cultural domination and social memory have merit. Each captures part of the broader historical experience, moments of its evolution. Yet neither really resonates with the process in which history is socially constructed by acting groups. Missing in these general explanations are grounded accounts of how historical actors and narrators actually behave, how they interact in real situations, and how they construct history. A theory of public history centered on collective action remedies these problems. Collective memory in general and public history in particular are social processes, social worlds like others that are usefully conceived as organized ensembles of collective action.[28]

The study demonstrates that the construction and maintenance of historical narratives is a contested, chancy, changing process. Narratives have pragmatic origins. They are produced by groups with an agenda. Public history is constructed, in the main, not for the purposes of posterity or objectivity but for the aims of present action (conquest, social reform, building, political reorganization, and economic transformation). Narratives make claims for the virtues of their individual and institutional authors, often as counterpoint to rival claimants. They characterize the past in certain ways for the purpose of shaping the future. The ability of narratives to effect change depends in the first instance on their institutional power, whether they are produced by a powerful church, conquering state, fledgling town, or contending voluntary associations. Whatever their origins, the effects of historical narratives depend on history itself, on the interplay of actors, social circumstances, and situational contingencies. History must be understood as an amalgam of events and narratives—what happened and what is said to have happened inseparably connected in a moving social process. In *Through The Looking Glass*,[29] the White Queen says to Alice, "It's a poor sort of memory that only works backwards." Studies of collective memory show that this seeming paradox in fact describes how the past is represented in the present for future purposes.

With this Alice-in-Wonderland or collective-action theory of the socially constructed past, I had reached a satisfying answer to my question. The ache of disorder was relieved, the burden of uncomprehended events lifted. Others must judge whether my explanation of collective memory satisfies their questions. I hope it does.

NOTES

1. Edmund Wilson, "The Historical Interpretation of Literature," in *Critiques and Essays in Criticism, 1920–1948*, ed. R. W. Stallman (New York: Ronald Press, 1949).

2. Edmund Wilson, *To the Finland Station: A Study in the Writing and Acting of History* (New York: Anchor Books, 1940).

3. C. Wright Mills, *The Power Elite* (New York: Oxford University Press, 1956).

4. Erich Fromm, *Escape from Freedom* (New York: Farrar and Rinehart, 1941).

5. William H. Whyte, *The Organization Man* (New York: Anchor Books, 1957).

6. Gordon Allport, *The Nature of Prejudice* (New York: Anchor Books, 1954).

7. Melville Dalton, *Men Who Manage* (New York: Wiley, 1959).

8. Joseph Bensman and Israel Gerver, "Crime and Punishment in the Factory: The Function of Deviancy in Maintaining the Social System," *American Sociological Review* 28 (August 1963): 588–98; Erving Goffman, *Asylums: Essays on the Social Situation of Mental Patients* (New York: Anchor Books, 1961); Gresham Sykes, *The Society of Captives: A Study of a Maximum Security Prison* (New York: Atheneum, 1965).

9. Peter Berger, *Invitation to Sociology* (New York: Anchor Books, 1967).

10. Floyd Hunter, *Community Power Structure: A Study of Decision Makers* (New York: Anchor Books, 1953).

11. Louis Menand, "College: The End of the Golden Age," *New York Review of Books*, October 2001, 44.

12. C. Wright Mills, *The Sociological Imagination* (New York: Oxford University Press, 1959), 5–7.

13. Alvin Gouldner, *The Coming Crisis of Western Sociology* (New York: Basic Books, 1970).

14. Karl Marx, *Capital, V. 1* (New York: Vintage Books, 1978).

15. Max Weber, *The Protestant Ethic and the Spirit of Capitalism* (New York: Scribner, 1958), 35.

16. Ralf Dahrendorf, "Out of Utopia: Toward a Reorientation of Sociological Analysis," *American Sociological Review* 64 (September 1959): 123.

17. John Walton, *Storied Land: Community and Memory in Monterey* (Berkeley: University of California Press, 2001).

18. Carl Becker, "What Are Historical Facts," in *Detachment and the Writing of History: Essays and Letters of Carl Becker*, ed. Phillip L. Snyder (Ithaca, N.Y.: Cornell University Press, 1958), 61.

19. John Walton, *Western Times and Water Wars: State, Culture, and Rebellion in California* (Berkeley: University of California Press, 1992).

20. Jeffrey K. Olick and Joyce Robbins, "Social Memory Studies: From 'Collective Memory' to the Historical Sociology of Mnemonic Practices," *Annual Review of Sociology* 24 (1998): 105–40.

21. Maurice Halbwachs, *The Collective Memory* (New York: Harper, 1980).

22. See Hayden White, *Metahistory: The Historical Imagination in Nineteenth-Century Europe* (Baltimore: Johns Hopkins University Press, 1973); Hayden White,

Tropics of Discourse: Essays in Cultural Criticism (Baltimore: Johns Hopkins University Press, 1978); David Lowenthal, *The Past Is Another Country* (Cambridge: Cambridge University Press, 1985); Michel-Rolph Trouillot, *Silencing the Past: Power and the Production of History* (Boston: Beacon Press, 1995).

23. See Antonio Gramsci, *Selections from the Prison Notebooks* (New York: International Publishers, 1971); Raymond Williams, *Marxism and Literature* (Oxford: Oxford University Press, 1977); Richard Maddox, *El Castillo: The Politics of Tradition in an Andalusian Town* (Champaign-Urbana: University of Illinois Press, 1993).

24. Lloyd Warner, *The Living and the Dead: A Study of the Symbolic Life of Americans*, Vol. 5, *Yankee City Series* (New Haven, Conn.: Yale University Press, 1959), 164.

25. James Fentress and Chris Wickham, *Social Memory* (Oxford: Blackwell, 1992).

26. Trouillot, *Silencing the Past*.

27. John Steinbeck, *Tortilla Flat* (New York: Covici, Friede [1935]).

28. Howard S. Becker, *Art Worlds* (Berkeley: University of California Press, 1982).

29. Lewis Carroll, *Alice's Adventures in Wonderland* and *Through the Looking-Glass* (New York: Signet Classic, 1960).

HERBERT J. GANS

8

MY YEARS IN ANTIPOVERTY

RESEARCH AND POLICY

This chapter is a partial account of my forty years in antipoverty research and policy. The story begins with my coming to America as a refugee in 1940 and becoming concerned with inequality a few years later. However, I required another fifteen years, as well as a sudden invitation to conduct research in a relatively poor community, to be truly gripped by American poverty.

My subconscious may tell another story, but except for coming here as a poor thirteen-year-old, my research, writing, and other antipoverty activities have not been shaped significantly by my personal life. My work in this area has not really changed my personal life either, but in the academy, the boundary between work and personal life is fuzzy and porous to begin with. In any case, both my life and my work have been pushed and pulled to a great extent by events and by the larger agencies and forces that generated them.

I was born in Cologne, Germany, and grew up in a comfortably middle-class, German-Jewish family, but in 1939 we left Nazi Germany with little more than our clothes. After staying seventeen months with relatives in England, the four of us arrived in Chicago in September 1940. The Great Depression was still on, and my parents were lucky to find even menial jobs.

My mother, who had had full-time household help in Germany, became a domestic. My businessman father sold Fuller brushes door to door. I had the easiest job, working as a newspaper delivery boy after school. For a few months, I was also a candidate for a slot on a weekly radio quiz show called "The Quiz Kids," each appearance on which would have paid me more than both my parents earned that week.

We began life in Chicago in a rooming house and then graduated to a basement apartment that flooded regularly after a heavy rain. Some days, when my father worked near Chicago's famous shopping street for the poor, Maxwell Street, he bought tin cans for 5 cents that had lost their labels, resulting in a surprise supper.

We were clearly poor, but I do not remember feeling poor. For one thing, I did not really know any poor people. Although I attended a large, multiclass public high school, I had almost no contact with the poor students, was friendly in class with some of the rich ones, and belonged to the clique of lower-middle-class students who wrote and edited the school's publications.

Also, during my four years in high school, the Depression ended, at least for whites, enabling my parents to graduate to stable though poorly paid white-collar jobs. There was now enough money to move out of the basement apartment.

Perhaps most important, like many other refugees for whom immigration involves drastic downward class mobility, my family began almost at once to try heading back up.[1] Formerly middle-class people who have been able to retain their middle-class cultural capital are never poor in the same way as people born into poverty or the permanently poor. For example, I had been an academically successful student in Germany and England and was able to do equally well in America.

In any case, there was never any doubt that both my brother and I would go to college, even though none of us had the vaguest notion of what that would take or how we would pay for it. I was expected to become a high school teacher, although after I began to write for and edit the high school paper, I wanted to become a journalist.

I also benefited from what some sociologists would today call a neighborhood effect. Partly because the family that gave us the affidavit that enabled us to come to America lived in a mansion district called Kenwood, we ended up in nearby Woodlawn. Woodlawn was then a poor Irish neighborhood but adjacent enough to two upper-middle-class neighborhoods that the local high school, Hyde Park High, was academically one of the best in the city.

My luck extended even further, for although I could not afford to go away to school and had to attend the college closest to home, that college happened to be the University of Chicago. True, I had saved only enough money to pay the tuition for part of the first year, but the year being 1945 I already knew I would be drafted into the army as soon as I was eighteen. Thanks to the GI bill and the end of World War II, I was back at the University of Chicago by the fall of 1946.

Other factors in my limited awareness of American poverty were the country's and city's economic hierarchies and the cultures attached to them. Poverty was still publicly invisible, and the concept itself was certainly not bandied about. The Chicago newspapers were mostly conservative, and the high school curriculum avoided everything remotely political or otherwise controversial. Moreover, today's adolescent youth cultures and the entertainment and other expenses that go with them did not exist in the wartime America of sixty years ago, and I had enough money from my after-school earnings to buy what little I felt I needed.

It may seem incredible today that one could be poor, live in a poor neighborhood, and not feel poor, but among those who are not utterly destitute, it still happens today. It may even be a useful survival mechanism in a society that does so little to help poor people. Certainly I would have gained nothing by being aware of my poverty.

However, my low-income status may have expressed itself in more covert ways, for in the middle of my high school years, I became interested in inequality and equality. At that time, I spent several summers at a Jewish work-and-education camp near Chicago. There I learned about the kibbutz, the economically and socially egalitarian agricultural collective that was then the best known institution in what later became Israel.

I remember being impressed by the fact that all work was rotated so that no one could monopolize the pleasant jobs, that all property was held in common, and that no one needed (or received) money or even owned a personal wardrobe.[2] Although I do not remember suffering from unfair treatment, I assume now that I saw enough unfairness in my own surroundings and in America to be impressed by a community in which everyone seemed to be equal.

Subsequently, I developed an interest in egalitarian and utopian ideas. This interest continued all through college and graduate school, and I have returned to it from time to time ever since.[3] It also led to an interest in more feasible forms of social improvement. Living in a city run by an ever-present political machine meant that I almost had to become interested in politics as well. I did so, learned about Left politics, and developed my eventual and continuing identification with left liberalism.[4]

Neither social improvement nor politics was high on the agenda of either sociology or the other social sciences at the University of Chicago. Still, I learned something about social change in my sociology and other social courses, as well as about how to do research. There were no courses on American poverty, but with the help of W. Lloyd Warner and of course Marx, I discovered social class and also a new way of making sense of inequality and unfairness.[5]

My GI bill money ran out after I received my master's degree in 1950, so I spent three years working and in effect being paid to learn to become a city planner. That experience and my discontent with mainstream social science eventually helped me decide to pursue a doctorate in planning (at the University of Pennsylvania) rather than in sociology (at Columbia University). Pennsylvania's doctoral program was ideal, for it was run by a social science–trained planner (and polymath), Martin Meyerson, whom I had already worked with at Chicago and who had supervised my master's thesis there. At Pennsylvania, I was also able to take further sociology courses and study social planning, or what sociologists now call social policy. City planning itself, however, was almost entirely concerned with physical or spatial planning. By the mid-1960s, I began dropping out of that and ever since have identified myself as a sociologist who also works in and writes about social policy.

After I received my doctorate in 1957, I finally became intellectually and otherwise involved in problems of poverty. While waiting to start a study of the third Levittown, about to be built near Philadelphia,[6] I was invited to join a study of the social and emotional effects of slum clearance on the soon-to-be-cleared population of Boston's West End. I was the "inside man," the participant-observer who would study the West Enders and their community and report what I had learned to the researchers who were preparing the larger study, which would be based on data from in-depth interviews.[7]

The West End housed mostly moderate-income people, but I also met a large number of poor ones. They, their poverty, and related problems began to touch me, but what really hit home at the time was the unjust treatment urban renewal was about to impose on them.[8] The injustice took several forms. The destruction of the West End community was made possible by some governmental data fudging to justify the official stigmatization of the area as a "slum." As a result, the West Enders lost their low-rent apartments and had to relocate themselves from a familiar community to new ones, where they were forced to pay higher rents. To rub it in, the West End's destruction was paid for by public funds so that the West Enders were also subsidizing the luxury housing that was to be built on the cleared acreage.

Just before the Boston Redevelopment Authority began to send out eviction notices, I seriously thought of dropping my research to join a small local protest group to fight the West End's destruction. Had I done so, my life and my subsequent career would have changed drastically. But I decided, with heavy heart, that the local group had no chance of stopping the clearance process and that I could be more effective by finishing the study and reporting on what had happened to the West Enders. I also learned a lesson that has been useful ever since: that a social scientist's political clout lies in the ideas, findings, and other data he or she can command.[9]

The book I wrote about my fieldwork, *The Urban Villagers*, supplied some scholarly legitimization for the critique and subsequent demise of the federal slum-clearance program, but it also affected my personal life. To my utter surprise, the book sold very well. At the time, authors' contracts were written to enrich only the publisher, but I became far better known in the discipline in a much shorter time than would otherwise have been the case. For a few years, I was also one of a handful of sociologists in contact with the journalists, writers, and literary figures who were writing about America for the general public.[10]

These writers all lived in New York, but by the early 1960s, so did I. A divorce (not caused by or connected to my research) led me to move from Philadelphia to New York in 1961. There I also got to know other people I could never have met in Philadelphia, among them Michael Harrington, Bayard Rustin, and others leaders of America's small democratic socialist movement. In addition, I met the founders and first officers of Students for a Democratic Society (SDS) and a number of other people who later played important roles in the antipoverty and civil rights movements.[11] My being a sociologist was useful, for I had some ideas and knowledge about poverty and social change that were sometimes helpful to them as activists.

The Urban Villagers was published in 1962, the same year as Michael Harrington's *The Other America*,[12] and thus appeared about the same time that America's liberal elites, as well as the Kennedy administration, discovered or rediscovered American poverty. Not long after the message of *The Other America* hit home, the call went out for social science experts on poverty. Partly because few such experts then existed and partly because my book had just appeared, I was perceived to be one of them. As a result, I began to be recruited to join seminars, appear on panels, attend conferences (many of which were held in ex–robber baron mansions), and write articles about poverty and related topics. Between 1962 and 1970, thirty of the forty-six articles I published were entirely or largely about poverty and antipoverty policy. In the process, I became part of what would eventually become an unofficial and informal antipoverty policy community. One of the efforts of that community was to try to broaden the emerging federal antipoverty policy and to ensure that it would actually help poor people. No one had time or money for research; instead, most of my work, much of it done after hours, involved going to meetings and, above all, writing [13]

I was not even sorry that I had done no empirical research about the poor other than while studying the West End. In fact, the West End research had already persuaded me that antipoverty research should be devoted primarily to understanding the poverty-makers: the people, institutions, and social forces that made and helped to keep people poor.

The available research opportunities were, however, focused on the poor themselves—their characteristics, their problems, and above all the troubles they caused the more affluent population. I saw some merit in studying their problems insofar as these were caused or exacerbated by poverty, but I did not think that the troubles they caused the more affluent could be called antipoverty research. Consequently, little of the research ever helped poor people escape poverty.[14]

Among the activists, the primary issue of the early 1960s was not poverty but civil rights. Many of the people and organizations with whom I came in touch were concerned particularly with poor blacks. Also, Bayard Rustin had already proposed that once civil rights legislation had become the law of the land, further progress would best be achieved by reducing the economic inequality of the black community. Rustin's proposal then spawned policy questions about what ought to be done to foster more economic equality.[15]

By the mid-1960s, the issues on which we had begun to work near the start of the decade heated up and were exposed to the national spotlight. One of the groups in which I participated was an informal advisory group to CORE (Congress on Racial Equality), then a prominent left-wing civil rights organization. Organized by S. M. Miller, the group is now remembered as the place in which Richard Cloward and George Wiley first discussed the idea for a national welfare rights movement.[16]

A more prominent interaction of civil rights and poverty took place in the national debate over the Moynihan report. The author, whom I had already met at earlier meetings on antipoverty policy, argued that despite the ravages of unemployment, the problems and pathologies of the black community were also caused by the fragmentation of the black family. I had always thought that these problems and pathologies were themselves effects of poverty, and I said so in a widely disseminated review of the report that first appeared in *Commonweal*.[17]

The underlying issue, which, as it turned out, dominated my antipoverty activities during the last half of the 1960s, was whether and how much the black poor ought to be blamed for their own poverty. The issue crystalized intellectually around Oscar Lewis's[18] notion of a culture of poverty, but it was first and foremost a policy issue.

If the poor or their alleged culture could be blamed for their own poverty, then they either did not deserve help or they had to be transformed culturally and psychologically. And even if that cultural transformation were financed with federal funds, it would cost less than the large amounts of money and political capital needed to supply the jobs, the income grants, and the better housing and schools that the poor really needed.

The *Commonweal* review led to an invitation to the White House conference To Fulfill These Rights, organized in part to publicize the Moynihan report, and then to a multiyear seminar on poverty headed by Pat Moynihan. The seminar devoted itself mostly to a debate over the culture of poverty; I was on the side that questioned the existence of such a culture.[19]

Even before the debate over the "broken" black family and the culture of poverty had ended, the ghetto disorders, called "riots" on the Right and "uprisings" on the Left, began. Now the trouble the poor were causing was called ghetto "violence," but once the ghettoes were "quiet" again, welfare recipients and the female-based families whom Moynihan had targeted in his report were restored to their previous positions as villains or victims.

For me, these events meant opportunities to make my ideas known, and in somewhat different arenas than before. Among other things, I was asked to testify as an urban expert to a Senate Committee on the Urban Crisis.[20] Then I became a consultant to the Kerner Commission.[21] One of my tasks for the commission was to draft chapter 9 of the Kerner Report, which debunked the neoconservative argument that blacks could escape poverty and racism without government action.[22]

In 1967, another personal change took place in my life that also affected my work. I remarried that year and became a father in 1970. As a result, I traded in a series of research positions that had allowed me to write most of the time in order to take up the first full-time teaching job of my now nearly fifteen-year-old post-doctorate career.

My new wife, Louise Gruner, was a lawyer and shortly after our marriage went to work in the federal Legal Services programs for the poor.[23] For the next two decades, she and her colleagues brought class-action and other suits to help poor people obtain their constitutional rights—and I became familiar with an entirely new set of poverty-related problems and antipoverty programs.

Although I did not time it that way, the War, or what we called the Skirmish, on Poverty was ending just as I was becoming a full-time academic.

Many of the old programs continued to exist in watered-down or emasculated forms and some still exist, but the policy innovations in which we were involved, directly or as critics, had dried up.[24]

I continued to write about race and poverty, but much of it in despair about the decline of antipoverty and antidiscrimination efforts. Actually, my despairing mood had begun earlier, about the time that Lyndon Johnson switched wars, and I wrote some satires reflecting my disappointments with the War on Poverty. In addition, I became interested in what Michael Katz later called "the language of poverty." One of the products of that new interest was a short satire about the hard-core unemployed in which an animal biologist searched the heads of the jobless for the hard cores he thought would explain unemployment.[25]

About that time, I also wrote an article entitled "The Positive Functions of Poverty," which appeared in the *American Journal of Sociology* in 1972. In it, I showed how useful the poor were to the nonpoor. Although I did not realize it at the time, I was also implying that the War on Poverty ended because so many Americans benefited from keeping poor people poor.[26]

The major product of my despair was, ironically enough, a fairly optimistic book of essays called *More Equality* (which Pantheon published in 1973) in which I argued—and now think I tried to persuade myself—that a revival of interest in equality during the late 1960s could become a new rationale for antipoverty policy. I also used the book to return to my past interest in equality but then decided that the world was too dark to justify utopian speculations.[27]

In the mid-1970s, poverty and even race had stopped being liberal hot-button subjects, and the foundations, as well as the federal government, virtually stopped funding antipoverty research. When increased unemployment, the arrival of crack, and the concurrent rise in the rate of murder and other street crimes hit the cities in the 1980s, interest in and money for antipoverty research became available again. By then, the field had been more or less taken over by quantitative researchers, particularly economists. Much of their work added more numbers about the characteristics, troubles, and trouble-making behavior of the poor and updated the blaming-the-victim analyses of the past. For me, these were old issues, and I had nothing new or useful to say about them.[28]

My return to the intellectual antipoverty wars followed the publication of William J. Wilson's *The Truly Disadvantaged* in 1987. Like others of my generation, I was pleased that Wilson was able to create the immense public stir that he did and to make people pay attention to problems and policy proposals that in our time had fallen on deaf ears.[29] Some of us were unhappy about Wilson's description of poor blacks as an underclass, although he generally used the term as Gunnar Myrdal had originally defined it: as a new class made up of the people who were no longer needed by the economy.

Wilson's book appeared at the height of the crack epidemic, however, and the new crime and violence that accompanied the epidemic also popularized a new definition of underclass. It replaced Myrdal's definition with one that stigmatized the poor, particularly the black poor, and for many of the same imagined shortcomings that had previously been included in the culture of poverty. Underclass was just the newest way to blame the victims.

The stigmatizing definition of underclass had actually first appeared in the 1970s, but I only became aware of and angry about it when it became a popular term. Eric Wanner, the president of the Russell Sage Foundation, shared some of my sentiments, and in 1989 I was invited to be a visiting scholar at the foundation. I spent my year by starting work on my *War Against the Poor*.[30] Half of the book was an empirical analysis of the formulation, history, and diffusion of both the Myrdalian and stigmatizing definitions of the term "underclass."

Although the stigmatizing version of underclass was spread mostly by the news media, a surprising number of social scientists used it as well. I joined other social scientists who argued with them and with the prominent foundations who funded research by using the stigmatizing term. The foundation studies came to nought, but so did our critiques. "Underclass" quickly became part of the mainstream language of poverty.

I am writing this chapter just after the end of the late twentieth-century economic boom, as too many former welfare recipients are losing their only recently won jobs and the remaining welfare recipients are beginning to lose their benefits. As I have tried to suggest, my antipoverty work has been shaped to some extent by attacks on the poor. If new attacks are launched *and* if I have new and useful ideas to contribute, I could be back on antipoverty's intellectual barricades again.

NOTES

1. Needless to say, becoming poor was a small price to pay for the ability to leave Germany and avoid death at the hands of the Nazis.

2. This portrait was romantic and designed to sell kibbutz ideology. Later, I wanted to study a kibbutz, not to debunk the romantic portrait but to look it over before deciding whether to live there. I joined up with two other fledgling social scientists with the same purpose, but only one of us ever undertook a study.

3. My interest in egalitarian issues was so strong that when R. H. Tawney, the famous British socialist and economist, lectured at the University of Chicago. I considered studying with him at the London School of Economics. The Tawney book that attracted me to him was The Acquisitive Society (New York: Harcourt, Brace, and Howe, 1920).

4. Neighborhood factors were at work once more: in the late 1940s, campus Stalinists, Trotskyists, and democratic socialists were engaged in an energetic pursuit of converts, which indirectly provided the political education that was not available in any classroom. For a while I thought of myself as a democratic socialist.

5. A little history is needed here because, in the 1940s, "class" was not in the American vocabulary. I had already read some Marx in college and wrote my first graduate school paper on historical materialism, but living in a working-class neighborhood made me wonder about the fit of Marx's working class to American conditions. Weber was only just beginning to be translated into English, and Warner's analysis, when corrected for his own social and political conservatism, made a lot of sense to me. Some of it still does.

6. As a result of discussions about the causes of political apathy with David Riesman, then working at Yale on The Lonely Crowd (New Haven, Conn.: Yale University Press, 1950), I wrote my master's thesis about political participation. I did the research in Park Forest, a planned new town near Chicago, which then evoked my curiosity about both planning and new towns.

7. I took the job in part because I had always wanted to study a working-class community. My course work with Warner and Meyerson had stimulated my interest in institutional and professional class biases, including those of the planners, many of whom were eager to tear down the houses of the poor and the working class.

8. I had already spent a year (1953) in Washington, working for the federal housing agency responsible for slum clearance. However, my job was to check application documents, and I remained unaware of the injustice about to be committed in the name of urban renewal.

9. I acted on that principle, writing an unsolicited report to the chair of Boston's Redevelopment Authority, outlining what was being done to the West Enders and what could still be done to reduce the financial, social, and emotional costs they would otherwise pay. The report was never acknowledged, but I published it in the planners' flagship journal, after which many planners stopped talking to me. Later, the article grew into the final two chapters of The Urban Villagers. Herbert J. Gans, Urban Villagers: Group and Class in the Life of Italian Americans (New York: Free Press, 1962).

10. Some I had already met in my graduate school days, when David Riesman introduced me to Nathan Glazer and his colleagues at Commentary, then a liberal magazine. Thanks to Glazer, I published my first article in Commentary in 1951, and thereafter I published in that journal (until it became a right-wing magazine) and in a few other general intellectual magazines as often as I could. A decade later, some of them would contact me to write about poverty. Herbert J. Gans, "Park Forest: Birth of a Jewish Community," Commentary, April 1951, 330–39.

11. Some I had met through Leonard Duhl, a psychiatrist who was working hard to bring his field together with the social sciences and to enroll both in antipoverty and other social policy projects. He was working as a program officer at the National Institute of Mental Health, financed the West End study, and had recruited me to take the fieldwork position that led to *Urban Villagers*. Now he was also working with Robert F. Kennedy, his issues staff, and others who were doing the groundwork for the oncoming War on Poverty.

12. Michael Harrington, *The Other America: Poverty in the United States* (New York: Macmillan, 1962).

13. Some dedicated English teachers, as well as my education and army experience as a journalist, had taught me to write a bit more clearly than many other academics. The same interests that attracted me first to journalism and then to fieldwork also drove me to write about topical issues while I was also doing academic research.

14. This lack of interest in the poverty-makers remains alive and well in antipoverty research. The latest hot topic, the amount and uses of social capital among the poor, is often just checking on whether and how they are pulling themselves up by each other's bootstraps.

15. Bayard Rustin was one of Martin Luther King's principal advisers. Fifteen years or so later, William Julius Wilson resurrected and updated a major theme of Rustin's analysis, first in *The Declining Significance of Race* and then in *Truly Disadvantaged*. William Julius Wilson, *The Declining Significance of Race: Blacks and Changing American Institutions* (Chicago: University of Chicago Press, 1978); *Truly Disadvantaged: The Inner City, The Underclass, and Public Policy* (Chicago: University of Chicago Press, 1987).

16. The group is discussed in Nick Kotz and Mary Lynn Kotz, *A Passion for Equality: George A. Wiley and the Movement* (New York: Norton, 1977), chap. 19.

17. The article was included with a variety of other reviews, critiques, and related documents about the report, with analysis and commentary on the controversy, by Lee Rainwater and William Yancey, *The Moynihan Report and the Politics of Controversy* (Cambridge, Mass.: MIT Press, 1967). The role of CORE's advisory group of social scientists in the controversy, particularly the White House conference, is discussed on pages 210–11 and 302. The title of my piece in the Rainwater and Yancey book was "The Negro Family: Reflections on the Moynihan Report," 445–57. It was a slightly longer version of the article by the same title that appeared in *Commonweal* 83 (1965): 47–51.

18. A concise statement of Oscar Lewis's conception of the culture of poverty appears in his "The Culture of Poverty," in Moynihan, *On Understanding Poverty*, 187–200.

19. The papers that came out of the seminar and the debate appear in Daniel P. Moynihan, ed., *On Understanding Poverty* (New York: Basic Books, 1969).

20. The testimony to the Senate committee is reprinted, together with some of the other articles I wrote about poverty and antipoverty policy, in Herbert J. Gans, *People and Plans* (New York: Basic Books, 1968).

21. This was also a period when publicly active social scientists were invited to join somewhat more mainstream national organizations. One was the national board of the Americans for Democratic Action, where I helped organize a symbolically successful resolution in favor of more economic equality. Another was the League for Industrial Democracy, a small but influential organization of conservative socialists that had spawned and then broken with SDS. I was also elected to the Councils of the American Sociological Association and of the Society of Social Problems. In all of these organizations, I helped put social policy issues about race and poverty on the agenda whenever the opportunity presented itself.

22. I never received either an author's credit or the nominal payment as a government consultant, however. As an antiwar protester, I had refused to pay my taxes the previous year, and even my existence could therefore not be publicly acknowledged. "Kerner Report" was the informally used title. The correct reference is "Report of the National Advisory Commission on Civil Disorders" (Washington: Government Printing Office, 1968). There's a more accessible recent reprinting, entitled *The Kerner Report:The 1968 Report of the National Advisory Edition on Civil Disorders* (New York: Pantheon Books, 1988).

23. The Legal Services program began as part of the War on Poverty. Although its budget has been shrunk drastically over the years and its ability to bring class-action suits ended, the program is one of the few of the original programs of the Office of Economic Opportunity that the Republicans were never able to eliminate completely.

24. There were exceptions, for example, the Family Assistance Plan that Moynihan proposed while working for Richard Nixon. I was involved marginally in the political struggles around it.

25. The little piece first appeared in *Society* in 1969 and is reprinted in Herbert J. Gans, *Making Sense of America* (Lanham, Md.: Rowman and Littlefield, 1999), 309–10. Michael B. Katz, *The Undeserving Poor: From the War on Poverty to the War on Welfare* (New York: Pantheon Books, 1989).

26. I wrote it not only as another kind of antipoverty analysis but also as a demonstration that Mertonian functionalism, then being attacked as a conservative paradigm, could be used for radical analyses. It is the most frequently reprinted of all my articles. Herbert J. Gans, "The Positive Functions of Poverty," *American Journal of Sociology* 78, no. 2 (1972) 275–89.

27. Herbert J. Gans, *More Equality* (New York: Pantheon Books, 1973).

28. Instead, I had spent part of the 1980s on a study of work sharing, an old policy idea to divide the existing supply of jobs among more people by shortening work hours, thus increasing the total number of jobs. Western Europeans were trying out various work-sharing policies and are still doing so, but Americans have shown no interest in them whatsoever.

29. Wilson, *The Truly Disadvantaged*. It goes without saying that the issues we discovered in the 1960s would have been old hat to the scholars and activists who raised them in the 1930s. I imagine this regress can be carried back to biblical times, if not

before. For a fine history of twentieth-century antipoverty research and policy analysis, which emphasizes the period about which I am also writing, see Alice O'Connor, *Poverty Knowledge* (Princeton, N.J.: Princeton University Press, 2000).

30. Herbert J. Gans, *War Against the Poor* (New York: Basic Books, 1995). I was fortunate that Michael Katz, the dean of American historians of poverty, who had previously written about the language of poverty and stigmatizing terms for the poor, was also a visiting scholar that year.

GENDER

Part II

BLEE | HÉCTOR L. DELGADO | SUSAN A. OSTRANDER | MARK S. MIZRU

.IS MOEN | ARLENE SKOLNICK | JANE MANSBRIDGE | CYNTHIA FUCHS

RISTOPHER WINSHIP | SHERRYL KLEINMAN | JODY MILLER | JOSHUA

SAN A. OSTRANDER | MARK S. MIZRUCHI | WILLIAM H. FRIEDLAND |

NE MANSBRIDGE | CYNTHIA FUCHS EPSTEIN | DOROTHY E. SMITH | BA

'L KLEINMAN | JODY MILLER | JOSHUA GAMSON | SHULAMIT REINHAR

| MARK S. MIZRUCHI | WILLIAM H. FRIEDLAND | HOWARD SCHUMAN

YNTHIA FUCHS EPSTEIN | DOROTHY E. SMITH | BARRIE THORNE | ROE

| JOSHUA GAMSON | SHULAMIT REINHARZ | VERTA TAYLOR | KATHLE

EDLAND | HOWARD SCHUMAN | JOHN WALTON | HERBERT J. GANS | F

SMITH | BARRIE THORNE | ROBERT R. ALFORD | GARY L. ALBRECHT |

NHARZ | VERTA TAYLOR | KATHLEEN M. BLEE | HÉCTOR L. DELGADO

HN WALTON | HERBERT J. GANS | PHYLLIS MOEN | ARLENE SKOLNIC

. ALFORD | GARY L. ALBRECHT | CHRISTOPHER WINSHIP | SHERRYL K

USAN A. OSTRANDER | MARK S. MIZRUCHI | WILLIAM H. FRIEDLANE

CHS EPSTEIN | ROBERT R. ALFORD | GARY L. ALBRECHT | CHRISTOPH

RTA TAYLOR | KATHLEEN M. BLEE | HÉCTOR L. DELGADO | SUSAN A.

PHYLLIS MOEN

9

UNSCRIPTED

CONTINUITY AND CHANGE IN

THE GENDERED LIFE COURSE

CONTINGENT CAREERS

In 2001, Katharine Graham, former publisher of the *Washington Post* and *Newsweek*, died as a consequence of a fall while on a trip to give a speech. She had published a Pulitzer Prize–winning autobiography in 1997,[1] depicting a life that was as unscripted and accidental as my own. Graham, whose father and husband were publishers of the *Washington Post*, became the publisher of that newspaper herself quite suddenly and unexpectedly when her husband committed suicide. Graham said that "the only reason I had my job was the good luck of my birth and the bad luck of my husband's death."[2]

I certainly did not have the good luck of a privileged background, but I, too, found myself propelled into the breadwinner role, which included getting a doctorate and becoming a sociologist, by the bad luck of my husband's death, suddenly and unexpectedly as a result of cancer when he was thirty-four and I was thirty-two. Like Katharine Graham, I had been a full-time homemaker when my children were young. As they reached school age and in tandem with the growing women's movement in the late 1960s and early 1970s, I had gone back to school to get first a bachelor's and then a master's degree. But I did so almost unobtrusively, making sure I was home before the school bus and that dinner was always on the table. My real focus was on my family, not schooling. And then my world turned upside down.

Although I have achieved none of the prominence and influence of a person like Katharine Graham, in a way our experiences follow parallel tracks. Both of our life paths emphasize the significance of shifting biographical experiences within a shifting and gendered historical context that are constructing and reconstructing women's (and men's) life courses. My life, like Graham's, like so many women's lives, has been unscripted, contingent on others' goals, needs, experiences, and expectations—those of my parents, my husband, my children—as well as exposure to other scholars' ideas and behavior. And as with Graham, this life course notion of linked lives is most poignantly demonstrated by the fact that my own occupational success is tied inextricably to the tragedy of my first husband's death.

My personal biography has motivated my scholarly interest in careers, lives, and the gendered life course, as well as in the ways institutions perpetuate women's and men's distinctive experiences, opportunities, inequalities, and vulnerabilities. Such deeply embedded beliefs about motherhood, fatherhood, family, and work continue to shape lives, even in the face of changing opportunity structures. But circumstances change. People change. I draw on my own experiences to show how life course transitions and trajectories, social relations, and the milieu of the second half of the twentieth century have shaped my biography, as well as my intellectual agenda.

SOCIAL RESEARCH AND THE GENDERED LIFE COURSE

My first exposure to social science was as a senior in high school in Atlanta, Georgia, in 1959–60. I was part of a vast survey of students called Project Talent, which documented our abilities, motivations, and goals, as well as our home environments. As I saw it then, the goal was to follow this cohort of young people into adulthood to see if they "turned out" as expected. After marriage and motherhood, I received newsletters and exhortations to continue in the study. But I never did. I knew that as a young wife and mother, a college dropout, I was not "turning out" as my tests and abilities would have predicted. I didn't want to be held up against peers and found wanting, even as I found my own lifestyle (as an isolated, full-time homemaker) and future occupational prospects wanting.

Graduating from high school at seventeen, attending college for a year and marrying at eighteen, becoming a mother at nineteen, I was living what I was to study years later: the gendered life course. Unaware, I was following a soon-to-be outdated script, feeling the nameless unease so well described by Betty Friedan in *The Feminine Mystique*[3] (published during this time period but not discovered by me for more than a decade). What I came to see, but could not grasp at the time, was how women's biographies were to be transformed by both personal and public events.

For me, Project Talent underscored my "failure" by conventional (male) standards. Thinking of what could have been epitomized the fork in the road that I had taken, almost unwittingly, and certainly without any appreciation of its consequences. My boyfriend, Arnie Moen, wanted me to meet his parents during the summer of 1961. We planned to take a Greyhound bus to his home in northern Minnesota. My mother balked at that idea, saying it would not be proper for an unmarried couple to travel so far on their own. Our solution was to get married. Deborah came along ten months later. What I was reading about raising children warned of the dangers of an only child, which meant a sister, Melanie, two years after that. The "choice" to marry was really a means to an end—a trip to Minnesota. Deborah was evidence of how poorly we were prepared for birth control (this is before the pill). Melanie was a conscious plan—for the possibility of a son, to stave off the horrors of the spoiled single child, to fit into the "ideal" two-year spacing touted at the time. But I was suddenly twenty-two, with no hope of escaping what was becoming a script of predictable and unpredictable contingencies, constructed around my husband's career, my children's needs, and the absence of any options to reconcile my family goals with my occupational dreams. Who could know that in ten years I'd be a widow, with two daughters aged ten and twelve, and that this singularly devastating event would change my life?

LEARNING SOCIOLOGY FROM SOCIOLOGISTS

My own unscripted life course made me especially receptive to my mentor, Reuben Hill's,[4] interest in the family life cycle and to the most influential book I read as a graduate student, Glen H. Elder, Jr.'s, *Children of the Great Depression.*[5] A group of us, as NIMH (National Institute of Mental Health) family-impact trainees, invited distinguished scholars to visit and give a talk, one of whom was Glen Elder. When I met him at the airport, I was surprised he was so young, given my assessment of the importance and potential impact of his book. Elder's ideas about linking social change with individual biographies made imminent good sense. I then proceeded to get lost on the way to a reception at Reuben Hill's house, which gave me the opportunity to get to know Elder. Having the privilege of talking with him after having immersed myself in his writing really brought home to me the importance of historical times and unexpected events in the shaping of life chances and life quality.

For Elder's book, the defining event was the Great Depression of the 1930s. For my own scholarly agenda and for my own life, it was the women's movement, though it took me a while to recognize this defining event for what it was in my work and my life course. For me, it is the *unevenness of social change* that is paramount. Some societal transformations seem to appear overnight (as the transition to cell phones seems to have taken the United States by storm): such was the event of the Great Depression, the bombing of Pearl Harbor, the terrorist attacks of 2001. But most transformations are more subtle, characterized by lagging rules, roles, and relationships—in policies and practices, in belief systems, and in mixed messages. My life and my work exemplify the cultural and structural lags in opportunity, expectations, and identity that women like myself and Katherine Graham have experienced in the face of changing circumstances and possibilities. Whereas most white, middle-class, and many working-class men's life courses followed a lock-step script from education through uninterrupted, full-time (or more) employment to the leisure of retirement in the latter half of the twentieth century, most women's lives, as well as most minority and poor men's, have been unscripted, typically contingent on the lives and resources of others, as well as on chance events. Because I was interested as much in social policy as in sociology, I saw Elder's life course approach as a way of linking policy shifts (or their absence) with changing individual and family options and constraints. My growing interest in the life course was not only as a way of understanding what was or what is, but also as a window on what could be.

Elder's framing of questions—along with a colleague's (Jeylan Mortimer's) focus on work and family and Reuben Hill's conceptualization of family stress processes, stages of family development, and family members' sense of being "on" or "off" time (in terms of consumption items like a house or a new refrigerator)—have had a direct and lasting impact on my own scholarship. Along with firsthand biographical knowledge of gender schema and women's changing roles, these intellectual strands came together to shape my own thinking about gendered career paths and, more broadly, the gendered life course.

INTELLECTUAL BEGINNINGS

My research agenda has, in many ways, paralleled my own life course progression. That can be both good and bad. One of my high school teachers said to always write about what you know, and I believe that is good advice. I have first-hand experience with the way gender constrains women's (and men's) expectations and options. The danger, of course, is to study *only* ourselves, in ways that are more personal than analytic, thereby remaining at the level of concentration on private troubles rather than public (and sociological) issues and interests. As a graduate student, newly widowed at age thirty-three, I was tempted to study death and dying. Fortunately, the then head of graduate studies in the sociology department at the University of Minnesota, Richard Hall, was skeptical. "You don't want to immerse yourself in that," he said, in so many words. The goal, he implied, was to get over the traumatic event of losing my husband so early and unexpectedly, not to make death and widowhood my life's work.

Heeding his advice, I took up another personally relevant but less emotionally valenced topic: the family economy. Because of Reuben Hill's theoretical focus on the life cycle I was sensitized early to the importance of time and the internal social clocks we all have ticking within us. I was "off time" in terms of being a widow, and in being in graduate school with two children. My studies at the University of Minnesota with Bob Leik, Jeylan Mortimer, Roberta Simmons, Steve McLaughlin, and of course Reuben Hill led to the establishment of my own research agenda: viewing the family economy as operating at the intersections of work, family, gender, social policy, and time.

However, the climate in graduate schools in the late 1970s fostered an ambivalence about the study of gender. Both students and faculty discouraged me from doing a "women's" dissertation, saying that no one would want to hire someone who was solely interested in studying women. Accordingly, for my dissertation I investigated the effect of the recession in 1974–75 on the likelihood of families at different life stages undergoing the unemployment of the family head, in other words, husbands and fathers.

As soon as I had a job (at Cornell University), I moved back to my larger interests in work, family, policy, and gender, including the gendered nature of work versus family role strains (which I knew only too well). I can remember sitting in faculty meetings that were running late, afraid to leave but envisioning one of my daughters waiting on a corner for me to pick her up, probably freezing. Sometimes I would leave with an excuse such as having to get my car from the garage, knowing that single parenthood, or more precisely *motherhood*, should not be seen as limiting my professional commitments. I had a more senior male colleague, however, who would make a big show of having to pick up his child from day care, and people would comment on what a good "modern" father he was.

When I was in graduate school at the University of Minnesota in the late 1970s, there were two women on the faculty: Roberta Simmons, who was tenured, and Jeylan Mortimer, who was a young assistant professor. Having two children of my own, I was eager to figure out how to combine an occupational career with my family responsibilities. I remember asking Roberta how she did it since by having tenure she had obviously succeeded in "managing." She said that she and her husband (a physician also on the faculty at the University of Minnesota) always hired help, including a full-time, live-in housekeeper and nanny. Since I was one rung above poverty, this didn't offer me much solace. Moreover, as a feminist, I recognized that, in essence, hiring a "wife" couldn't be the solution.

LEARNING BY DOING

As a new assistant professor and a novice sociologist, I was caught up with the realization that the social organization of work is incompatible with the social organization of child rearing, though I could not articulate it in this way for years. I first thought that changing work-hour options would be the solution. Shortly after coming to Cornell, I realized I needed to get grants in order to use large data sets (like the Panel Study of Income Dynamics, which I had used in my dissertation). At that time one had to pay real money to use the mainframe computer at Cornell (there were no PCs yet), and I used up a year's allocation of funds for computer use in manipulating this data set in one weekend. I applied for a grant to the U.S. Department of Labor to study women and part-time work (actually sending a letter of inquiry to "Whom it May Concern" at the Labor Department, having no idea about how to actually get a grant). The reason I even considered applying for a grant also points to my socialization in graduate school.

Somehow, I had enough sense to volunteer to work with Jeylan Mortimer, Steve McLaughlin, Bob Leik, and Reuben Hill as they wrote a grant proposal to study women's labor force participation. All I really did for them was a little library research on the existing literature, but sitting in on their meetings as they went about drafting the proposal taught me volumes. I observed people in the process of constructing a research design and proposal, which suggested that it was not a mysterious process but something I could do as well.

Another important lesson came when they did not get the grant. I learned that being rejected wasn't the end of the world. This was really brought home the following year when I went into Jeylan Mortimer's office and saw that she was obviously upset. She explained that she had just been notified that her proposal (to do a follow-up study on the people she had studied in her dissertation) had been rejected. I can see now how such news would be particularly devastating for a young assistant professor trying to do the work necessary to publish, which in turn was necessary to get tenure. My most important professional development lesson in graduate school came the next day, when I once again went to Jeylan's office. She was typing "a reapplication": "I am resubmitting my proposal," she cheerfully told me. What I learned was that succeeding was a process with ups and downs, and probably persistence was at least as important as creativity.

As a consequence of this insight, when writing my dissertation I made myself work on something every single day, even if it was only typing up mock tables to be filled in when I actually had the results. It also meant that as an assistant professor I felt I, too, could submit grant proposals. And that I, too, would refuse to be devastated by rejection from journals or from funding agencies (or, rather, I could be devastated for a day, maybe two, but then had to get back to work).

It turned out that I did in fact get the grant from the Department of Labor (which led to meeting my wonderful future husband, Dick Shore, but that is another story). What is important is that I used cross-sectional data (from the Quality of Employment Survey) to study women who worked part time and full time, and I found all kinds of differences between them. I never published those results, however, because I was also looking at longitudinal data from the Panel Study of Income Dynamics, and I came up with an entirely different story. What I found was that the women working part time one year were often either working full time the next year or had dropped out of the work force. The same was true of women working full time and of full-time homemakers.[6] In other words, there are seldom *permanently* part-time or full-time women workers or women who are continuously full-time homemakers. Women move in and out of these categories in tandem with changing opportunities, in addition to the changing opportunities of their partners and changing needs of their children or aging relatives. This insight about the dynamic nature of roles and behavior, as well as the social construction and perpetuation of gender, led me to incorporate time and context into my subsequent research agenda. I have focused on the way gender and age, as fundamental dimensions of social organization and inequality, persist as key components of virtually all contemporary organizational and interpersonal arrangements.

CONCLUSIONS

An important proposition of life course analysis is that an understanding of one life phase requires it to be placed in the larger context of life pathways.[7] In other words, past experiences matter. Although educational and other credentials help to shape career paths, a changing opportunity structure is paramount, as are changing family circumstances.

I have maintained an ongoing interest in work, family, and social policy, as well as in multiple roles and women's health.[8] But as my own career has developed and my understanding of life course issues has deepened, I have moved from investigating work and family *roles*, to the study of work and family *career paths*:[9] in particular, how they are shaped both by the changing options brought about by (1) the shift to a service economy, the women's movement, and the resulting policy initiatives related to gender equality; (2) demographic changes due to increasing longevity, declining fertility, and the aging of the baby boom cohort; (3) more recent shifts to a global economy and the dismantling of the traditional "contract" between workers and employers (trading commitment and long hours of work for advancement, seniority, and job security); and (4) what Robert Merton calls the "social givens"[10]—the now outdated but persistent, taken-for-granted notions about gender, age, and the lockstep, breadwinner versus homemaker career template. This obsolete schema continues to permeate all institutions—from the social organization of education (as preparatory for occupational careers, not lifelong learning), to the division of household (and societal) care work (as unpaid or low paid "women's work"), to the structure of pension policies (rewarding continuous, full-time labor force participation throughout what are essentially the childbearing and child-rearing years). These four uneven, and even indeterminate forces in American society operate in the media, schools, workplaces, communities, social policy development, and households, offering women and men, girls and boys, mixed messages about life course possibilities, along with incompatible sets of opportunities and constraints. What led to these insights is that I have experienced these contradictions and incompatibilities firsthand. But studying these social forces has also enabled me to put my own biography in perspective.

What the life course approach provides is a way of linking early experiences with subsequent life paths, as well as a way of seeing (1) how accidental (or deliberate) events can shape directions and possibilities and (2) how the life course is socially structured and regulated by public and private (workplace) policies and practices. But institutions lag behind changing realities of the contemporary life course, reproducing gender schema at work and at home. My current agenda, in life and in scholarship, is to identify and understand what I perceive as the emergence of a new life stage, *midcourse*, one that is truly midcourse between earlier adulthood and old age. This, too, is a stage defined by past experiences and future possibilities, along with ambiguous messages about and uncertain options linked to the intersections of gender and age. There is a new stage of the life course in my own personal biography, a new research agenda—it is my privilege to live in exciting times. Living at the margins rather than in the mainstream of society, again drawing on Merton, generates ambiguity but also opportunity. My life, like that of growing numbers of women, illustrates both processes as we engage in redefining and broadening established pathways.

NOTES

1. Katharine Graham, *Personal History* (New York: Knopf, 1997).

2. Ibid., 417.

3. Betty Friedan, *The Feminine Mystique* (New York: Norton, 1963).

4. Reuben Hill, *Family Development in Three Generations* (Cambridge, Mass.: Schenkman, 1970).

5. Glen H. Elder, Jr., *Children of the Great Depression* (Champaign-Urbana, Ill.: University of Chicago Press, 1974).

6. Phyllis Moen, "Continuities and Discontinuities in Women's Labor Force Participation," in *Life Course Dynamics: 1960s to 1980s*, ed. Glen H. Elder, Jr. (Ithaca, N.Y.: Cornell University Press, 1985), 113–55.

7. Glen H. Elder, Jr., "The Life Course Paradigm: Social Change and Individual Development," in *Examining Lives in Context: Perspectives on the Ecology of Human Development*, ed. Phyllis Moen, Glen H. Elder, Jr., and Kurt Lüscher (Washington, D.C.: American Psychological Association, 1995), 101–39; Janet Z. Giele and Glen H. Elder, Jr., *Methods of Life Course Research: Qualitative and Quantitative Approaches* (Thousand Oaks, Calif.: Sage, 1998).

8. For example, see Phyllis Moen, Donna Dempster-McClain, and Robin M. Williams, Jr., "Social Integration and Longevity: An Event History Analysis of Women's Roles and Resilience," *American Sociological Review* 54 (1989): 635–47; Phyllis Moen, Donna Dempster-McClain, and Robin M. Williams, Jr., "Successful

Aging: A Life Course Perspective on Women's Roles and Health," *American Journal of Sociology* 97 (1992): 1612–38; Phyllis Moen, *Working Parents: Transformations in Gender Roles and Public Policies in Sweden* (Madison: University of Wisconsin Press, 1989); Phyllis Moen, *Women's Two Roles: A Contemporary Dilemma* (Westport, Conn.: Greenwood, 1992).

9. For example, Shin-Kap Han and Phyllis Moen, "Work and Family Over Time: A Life Course Approach," *Annals of the American Academy of Political and Social Sciences* 562 (1999): 98–110; Shin-Kap Han and Phyllis Moen, "Clocking Out: Temporal Patterning of Retirement," *American Journal of Sociology* 105 (1999): 191–236; Shin-Kap Han and Phyllis Moen, "Coupled Careers: Pathways Through Work and Marriage in the United States," in *Careers of Couples in Contemporary Societies: A Cross-National Comparison of the Transition from Male Breadwinner to Dual-Earner Families*, ed. Hans-Peter Blossfeld and Sonja Drobnic (Oxford: Oxford University Press, 2001), 201–31; Phyllis Moen, "The Career Quandary," *Population Reference Bureau Reports on America* 2, 1 (February 2001); Phyllis Moen, "The Gendered Life Course," in *Handbook of Aging and the Social Sciences*, ed. L. George and R. H. Binstock (San Diego, Calif.: Academic Press, 2001), 179–96.

10. Robert Merton, *Social Theory and Social Structure* (New York: Free Press, 1968).

ARLENE SKOLNICK

10

CONFESSIONS OF AN

ACCIDENTAL SOCIOLOGIST

In the fall of 1969, I found myself newly arrived and unemployed in a southern California beach town. We had fled there—my husband, Jerry, and I and our two young sons, Mike and Alex—from the seemingly endless turmoil of Berkeley at the time, especially the tear gas drifting from the campus to our house and my older son's elementary school.

Jerry had taken a job at a newly formed branch of the University of California. I was planning to continue what had seemed a viable academic career as a researcher, as I had done at Berkeley's Institute of Human Development (IHD). Now, however, in a much smaller and newer university and in a different fiscal climate, it seemed as if that plan wasn't going to work. The funding for the project I had been invited to join did not come through. Weeks of looking around did not turn up any other possibilities.

Despite the sunshine, the sea air, and the beaches, I began to feel discouraged and depressed. One particularly low moment remains vivid. I had gone to talk to the chair of the psychology department, a man I shall call Ted, to see if he knew of any possibilities. Ted and his wife were new friends; Jerry and I had seen them several times at social events and had gone to dinner with them. We looked forward to getting to know them better.

After a few minutes of small talk, Ted asked me a perfectly reasonable question: what were my research interests? I suddenly found myself unable to utter a word. I don't remember what happened next. Looking back, I believe it was something like a bad case of stage fright. I felt I was being called to perform in a role whose lines I had not yet learned.

Meanwhile, during these weeks I had spent searching, Jerry had been busy being a new professor on campus—teaching, meeting colleagues, giving talks. I hadn't the heart to tell him how I was feeling, and I was able to act upbeat as I carried on with everyday life. Eventually, however, I did tell him of the growing discrepancy between the two of us in adapting to our new surroundings.

After a while, he had an idea for a possible solution: the two of us could work on a book, a text reader in family sociology. A sociologist whose first job was at Yale Law School, Jerry had coedited a casebook on family law (with Fowler Harper) and had taught family sociology. More recent, he had edited, with Elliot Currie, a successful text reader on social problems, *Crisis in American Institutions*.[1] The book adopted what was then a novel approach to understanding social problems: instead of focusing on individual deviance as the source, it examined social structures and institutions. Jerry suggested that we coedit a similar book on the sociology of the family.

To me, this did not at all seem like a solution. "But I don't know anything about the family," I complained, "I'm a psychologist." That may sound strange now, but thirty years ago, academic psychology and sociology were much further apart than they are today. The family was starkly divided between them: marriage and family belonged to sociology, and children and parent-child relations belonged to psychology. It felt presumptuous to be thinking of writing a text in a field for which I had no credentials. Nevertheless, I agreed to look into the family literature.

In fact, as my attack of speechlessness revealed, I did not have a firm identity as a psychologist—that is, as a particular kind of psychologist, with a well-defined research agenda. As a graduate student at Yale, I had taken an eclectic array of courses. I managed to earn my doctorate without running a single rat through a maze, even though this was the heyday of behaviorism, and rats were seen as stand-ins for humans. My dissertation was a social-psychological experiment, testing a particular wrinkle in cognitive dissonance theory. Like most of my fellow students, I was aiming at speedy progress toward a doctorate rather than pursuing a deep personal interest.

Toward the end of graduate school, I had become interested in clinical psychology, and I eventually became qualified as a clinical psychologist. Yet I did not completely identify with being a clinician. The handful of patients I had seen as a fledgling therapist convinced me that I was temperamentally unsuited to that aspect of clinical work. I did enjoy psychological testing—deciphering a battery of Rorschachs, Thematic Apperception Tests(TATs), and other tests to produce a psychological portrait of a person.

At IHD, I had been hired as a clinician but had also gone on to publish articles based on the longitudinal data there. I compared motivational scores on the TAT, such as achievement and affiliation, to past and present evidence of real-life behavior. But this work was tied to the IHD database and didn't seem to suggest a line of further studies.

There was something else behind my lack of a practiced academic persona. A journalist once asked me how I had escaped the feminine mystique, but in fact my escape was only partial. Looking back, I see that I was a hybrid—a cross between Betty Friedan's overeducated housewives and the career-focused younger generation that made the feminist revolution.

Even as the women's movement was taking off in the early 1970s, it was still a bit deviant for a wife and mother to be concerned with a professional career. Faculty wives' clubs were a more significant presence on campuses than women faculty. Of course, there were some women who accomplished high-level academic careers even at the height of the Ozzie and Harriet years. But I could not identify either with the "spinster" professors I had known in college or with the few superwomen who could go full speed ahead on a male career path, all while raising three or four children.

Growing up, however, I was naively unaware that being female might constrain my future. The culture as I encountered it did not present a monolithic vision of what a woman's life could be. Gender wasn't an issue until I reached graduate school. My high school, New York City's High School of Music and Art, was more like an outpost of Greenwich Village than the typical American high school, with football teams and cheerleaders. There was no hint that male students were inherently more talented as musicians or artists. Nor, for that matter, was there any apparent distinction in academic accomplishment or recognition. Yet at graduation I was demoted to salutatorian while a boy with lower grades was named valedictorian. It made only a slight dent in my (unraised) consciousness at the time. Mostly, I was delighted at the honor, even if it was second prize.

My gender blindness remained unchallenged at Queens College. My parents, who had literally celebrated my good grades in elementary and high school, began to warn that too much education might not be a good thing for a woman. But Queens College was a cultural force in the opposite direction. I was an English major. In the humanities, there were at least as many women who were recognized scholars in their fields as men, and my advisor and mentor was a leading Ruskin scholar who simply assumed that I would be going on to graduate school. Also, my social circle consisted of other women who were planning professional careers. None of us thought of this as a reason to delay marriage, much less to remain single.

I did not graduate with an engagement or wedding ring on my finger. But as I was preparing to go to France on a Fulbright scholarship, I met Jerry, then a Yale graduate student. Almost instantly, we became engaged. I left for Paris, assuming that Jerry would join me. Jerry's draft board had other ideas. They told him that if he left Yale, even for a semester, he would lose his student deferment. So I left France after a few months and started married life in New Haven, expecting to resume my graduate studies.

It hadn't occurred to me that my gender would be relevant, much less an obstacle. But Yale in the late 1950s was an unpleasant surprise. I soon learned through the graduate student grapevine that the English department was not friendly to women, particularly women of the New York, non-WASP (white, Anglo-Saxon Protestant) variety. The same was true of the history department (history had also been an important interest for me in college). Eventually, however, I found that the psychology department did welcome women graduate students. I had not majored in psychology in college, but there was a sort of back door that had been discovered by a friend: she had signed up for a master's degree in teaching, which had no course requirements of its own. Having done well in the psychology courses she took, she was admitted to the department as a regular student. I followed her through the same back door.

Despite my determination to go to graduate school, I didn't have a clear image of what I would do afterward. I didn't aspire to an academic career. When I started, graduate school for me was a continuation of college. In fact, I would have been happy to be a perpetual student or, better yet, a writer and critic like the New York intellectuals.

There was also the matter of location. Where we lived was an important issue for both of us. At Yale, Jerry and I became part of a circle of cynical ex-New Yorkers, graduate students and assistant professors who did not easily fit into the customs and manners of Ivy League academia at that historical moment. We dreamed of returning to New York or London or Paris. Having fallen in love with the Bay area on a trip there, I also dreamed of a life in California, and I was delighted when Jerry was offered a job at Berkeley. Several times over the years, we were offered joint academic appointments in places we would otherwise not have chosen to live, and so we declined.

The move to Berkeley came just after I had gotten my doctorate and when I was in the later stages of pregnancy. Michael was born, early, three weeks after we arrived. A few months later, I was hired by the Institute of Human Development. Luckily, there was a good fit between my needs as a new mother and the flexibility of the work.

The institute is renowned for its longitudinal studies, begun in the early 1930s and still ongoing. Our arrival in Berkeley came after the first adult follow-up had been completed and just as the massive array of past and recently collected data was ready to be analyzed. I was assigned to create clinical assessments of the longitudinal study subjects. This resulted in a good deal of ongoing work for me at the institute, and it also immersed me in detailed descriptions of individuals and their families. At the time, this rich qualitative data served only as raw material to be processed into a set of variables to be analyzed statistically. But I remained deeply impressed by the richness of the data and the distinctiveness of individual lives.

By the time we left Berkeley for southern California, the institute had become something of a home base for me. I had found the atmosphere of a research institute far more congenial and intellectually stimulating than solo practice as a clinician. Moreover, the institute was in its prime in the 1960s and 1970s, sustained by the state of California and with large grants from other public and private funders. Looking ahead, I took it for granted that financial support would continue to flow indefinitely and that the longitudinal studies would go on throughout the lives of the original subjects and even into the next generation. These assumptions proved to be correct, although the various fiscal crises of the 1970s and beyond brought harder times.

There was another feature of the institute that suggested a workable career path for me. Despite the presence of John Clausen as director, Glen Elder, and other male faculty members, IHD was something of a matriarchy. The group of women psychologists who had been part of the generation that founded the longitudinal studies was still very active, including Jean Macfarlane, Nancy Bayley, Mary Cover Jones, and others. These distinguished women never became tenured members of the psychology department. In addition, there was a fairly large second generation of researchers and staff, also mostly female, who followed in their footsteps.

By the end of our academic year in southern California, we were headed back to Berkeley. Jerry eventually became convinced that whatever the considerable merits of the new location, the University of California at Berkeley was special, particularly in his field—law and society. I returned to the institute.

Ironically, by the time we had decided to leave, I was already immersed in the family book. The early 1970s turned out to be a propitious moment to begin studying and writing about the family. As I looked into the sociological literature, it was clear that a huge gap had opened between social reality and the dominant social science views of the family. That fact that I was an outsider to the field turned out to be an advantage rather than a handicap. I had not been fitted with the prevailing theoretical lenses, and I had no personal ties to mentors or teachers who might feel betrayed by my revisionist views.

It also helped to be in Berkeley. The gap between theory and reality was more conspicuous there than anywhere else at the time. Since the 1960s, the town had been the epicenter of the social and cultural earthquakes that would soon shake the entire country—student protests, communes, open marriage, feminism, the gay movement, the divorce revolution. Marriages of friends and colleagues were breaking down or opening up all around us. Lives were changing on a grand scale.

In the midst of this turmoil, Jerry and I were swimming against the tide, trying to settle into work and family life. The family book was as much an attempt to make sense of our own lives, our marriage, and what was happening around us as it was a solution to my job problem.

Most sociological writings on the family at the time seemed not only to describe a bygone world but also to insist that significant changes in sex, gender, and male-female relationships simply couldn't happen. I remember one article from the late 1960s, which, using a sex survey conducted a few years earlier, found no evidence that rates of premarital intercourse had recently increased. The author concluded that such increases were highly unlikely because few men would be willing to marry nonvirgins.

As Glen Elder put it, the study of the family in the postwar era was "shaped more by simplistic abstract theory and ideological preference" than by the detailed study of families in particular times, places, and circumstances.[2] Parsonian functionalism was then still in its heyday, and what Dennis Wrong called "the oversocialized view of man" prevailed.[3] In general, the stability and legitimacy of all major institutions went largely unquestioned. It was assumed that the traditional nuclear family was a timeless entity but that it had evolved into a more "differentiated," specialized institution in response to industrialization.

The prevailing social theories were also being challenged by new thinking in other fields. In psychology, the cognitive revolution was on its way to dethroning behaviorism, and formerly taboo words—"mind," "consciousness," and "image"—were respectable again. It seemed clear that socialization had to involve more than simple conformity or the internalization of norms.[4]

Another major challenge came from the past. Newly interested in the everyday lives of ordinary people, historians had been drawn to the study of the family and had devised new methods to do so. The findings of the new history undermined nostalgic assumptions about families in past time, especially notions about some lost golden age of family stability and harmony. Also, families in past times turned out to be as diverse and complex in the past as they are today.

Still another breakthrough came from observations of live family interaction. At first, the aim was to discover how schizophrenic families—that is, the families of schizophrenics—differed from other families. At first, it seemed that specific patterns of communication seen in the families of schizophrenics, such as double binds, were the source of pathology in the offspring. When similar patterns were found in ordinary families, one researcher concluded that what had been found was not the pathological family but simply the family. Finally, child abuse and other forms of family violence were "discovered" in the 1960s. Today these insights about the dark side of family life have become familiar to most people, probably too familiar. The "dysfunctional family" has become as much a cultural cliché as its idealized opposite.

Back in the 1970s, though, reading about these new ideas in disparate fields turned out be highly enjoyable and eye-opening. There was something playful and liberating in working outside of any institutional setting or particular academic framework. After a while, the prospective book began to take shape. It would challenge existing myths about the family, describe important changes in the American family, and show how family life is bound up with the social and economic circumstances of particular times and places.

Fortunately, Jerry and I were able to find enough articles that reflected these ideas about families to put together into a book. *Family in Transition*,[5] as we called it, was surprisingly successful. It not only sold well but also steered my career in a different direction.

For a brief period in the mid-1970s, it appeared as if the country was ready to confront old and new family issues in a pragmatic way. An array of foundations, family professionals, policy intellectuals, and government task forces began to take stock of the state of the nation's children and families. I suddenly began to receive invitations to speak at meetings and conferences on the family, and I also became involved in a series of projects dealing with family policy and family law. I had morphed into a family sociologist.

Meanwhile, I continued to work on the longitudinal studies at IHD, now focusing on the marriages and relational careers of the study members. A second adult follow-up took place in the early 1970s, when the study members were in their forties, providing an opportunity to study marriages over a decade-wide span, as well as in greater depth than usual. Among the findings were the following: spouses tend to be similar in personality, rather than complementary, and the greater the similarity, the higher the level of marital satisfaction; study members who were divorced, those who remained in unhappy marriages, and those who were happily married were different in personality even in adolescence; marital relationships could change a good deal over time, for better or for worse.[6]

Based on sales of *Family in Transition*, our publisher asked me to write a textbook on the family. The size of the advance made it an offer I couldn't refuse. *The Intimate Environment*, as I called it, was revised through five editions. Another publisher, who knew of my doctorate in psychology, offered another large advance for a textbook, which eventually was published as *The Psychology of Human Development*.[7]

I enjoyed writing textbooks. For me, they were like extended essays, with pictures and lots of asides. They gave me an excuse to read, browse widely, and patch together ideas from disparate fields. I enjoyed covering the obligatory topics, rethinking old issues, and arguing a point of view. The constraints made the writing itself flow more freely, unlike my previous efforts at fiction. And I could write at home and be available to the children.

Taking the role of critic in an adjacent field led me to cast a colder eye on my original one. Although some theorists were emphasizing the child's active role in its own development, academic psychology seemed wedded to deterministic assumptions about socialization. Children tended to be viewed abstractly as the raw material for the adults they would later become. The child's perceptions, intentions, or individuality as a particular person were ignored.

Moreover, developmental researchers held to an almost Calvinistic fatalism about the continuity of personal traits and influence of early experience on later development. But over the years at IHD, I repeatedly encountered evidence of how much individuals could and did change. Of course, some people's lives did show continuity, for better or for worse. But others followed crooked pathways through life.

Until recently, such "anomalies" were dismissed by most researchers as error variance. One of the most surprising of such findings was the variation in individual IQ (intelligence quotient) scores over time. Jean Macfarlane had written a paper on the subject in the 1940s; she presented some examples of children whose Stanford-Binet scores had fluctuated wildly and showed how these swings were linked to episodes of bad health, trouble in the family, and the like. In another article, Macfarlane described how surprised the IHD staff was when the study members returned at age thirty for the first adult follow-up.[8] Half were more effective adults than the staff had expected them to be. A smaller proportion had failed to live up to high expectations.

My own research on marriage confirmed Macfarlane's observations about change. As I followed the marital lives of particular couples, I was impressed by the great variation over time among individuals and couples. For example, in the study mentioned earlier, of the eighty-two couples who had marital satisfaction ratings at both times, thirty-eight had marriages that changed markedly. In most of these families, the case materials suggested that change for better or worse was linked to life events and shifts in circumstances—illness in the family, money troubles or success, or children growing up.

The more I worked with the longitudinal data, the more I came across people whose lives departed in one way or another from theoretical expectations. For example, I looked into the case histories of people whose marriages scored high on a composite of a number of different measures of marital quality, I was surprised to find that the wife in one of the "best" marriages grew up "hating men" and planned never to marry.

Other long-term longitudinal studies were also turning up evidence that change and discontinuity were as much part of the story of human development as consistency and continuity. To some psychologists, however, such views were heretical. One of my colleagues wrote to a leading developmental journal to complain that recent references (mine) to Macfarlane's writings did not represent the findings of the Berkeley longitudinal studies; Macfarlane, he complained, was a clinician, not a statistically competent researcher.

My old experience as a dissident in family studies gave me the nerve I didn't come by temperamentally to persist in my heresy. I had come across a relatively simple statistical method to analyze life course trajectories, developed by another colleague, William Runyan. This method looks at the life course as a series of different pathways through life and their relative frequencies in a population. In contrast to the more standard statistical techniques, the emphasis is on individuals rather than variables and on variation rather than central tendencies.

I used Runyan's technique to look at the relational careers of longitudinal study members who had data from infancy onward. Briefly, I found that a majority of study members did not follow the continuous pathways predicted by developmental theory—that is, good (or bad) early relationships in the family were not necessarily followed by good (or bad) peer relationships in childhood and adolescence and by good (or bad) marriages.[9] The number was relatively small and the study crude, but I got a great deal of satisfaction out of vindicating Macfarlane's insights.

In the years since my detour into family studies, I have rarely looked back at roads not taken. My career has been an eclectic mix of research, writing, textbook writing, speaking, teaching, and taking part in study groups and public policy debates. The latest edition of *Family in Transition* (the twelfth) has just gone to press.[10] I continue to be engaged in trying to make sense of the ongoing process of family change.

Would I have had a more orderly (stepwise) career if I had come of age after the gender revolution? Would I have developed the more assertive and focused professional persona I needed in that interview? I tend to think so.

Yet in my reading of the literature on contemporary educated women's lives I am impressed by how many of the cultural and occupational constraints still exist and that even ambitious women are reluctant to pursue career goals in a single-minded way. I recently observed a focus group in which a number of students from an elite women's college discussed their futures. They were intensely ambitious for career success and leadership. Yet they were also fiercely determined to have close, highly involved relationships with their families, especially the children they were all planning for. Similar findings emerge from survey data and other research on the eighteen- to thirty-two-year-olds—labeled "Gen X" by the media—and not only among the women.

Would I have *preferred* to have a more orderly standard career? It's hard to say, given that my identity is so intertwined with the experiences I have had and the choices I have made. After *Family in Transition* came out, I had a new career path, a set of abiding new interests in the mysteries of family life, and a sense of intellectual excitement and purpose I hadn't had before.

There were clearly economic costs. A tenured academic position turns out be one of the last of the secure lifetime jobs that used to sustain much of the middle class. But that wasn't always apparent. For some years, writing textbooks brought in more family income than Jerry's professorship. But his lifetime tenure at an elite university allowed my economic contributions to fluctuate wildly.

Looking back, I'm struck by how much my difficulties and choices were shaped, far more than I knew at the time, by gender and by living in a particular historical moment, in particular places, at particular points in my life—and, especially, by contingency. We are now living in New York City as an unanticipated consequence of Jerry's acceptance of a generous early retirement offer that came about because of a fiscal crisis at the University of California. This led to a visiting professorship for him in New York, which led to a job offer at New York University Law School, which I urged him to accept because I had fallen in love with the much-changed place of my birth. This move led to my involvement in projects dealing with families and work and the future of the family.

Over the years, I have also been impressed by the power of cultural time, that is, the more subtle aspects of history, such as the cultural common sense and structures of feeling that prevail at a particular time. What ideas are taken for granted and what is considered outlandish or disturbing? For example, the shifts in ideas about a woman's place over the past three decades have been astonishing. These shifts, as much as events like wars and depressions, set one generation off from another.

I was part of that colorless, "silent" swath of people who came after what the media now call "the greatest generation"—the one that fought and endured World War II—and before the tidal wave of baby boomers overwhelmed us. In 1986, a writer named Benita Eisler wrote a book about this in-between generation, which was also her own.[11] Eisler did not pretend to be doing a sociological study, but her observations rang true to me. The most common generational trait she found in her interviewees was a hidden, "outsider" self, lurking behind a bland outward appearance. Her statement reminded me of something I had not thought of in years: the motto of some of the Jewish professors at Yale in the 1950s and 1960s, the first of their kind to arrive in the Ivy League in significant numbers—"Look British, think Yiddish."

In a somewhat similar vein, the feminist literary critic Carolyn Heilbrun has written of the condition of "liminality," a term she borrows from anthropology. To be liminal is to be in transition, on uncertain ground, "betwixt and between, neither altogether here nor there, not one kind of person or another, not this, not that."[12] Heilbrun identifies liminality as a prime characteristic of recent women's memoirs. Her concept surely fits this one.

NOTES

1. Fowler V. Harper and Jerome H. Skolnick, eds., *Problems of the Family*, rev. ed. (Indianapolis, Ind.: Bobbs-Merrill, 1962): Jerome H. Skolnick and Elliot Currie, eds., *Crisis in American Institutions* (Boston: Little, Brown, 1970).

2. Glen Elder, "Approaches to Social Change and the Family," in *Turning Points: Historical and Sociological Essays on the Family*, ed. J. Demos and S. S. Boocock (Chicago: University of Chicago Press, 1978), 1–38; Supplement to *American Journal of Sociology*, 84 (1978): S34.

3. Dennis Wrong, "The Oversocialized Conception of Man in Modern Sociology," *American Sociology Review* 26 (1961): 183–93.

4. Roger Brown, *Social Psychology* (New York: Free Press, 1965).

5. Jerome H. Skolnick and Arlene S. Skolnick, eds., *Family in Transition: Rethinking Marriage, Sexuality, Childrearing, and Family Organization* (Boston: Little, Brown, 1971).

6. Arlene Skolnick, "Married Lives: Longitudinal Perspectives on Marriage," in *Present and Past in Middle Life*, ed. D. H. Eichorn, et al. (New York: Academic Press, 1981).

7. Arlene S. Skolnick, *The Intimate Environment: On Exploring Marriage and the Family* (Boston: Little, Brown, 1973); Arlene S. Skolnick, *The Psychology of Human Development* (San Diego: Harcourt Brace Jovanovich, 1986).

8. Jean W. MacFarlane, "Perspectives on Personality Consistency and Change from the Guidance Study," *Vita Humana* 7 (1964): 115–26.

9. Arlene Skolnick, "Attachment and Personal Relationships Across the Life Course," in *Life Span Development and Behavior*, ed. D. L. Featherman and R. M. Lerner (Hillsdale, N.J.: Erlbaum, 1986), vol. 7, 173–206.

10. Arlene S. Skolnick and Jerome H. Skolnick, *Family in Transition*, 12th ed. (Boston: Allyn and Beacon, 2003).

11. Benita Eisler, *Private Lives: Men and Women of the Fifties* (New York: Franklin Watts, 1986).

12. Carolyn G. Heilbrun, *Women's Lives: The View from the Threshold* (Toronto: University of Toronto Press, 1999), 8.

JANE MANSBRIDGE

WRITING AS A DEMOCRAT

AND A FEMINIST

11

Democracy implies feminism, and feminism implies democracy. The two causes that have impelled my research are logically and reciprocally related. In my own life, though, each had separate roots, meeting and intertwining in the 1960s.

DEMOCRACY

I was always a bit of a misfit. I attributed my differences from others to my father's being English. That's why, I thought, we didn't have a TV set when everyone else did. That's why I had a funny accent, saying "bean" instead of "bin" for "been," so that the kids in third grade danced around me shouting, "'Been'—bean—stringbean!" (I was pretty skinny). I identified with people who didn't quite fit in.

My father had left England in part because he had come to hate the English class system. In lots of little ways, from rooting for the Brooklyn Dodgers to appreciating an old lady hooting her hymns in church, he taught me to value the plain and simple, to take the side of the underdog, and despise (or maybe just laugh at) people who gave themselves airs. So I grew up thinking equality was good, hierarchy suspect.

I also grew up in a New England town governed by a town meeting. Self-organized committees and other groups did much of the collective work. From the volunteer fire department to the churches—all Protestant and therefore run by committees—through the Girl Scouts, Boy Scouts, and Parent-Teachers Association (PTA), most of the town's work was done in groups, where people made decisions mostly by consensus but occasionally took a vote when they disagreed. The town meeting, where the townspeople themselves made the regulations that governed them and chose three selectmen to carry out those decisions, was not a big part of our lives. It seemed like a natural extension of the ways in which people were already making decisions that affected them in their churches, the PTA, and the other committees that helped do what the town needed done. So I grew up thinking that democracy was the obvious way to make collective decisions.

At the end of my junior year (1960) in college (Wellesley), I heard from a friend about a disarmament group at Harvard called Tocsin. At first I thought the very concept of disarmament wildly unrealistic. Then I began to read its literature and saw how close the world was to accidental nuclear war. I realized that the newspapers I read had not carried, or had not placed in conspicuous spots, the information both I and other citizens needed to know. In my senior year I started a small disarmament group at Wellesley. We worked under a disadvantage. In an era still shaped by McCarthy, none of us dared to subscribe to the "I. F. Stone's Weekly," the source of most of our information. When we asked the one faculty member who supported us to give a talk on disarmament in chapel, he felt he could only give a talk against apathy, using as an example failure to join groups such as ours.

In graduate school at Harvard, although the Vietnam War gradually began to fill the horizon, I was not active against it. I was married, carrying both a full graduate load and the second shift of household responsibilities. After my divorce in 1967, I took the class I was teaching at MIT to a sit-in against the war. I also joined an MIT collective of university teachers who were volunteering to help high school students hold teach-ins against the war. When three of us went to a nearby high school in Tewksbury one day in response to student requests, the police arrested us for trespassing on public property and lied in court later about what we had done. Although we were convicted, we thought it best not to appeal because the appeals judge was known to hate war protesters.

So these experiences set back a bit my earlier conviction that democracy was both obvious and relatively simple. Discovering the media biases in reporting the dangers of nuclear war; realizing that a majority of citizens, relatively uninformed, supported the war in Vietnam; and finding that the police in Tewksbury, presumably responsible to its elected government, had no hesitation in lying in court, I was forced to develop questions about the practice and outcomes of democracy in the United States.

Several years before this, in 1962, students at the University of Michigan had written the Port Huron Statement, calling for a democracy that would bring people "out of isolation and into community," encouraging "respect for others, a sense of dignity and a willingness to accept social responsibility." Inspired by the young University of Michigan philosophy professor Arnold Kaufman, who had coined the phrase, they called their ideal "participatory democracy."[1] Although the Port Huron Statement did not spell out the mechanics of participatory democracy, the decision-making practices of the small groups that were working against the war soon evolved in directions suggested by the Quakers and by a few civil rights leaders like Ella Baker, who advocated decision making from the bottom up. For many young activists, the ideal came to be making as many decisions as possible by those who would be affected by them, in conditions of equal power, face to face, and by consensus.

As the 1960s wore on, many thousands of small collectives—communes, food coops, bicycle repair collectives, law collectives, free schools—sprang up across the United States, all managing their affairs through some version of the small, face-to-face, egalitarian, consensual participatory democracy. As a member of a food coop, with friends in most of these other kinds of collectives, I was deeply immersed in the culture and institutions of participatory democracy. But not until I became heavily engaged in the women's movement did I come to feel the urgency of finding solutions to some of the practical problems that participatory democracy posed.

FEMINISM

My engagement with the women's movement had many causes. First, in high school I found that I wanted not to have to please men. When I went for six months to a girls' boarding school, I reveled in not having to worry about boys. I could immerse myself in books, go for walks in the fields and forest, choose my clothes in the morning, wave my arms and legs in any direction I chose, and not have to worry about what a boy might think. I didn't formulate this conclusion consciously, but when the time came to look at colleges, I found I was interested only in women's institutions. At Wellesley, I wore my gym suit almost every day, almost always with the same sweater and jeans, eliminating the need to buy shirts or other clothing. During the week, I threw myself into my classes, my papers, the library, and my friends in the dorm. On the weekend, I prettied myself up and saw boys. At the first mixer of my freshman year, I met the man I would marry in June of my senior year.

Second, my marriage ended in divorce. It was in 1967, at the beginning of the women's movement. My husband threw me out—not literally; he simply asked for a divorce, and kept the apartment, the towels, the sheets, and the accoutrements of daily life. We divided our record collection, and I looked for a roommate somewhere in Cambridge. Looking back, I marvel that I left so meekly, taking so little with me, not insisting that since he wanted the divorce he should have to move. My self-esteem was at rock bottom. I had begged my husband not to divorce me. He had slept around quite a lot when we were married (it was the era of "sexual liberation"), but I was willing to accept that rather than divorce. I felt about being on my own the way the sailors who did not go with Columbus must have felt about the world beyond the horizon—it was filled with unknown monsters and whirlpools that would suck you under. So when it all ended so badly, I felt that something had gone very wrong.

Soon after that, I was raped. One weekend, about two months after my separation, as I was bravely trying to do things right and not make the mistakes I had made when I was married, I realized I had left my appointment book in my office at Northeastern, where I had a part-time job. My old self would have just left it there until Monday. My new self, trying to be very responsible, got in the car, took a loaned dress back to a friend in Roxbury, fended off a man in front of her house who wanted to put his hand on my bottom, got back in the car, drove to the office, got the key from the superintendent in another building, climbed the stairs to my office, got my appointment book, came downstairs, and found inside the door of the empty building the man who had put his hand on my bottom half an hour before. He had a razor blade in his hand. He told me he had just gotten out of an insane asylum and would kill me if I did not do what he said. Afterward, he took my purse (with my wallet and address) and said he would kill me if I told anyone what had happened. In shock, I took the key back to the superintendent's office and kept quiet. Back in my car, I drove wildly, trying to lose anyone who might be following me. When I finally dared to go home, certain that I was no longer being followed, I took a shower for an hour, scrubbing myself all over, crying all the time.

These traumas, not as unusual as you might think, were surrounded by all the little things that Mary Rowe, at MIT, called "Saturn's rings"—each so small as to be almost invisible but together forming a massive environmental fact.[2] Women were not allowed in Harvard's Lamont Library, which had reserve books right in Harvard Square. We had to use the Radcliffe Library, fifteen minutes away. Women were not allowed in the Faculty Club, except escorted by a man, and then we had to come in the back door. (This all seems impossible today. Why the back door? What earthly good did it do the men to have the women come in the back door?) We were often ignored in seminars and lectures. (So I taught myself such techniques as leaning forward, speaking forcefully, and beginning by addressing the last speaker by name.) A graduate student, intending to be complimentary, said of me, "She thinks like a man." A faculty member, finding that he and I were in his office alone, pulled me against him for a kiss and pushed his pelvis against me. When I reacted with confusion and dismay, he backed off and apologized, and that was the end of that. Except, on my side, I didn't feel I could take another course from him or have him as an advisor.

So, when the women's movement arrived, I was ready. The most important cause of my active feminism was, I think, simply that I was in the right place at the right time. The Boston area from 1969 to 1973, my most active years, spawned a huge critical mass of feminist groups and activities—open-ended, various, and all hungering for people ready to work. I was in the doctorate stage of graduate school, which at Harvard then could stretch for many years, and I had no consuming relationships. I was relatively free and intensely interested. When a friend from MIT asked me if I wanted to join a consciousness-raising group, I jumped at the chance.

In my first group we started putting the pieces of our lives together into a coherent analysis. I was angry, fascinated, exhilarated. My group of twelve women was all white, various shades of middle class, and mostly nonacademic. I did not know most of the members and would not have chosen them as friends in another context. Each week for three hours in the evening, we discovered that our experiences had been far more similar than we ever would have guessed and that they were rooted in a pattern of inequalities we now recognized as unjust.

Every day brought new revelations. Another collective I joined gave an informal course on women's health. I gave the evening on "sexuality," drawing a vulva on the blackboard to show where to touch in order to masturbate. When our group wrote up what we'd done, I wrote the first draft of the sexuality chapter in what would become *Our Bodies, Our Selves*. In Bread and Roses, the Boston women's umbrella group that sprang up, scores of self-starting collectives worked on whatever inspired them. (In one collective, we put out the "New England Women's Liberation Newsletter"; in another, we did college organizing; one day with a friend I handed out "The Myth of the Vaginal Orgasm"[3] on the Cambridge Common.)

But issues of governance began to undermine our organization. Some people had had a major effect on the shape of the movement in Boston. Others resented their greater influence. We were all committed to not duplicating the hierarchy and exclusion that everyone had experienced both in the mainstream world (like my seminars) and in the New Left. We agreed not to speak to the media except in groups. No one would allow herself to be a "spokeswoman" for the movement. A writer from New York, sent to do a major story for *Life* magazine, grew frustrated and angry because no one would agree to be on the cover. Our insistence on equality made it hard for us to communicate easily because we refused to have a central organization. A group called Crumbs and Petals met to discuss the situation. We decided that to maintain both egalitarian decentralization and coordination we needed a women's center. The next month, our International Women's Day march veered from its publicly announced route, and we occupied 888 Memorial Drive, a little-used Harvard building, as a temporary women's center.

By this time, I had become seriously concerned with trying to make participatory democracy work. One of my students suggested that I read the anarchists.[4] When an anonymous donor gave us the funds for a down payment on a house for a women's center, and we marched out of 888 Memorial Drive in triumph, I joined the fund-raising collective, then the house-finding collective, then the collective working on governance. I was reading whatever I could find in political science, sociology, psychology, and anthropology on how to do this.

Meanwhile, the collectives of the New Left were breaking up all around me. To make a little money, I taught a seminar on participatory democracy. Because I couldn't find many good readings, I concluded that the movement needed, at the very least, a book like Gissell and Ilg's *The Child from Five to Ten*, based on research on child development that advised parents, for example, not to blame themselves or their five-year-olds for the tantrums likely at that age.[5] I thought that participatory groups faced inevitable dilemmas of time, emotion, and inequality that no one could solve, and that recognizing some simple structural constraints would at least help with the problem of blame.[6] This "at least" approach helped me tackle what all my advisors predicted would be (and was) a ten-year study.

Beyond Adversary Democracy,[7] the work I designed as best I could to meet the need I had experienced, was originally titled *Participatory Democracy*. By the time the book came out in 1980, fewer people cared about participatory democracy than when I started, and fewer collectives were trying to govern themselves in that way. But the title also changed because, in the course of studying the three direct democracies that were intended to form the core of the book—a town meeting, an alternative workplace, and my own women's center—I discovered that one central problem was philosophical. The members of the young participatory collectives and the political scientists who wrote about democracy at the national level had each fixated on a different form of democracy. The collectives thought they needed a kind of democracy that was, at bottom, based on common interests. The political scientists thought the nation needed a kind of democracy that was, at bottom, based on conflicting interests. These assumptions were implicit rather than explicit, for no one had teased apart what each form of democracy implied.

Beyond Adversary Democracy argued that the institutions and practices that flow from an assumption of common interests cling together logically. So do the institutions and practices associated with an assumption of conflicting interests. An unnoticed logic also derived from these assumptions. I came to realize that on issues involving primarily common interests, members of a polity do not need equal power to protect their interests equally. Those with more power, following their own interests, will make decisions that protect the interests of others. If we both want to get to Boston, I can fall asleep in the back seat and let you have complete control over the car because I know you want to get to Boston too. The assumption of common interests, I now saw, lay behind arguments for unequal power, from Plato's guardians to Lenin's vanguard to the U.S. Supreme Court.

Working out these relationships took several years and followed an inductive course. A critical moment came when I was interviewing the members of Helpline, the alternative workplace I had chosen to study because it was the most dedicated and successful participatory democracy of any I could find. The forty-one full-time workers at Helpline were heavily committed to equality, in salaries and in their practice of democracy. But at the end of each interview, I gave each person a sheet of paper depicting a series of concentric circles and forty-one little slips of paper, each containing the name of one member. I then asked if it made sense to arrange the members around a center of power. Thirty-four of the forty-one full-time workers thought the task made sense, and all of these distributed the names unequally. Then I taped the names to the paper (a significant moment) and asked people if they felt comfortable with that distribution. All but five said they did. When I asked them why, as egalitarians, they felt comfortable with the unequal distribution of power they had just portrayed, they gave me lots of reasons, which eventually gave me the clues I needed to realize that they thought they had the same underlying interests.[8]

I concluded that when equalizing power makes it harder to reach other goals, as it often does, and when a collective is dealing with issues in which the members have primarily common interests, the participants do not need to insist on complete equality of power. When they do, they are mistakenly importing norms appropriate for situations in which individuals have conflicting interests. I think this was my biggest contribution to helping participatory democracies govern themselves, although it may also help to have identified the specific advantages and disadvantages of consensus, people's fears of conflict, and the subtle forms of inequality that shape outcomes even when people are theoretically free to participate. I'm sure my experiences as a child made me particularly sensitive to people who felt marginal in town meetings. My experiences in graduate school certainly made me resonate to women's particular styles of being less powerful—speaking less at the meeting, expressing fewer opinions when they did speak, and feeling uncomfortable with taking power.

As I was writing the book, I realized that the kind of democracy we practice nationally in the United States worked from an assumption of conflicting interests and that this assumption—just like the opposite assumption of common interests in town meetings—is often mistaken. Of course, interests often conflict. But even national-level democracy could benefit from institutions and practices designed to encourage individuals to seek consensus. Democracies that have been functioning well for a long time, I concluded, learn to segue back and forth between practices and institutions designed for common interests and those designed for conflict. They choose among them according to how much conflict they expect to find in the issue at hand or in the issues most likely to come before their group or form of government. Both the collectives I studied and the nation-state developed problems when they did not recognize the limitations of their dominant mode of democracy and did not know how to harness the virtues of the other mode.

So a project that I had initially conceived as being perhaps useful only through description emerged with a philosophical conclusion that would challenge those of John Rawls and Jürgen Habermas.[9] En route, it provided the first analysis of the workings of what would later be called "deliberative" democracy; revealed the patterns of inequality that emerge in an open, face-to-face democracy; and gave some insight into the reasonable fears of those who decide not to speak out in a public meeting. En route I also dropped my own collective, the women's center, from the book, which was already too long. But I still think I ended up with a book that could help collectives that were trying to make participatory democracy work.

Why We Lost the ERA[10] also began with a problem I faced, as a feminist, in the workings of democracy. When, as a young assistant professor at the University of Chicago, I helped organize the first feminist organization on campus, we used the Equal Rights Amendment (ERA) as an organizing tool. I was puzzled by the failure of the state of Illinois to ratify the ERA—an amendment to the U.S. Constitution that my radical Boston self had thought too "liberal," too "white-bread" to bother with. One of my freshman students had produced a table, based on data from the NORC (National Opinion Research Center) General Social Survey, showing that, even among the most deeply sexist, 20% of the population—people who said in face-to-face interviews with (mostly) female interviewers that they would not vote for a woman for president even if she were qualified and their party nominated her—49% favored the ERA.[11] Most people, it seemed, supported the amendment because they were for equal rights, not because they supported changes that would benefit women. But our own movement seldom seemed to recognize this fact. I decided that interviewing legislators and activists would help the women's movement by illuminating this disjunction. Again I started work on a book, thinking that pure description would serve a useful purpose even if no deeper insights emerged.

As I dug deeper, through my interviews and participant observation, I began to realize that the very structure of a social movement works against the kind of listening I was advocating. Recruiting only volunteers, whose incentives are idealistic, sets up a dynamic that I came to call institutional deafness: not listening to people outside one's own group. It also encourages decisions by accretion: decisions made without discussion that go unchallenged because they fit what people want to believe. Like the town meeting and the participatory workplace I chose for *Beyond Adversary Democracy*, the ERA movement allowed a best-case analysis. More than in any other social movement I know, people in the women's movement believe in listening. Movement organizations often devote considerable resources to practices designed not to exclude anyone. If institutional deafness and decisions by accretion appeared in the women's movement, I thought they were likely to appear in any social movement that entered a battle while relying mainly on volunteers. Because social movements must rely on volunteers, their members should be aware of the dynamics that will inevitably emerge in deeply adversarial situations in order to struggle consciously against those pressures as best they can.

There was a manual for practice embedded in the ERA book, just as there was in the book on participatory democracy. Both books ask, among other things, to look for who isn't there and to think how outcomes may have been shaped by their absence. The lessons spring in part from my continuing sympathy with people who might think they have not been invited to this party.

Over the years, my work has changed me. Although I help run a program in women and public policy, I have also become a professional in a professional discipline. I now care deeply for the discipline of political science, which in its best incarnation is a group of people systematically trying to figure out how the human race can govern itself justly and with a minimum of violence. I care about getting it right, and I have tried to combine a historian's obsession with digging details from archives, a quantitative social scientist's obsession with making sense of numerical data, and a normative theorist's obsession with logical argument. I have become more of a theorist,[12] though I insist on going back every so often to interviewing, and when I can't do that, working with others' in-depth cases.

My most important work has been problem-centered. It does not sit in an established research tradition, although I hope it has helped bring about the field now known as democratic theory. I have been influenced by Judith Shklar more than by anyone else, but I had no real mentor. In Shklar's seminars at Harvard on the history of political theory, I learned more than ever to read closely, be careful of my inferences, and feel joy at an idea that made sense. Because I write to some degree in the political theory tradition, my work often requires normative analysis and prescription, which are foreign to sociology. Someone trying to describe my professional persona might say I was a "normative democratic theorist whose work was guided by empirical analysis." But in my own mind, I am still a feminist, still committed to equality, and still trying to figure out how to do democracy better.

NOTES

1. "The Port Huron Statement," reprinted in James Miller, *Democracy Is in the Streets* (New York: Simon and Schuster, 1987); Arnold Kaufman, "Human Nature

and Participatory Democracy," in *Responsibility: NOMOS III*, ed. Carl Friedrich (New York: Liberal Arts Press, 1960).

2. Mary Rowe, "Saturn's Rings," *Graduate and Professional Education of Women* (Washington, D.C.: American Association of University Women, 1974), 1–9, revised and expanded as "Barriers to Equality: The Power of Subtle Discrimination to Maintain Unequal Opportunity," *Employee Responsibilities and Rights Journal* 3, 2 (1990): 153–63.

3. "Sexuality" (as Jane de Long) with Ginger Goldner and Nancy London, in *Women and Their Bodies: A Course* (Boston: New England Free Press, 1970), first edition of *Our Bodies, Ourselves*, ed. Boston Women's Health Book Collective (New York: Simon and Schuster, 1973).

"The Myth of the Vaginal Orgasm" was a pamphlet at the time. It was later reprinted in *Notes from the First Year* by Anne Koedt (New York: New York Radical Women, 1968).

4. I owe those readings in anarchism to Stephen Soldz: for example, Serge Bricianer, *Pannekoek and the Workers' Councils*, trans. Malachy Carroll (St. Louis, Mo.: Telos Press, 1978); Errico Malatesta, *Anarchy*, trans. Vernon Richards (London: Freedom Press, 1974); Peter Kropotkin, *Anarchism: Its Philosophy and Ideal* (San Francisco: Free Society, 1898); and *Mutual Aid, a Factor of Evolution* (Boston: Extending Horizons Books, 1955).

5. Arnold Gesell and Frances L. Ilg, *The Child from Five to Ten* (New York: Harper, 1946).

6. Jane Mansbridge, "Time, Emotion and Inequality: Three Problems of Participatory Groups," *Journal of Applied Behavioral Science* 9 (1973): 357–68.

7. Jane Mansbridge, *Beyond Adversary Democracy* (New York: Basic Books, 1980); reissued with a new preface by the University of Chicago Press, 1983.

8. Jane Mansbridge, "Acceptable Inequalities," *British Journal of Political Science* 7 (1977): 321–36. The title came from a faculty seminar at the University of Chicago, where I was an assistant professor. After I had presented my analysis of the answers my interviewees had given, Lloyd Rudolph commented, "You're talking about which inequalities are acceptable." A reasonable closeness to common interests is, in the full analysis, only one of three necessary justifying circumstances for legitimately unequal power. The other two conditions are equal respect and sufficient opportunities for self-development among the members.

9. For that analysis, see Jane Mansbridge, "Using Power/Fighting Power," *Constellations* 1, 1 (1994): 53–73.

10. Jane Mansbridge, *Why We Lost the ERA* (Chicago: University of Chicago Press, 1986).

11. Ibid., table I, 21.

12. See, for example, Jane Mansbridge, "Should Women Represent Women and Blacks Represent Blacks? A Contingent 'Yes,'" *Journal of Politics* 61, 3 (1999): 626–57. For analytic work less in the tradition of normative theory, see Jane Mansbridge, "The Rise and Fall of Self-Interest" and "On the Relation of Altruism and Self-Interest," in

Beyond Self-Interest, ed. Jane Mansbridge (Chicago: University of Chicago Press, 1990); and Jane Mansbridge, "The Making of Oppositional Consciousness" and "Complicating Oppositional Consciousness," in *Oppositional Consciousness: The Subjective Roots of Social Protest*, ed. Jane Mansbridge and Aldon Morris (Chicago: University of Chicago Press, 2001).

CYNTHIA FUCHS EPSTEIN

12

DECODING DICHOTOMIES

AND PUSHING THE BOUNDARIES

A LIFETIME OF RESEARCH ON

WOMEN IN THE PROFESSIONS

This account of my research on the cultural and structural underpinning of gender distinctions—focusing on women's participation in the legal profession—begins more than three decades ago. At the time it was initiated, the research topic was unusual, as were the individuals I set out to study: the "deviant cases" of women practitioners in an elite profession. Since that time, women's roles in society—especially in the workplace and particularly in the top professions—have changed radically and research on them has proliferated, engaging several subsequent generations of researchers. Along with these changes has been the questioning of the analytic frameworks that had accounted for (and often justified) women's exclusion.

Therefore, I shall attempt in this brief chapter to write of my part in this transformation as a researcher who offered a competing framework for analyzing gender roles, who documented the changing context and roles of women, and who was an activist in the social movement that was partly responsible for the changes.

How does one write about a research agenda that has been part and parcel of one's everyday life for three decades? Personal history, at best, provides a selective narrative based on what one remembers and what one is willing to tell about it. Thoughts about the causes of one's decisions may conform to paradigms drawn from the available cultural frameworks, as when people think of important people in their lives as role models to explain the reasons for their aspirations. (Another generation would have attributed their motivation to their own pluck.) As Peter McHugh and Alan Blum[1] pointed out many years ago, our views of why we make certain choices are no more and no less than theories, not the "true" story. Since I am eclectic in my theoretical orientation (I believe that some combination of psyche, social control, opportunity, historical rooting, and cultural ideology shape us), I can point to many factors that made me into a sociologist whose focus has been on deconstructing binary ways of thinking about sex and gender in society—one lifelong research project. So here is a version of my journey, truncated and incomplete, but as true as I can make it.

My commitment to working for a better society—part of my upbringing—and the genesis of my research career came together at a historic moment. Because I came of age in the 1960s, the drama of the civil rights movement, the antiwar movement, the Zionist movement, and most important, the feminist movement shaped the research questions that were to guide my scholarship for the decades following.

My first focused research questions concerned the sources of inequality. These questions centered on women's access to the top jobs in society. My exploration began with the case of women lawyers' access to and participation in the legal profession in the United States—a case that I chose as a strategic research site for the study of exclusion. In time, my work came to focus on how binary distinctions in social life are a mechanism for maintaining boundaries between groups, with gender as the most universal dichotomy.

My study of the ways in which women have been stereotyped and cast in the role of other in the law began as a doctoral dissertation and took on its own life, making me a specialist in gender differentiation in the workplace. My first research reported on the discrimination the first women in the legal profession were encountering through the end of the 1960s. But because its findings were reported in a time of rapid social change, the research did not end with my dissertation, and it became a project of inquiry that was to go on for three decades. In fact I defended my dissertation at Columbia University in 1968 during student protests; students were literally scaling the walls outside the examination room, and although I was conflicted about being inside while many of my classmates were outside, I was determined to finish my degree and get on with my life after having been a graduate student for eight years. (The classmates scaling the walls also finished their degrees soon after.) The research for my dissertation was done at a time when the woman's movement, in which I was heavily involved, had burst onto the American scene. Thus, my project, a study of the dynamics of discrimination, became the first step in my continuing research on social change.

Sociology had hardly addressed my choice of topic—the role of women in the professions and, broadly, the role of gender in the workplace—when I started to explore it. Only a handful of social scientists had analyzed the paucity of women's roles in society outside the home and found it problematic. Most individuals, including social scientists, regarded the division of labor by sex as rooted in women's and men's natures or the pragmatics of their life situations, that is, their choices. However, a few pioneers (I offer their names to jolt historic memory), Jessie Bernard, Alice Rossi, and Mirra Komarovsky in the United States; Alva Myrdal and Viola Klein in Britain; Harriet Holter in Norway; and Elina Haavio-Manilla in Finland, looked to structural and cultural constraints as the source of women's near invisibility from the professional, scientific, artistic, and public administrative sectors of society. Their insights into the structural and cultural constraints on women's equality were to be discovered or rediscovered by subsequent academic generations. The term "gender" had yet to be used, and analyses of women in society were seen as part of the sociology of the family.

Furthermore, there were no women sociologists on the graduate faculties at which I studied. Only once, at Columbia, did I have an opportunity to sit in on a class with a woman. It was Margaret Mead, who in spite of her fame was not on the regular faculty but an adjunct lecturer in anthropology. However, I had the full support of several male mentors as I began my research on women in professional life.

An early set of influences, drawn from a community and a family oriented toward social justice, led me to think about gender discrimination. Among these influences was my involvement in a Zionist youth group during the early days of the founding of the State of Israel. The group subscribed to the socialist ideals of the Israeli kibbutz, with its model of equal participation of men and women in governance and the division of labor. This and a "progressive" education from grade school through college (the experimental Antioch College), emphasizing women's abilities, made me skeptical of the rationales that supported a division of labor by sex that provided few professional opportunities for women. After college, there were five years of frustrating dead-end jobs as a secretary, researcher, and writer of ceremonies and newsletters in nonprofit charitable organizations—a typical female work track at the time. However, working in the nonprofit sphere, particularly in one organization in which the top executives were women volunteers who clearly demonstrated leadership abilities and serious ambition, led me to question why women were generally regarded as lacking these traits and talents by gatekeepers to top jobs in other spheres.

After a few years, I decided to obtain a doctorate at Columbia University, where I studied with (and subsequently worked for) Robert K. Merton and William J. Goode. Both men encouraged my choice of dissertation topic: a study of women's exclusion from the prestigious professions, using the legal profession as a case in point. Women lawyers were rare and thus constituted a deviant case in their profession; they were survivors of a system that was generally hostile to women.

One key event on the way to formulating the women lawyers' project was the $1000 grant I received from the Institute of Life Insurance to study the changing American family. (A small grant can have a large outcome. I received it in January 1963 while in the hospital where I had just given birth to my son, Alex—extending the bonding experience to my work, as well as to my child.) Assembling materials on the family, I saw that women were rapidly entering the labor force but generally were limited to jobs sex-typed as female. This led me to look at women's work force participation cross-nationally. I saw that women always worked at sex-typed occupations but that the occupations viewed as "natural" for women differed from country to country. Yet everywhere rationales supported the division of labor by sex as consistent with women's and men's nature. For example, in the Soviet Union it was considered natural for women to be doctors because medicine was regarded as a nurturant profession; in the United States it was considered natural for men to be doctors because medicine was regarded as an abstract scientific profession. Of course, no society left the selection of training and career to nature. Males and females were given opportunities or denied them on the basis not only of their sex but also their class position, ethnicity, and age—all factors constituting an opportunity structure. Focusing on the United States, I saw how women who were interested in being doctors and lawyers faced extreme discrimination. The few who managed to circumvent the discrimination received little acknowledgement of their productivity and creativity. I observed that out of networks and without mentors, women were either prevented from participating in professional life altogether or they did so as silent and invisible partners whose contributions were used without credit or ignored entirely.

This work evolved into my dissertation, which analyzed the factors that contributed to women's inclusion in professional life and the factors that led to their exclusion. The dissertation also examined the social dynamics of status sets—the theoretical perspective outlined by Merton. I was interested in the ways in which acquisition of certain statuses was facilitated or impeded by possession of a dominant status (or a "master status," as Everett Hughes put it), in this case, the status of woman.

In the days before it was unlawful to discriminate on the basis of sex, women faced many obstacles to entering professional life. Leaders of all elite professions were clear and vociferous in their antipathy toward women and imposed quotas on women's admission to professional schools. Nearly all elite professional schools had either refused to admit women or imposed severe quotas on their entry—rarely more than 3% of each entering class. In the law, the few who surmounted the obstacles and graduated from school found it difficult to get jobs as attorneys. Gatekeepers who recruited lawyers for large or small firms, government work, and corporations for the most part refused to hire women. I decided to examine a sample of "survivors"—the few who managed to circumvent the discrimination.

When I began to assemble a reading list, I found there were slim pickings. One book was Betty Friedan's *The Feminine Mystique*,[2] which, readers may recall, attacked sociologists such as Talcott Parsons for suggesting that the conventional nuclear family, with a bread-winning father and stay-at-home mother, was a functional unit for society and that it was best for the family if women did not compete with their husbands in the occupational sphere. William J. Goode, who was her neighbor and sociological guide in the research for her book, introduced me to Friedan. I became a friend and a follower in the developing woman's movement.

By 1966, with my research underway, I joined with Friedan and a cluster of other academic and professional women to form the National Organization for Women in New York City. During that time, continuing my research, I began to write of the difficulties women faced as recruits to the professions, analyzing their problems in finding mentors or places in networks and in being defined as competent professionals. I attended the first Women and the Law Conference at Rutgers University, organized by Ruth Bader Ginsburg.[3] Through Betty Friedan's instigation, I also testified at hearings of the newly formed and empowered Equal Employment Opportunities Commission (EEOC) on establishing guidelines to interpret Title VII of the Civil

Rights Act. My testimony dealt with the consequences of continuing to permit "help wanted" advertisements in newspapers to be segregated as "help wanted—female" and "help wanted—male."

The long overdue report to the Institute of Life Insurance for the $1000 grant resulted in a manuscript of hundreds of pages, and I decided to submit one chapter of it as a paper to the American Sociological Association (ASA). After a long delay (and, as I understood, some question by the committee concerning the importance of the subject), it was accepted. The paper, "Encountering the Male Establishment: Sex-Status Limits on Women's Careers in the Professions," was discovered by the University of California Press's social science editor, Grant Barnes, who heard me present it at the ASA's annual meeting. In an unexpected and exciting telephone call after the meeting, he expressed interest in my work and asked whether I might consider writing a book. I sent him the manuscript of the report to the Institute of Life Insurance, and he immediately optioned it. Barnes believed that scholarship on women, almost nonexistent in sociological studies in the past, would be of growing interest. After extensive revision, *Woman's Place* was published in 1970. Based on the report and on preliminary findings from my dissertation research on women lawyers, the book sold widely (47,000 copies) and was to define my work of a lifetime. It was one of the earliest analyses of the structural and cultural impediments women faced in attaining prestigious and powerful public roles.[4]

However, my dissertation research was a qualitative study limited to women lawyers, chosen because I was interested in learning why so few women were to be found in the prestigious professions. That study, in some sense, was never to end in my professional life. The first work, building on my dissertation research, was a study of black professional women,[5] survivors of the double whammy of discrimination. Like my study of women lawyers, this was a deviant case analysis, explaining how a cluster of individuals surmounted the substantial barriers against them because they possessed statuses (as women and African Americans) that were considered to be inappropriate for the occupational community for which they qualified on the basis of ability and training.

During this same period I had been moving toward publishing my dissertation, with a contract in hand but a sense that my research needed to be updated. Thus, I began interviewing clusters of women lawyers who were moving into domains that had routinely excluded women or were entirely new to them. The leading exclusionary domain, of course, was the large, private, corporate, Wall Street law firms. The most striking new domain was that of the all-women law firms devoted to feminist issues such as employment discrimination—a specialty that came into being in the late 1960s when Title VII of the Civil Rights Act of 1964 became the basis for litigation. I also interviewed women judges and women professors and deans in law schools. Of interest to me were the subtle social controls women faced, undermining their participation and upward mobility in the profession, and the problems they encountered in integrating their careers with family life. A book, *Women in Law*, reporting on my dissertation research and on the subsequent research over the next decade, was published in 1981 and updated in 1993.[6]

The years of studying women in professional life have taken me beyond the borders of gender studies to the dynamics of stereotyping in all social spheres and to consideration of the potential for change in human development, the relationship between self and work, and the integration between cultural and social factors. More recently, they have led me to concentrate on the social construction of boundaries, especially those resulting in binary distinctions. As a fellow for six years at the Russell Sage Foundation (1982–88), one of my tasks was to explore gender distinctions. During those years I assessed a wide swath of social science studies of gender and explored the often hidden bases for what I called *Deceptive Distinctions*, the title of the resulting book.[7] I spent some time in the 1980s and 1990s working with Kai Erikson on a study of the then unified AT&T (American Telephone & Telegraph), working on gender and other boundary issues such as skilled and unskilled work, black and white relations in the workplace, and resistance to changes in the sex division of labor.

But my reputation as a sociologist of women in the law caught up with me again in the early 1990s when I was invited by the Association of the Bar of the City of New York's Committee on the Status of Women to discuss a research project that would shed light on a puzzling phenomenon they had encountered. The committee included several women who had achieved partnerships in the decade before but who noticed that almost no women were following in their footsteps up the ladder. (They had achieved their status in the late 1960s, after the first important lawsuits against employment discrimination by large law firms had been settled.) The committee offered to fund a project to study the issue. We agreed on a study of women's mobility in large private corporate law firms because we knew (1) the firms drew recruits from the top echelon of the top law schools and (2) the career track at these firms was clearly outlined and institutionalized. By interviewing women and men at the partnership rank, we could track career progressions. By studying associates at and after their fifth year, we had a sample of lawyers who were clearly interested in a career in their firm and had proven themselves sufficiently to achieve senior status. Thus we had a built-in control for quality and performance. The members of the Status of Women Committee persuaded ten firms to cooperate in the study, and in the end eight of them participated. Each firm assigned a partner to "broker" our study and win cooperation at every level, from the most senior managing partners to the associates. As a result, we were able to interview equal numbers of men and women partners (which meant we had almost all the women partners, given their low percentage among the lawyers in these firms).

This study, which employed several graduate students to go into the field with me to interview associates and partners, found that women had achieved equity in recruitment, an important achievement, but were disadvantaged on the route to partnership. We found that women were no longer questioned about their intellectual competence, as they had been in earlier years, but that the male gatekeepers questioned whether their image and personal style met the criteria for partnership. Furthermore, we found that women were often out of the loop because older male partners did not refer clients to them. Without these referrals, associates could not acquire the social capital to "make rain," that is, to get business for the firm—a necessary element in a positive assessment for partnership.

We also found that women in these firms faced dual burdens in time demands: an escalation of hours at work because of new and higher demands for billable hours and an escalation of expectations about their parenting responsibilities. Although doors to the firms had opened, the family was unchanged in its assignments of responsibilities for child care. The culture placed the career costs of child care solely on women's shoulders.

This study's findings mirrored what my research on the "difference literature" had revealed. Women seemed to have the same competence as men in all specialties of the law, and this was acknowledged by men, as well as women. However, both women and men often accepted the stereotype that women had a different style. This was not supported by our observations. We observed as many different interpersonal styles and personalities among women as among men, and we saw how much situational factors played into which style was presented and how the interactions were interpreted. Certainly women differed from men in several ways, based on their situation. For example, those who had children accepted more responsibility in caring for them than the men, and they internalized common stereotypes about women's caring nature, bringing into question studies based on self-reporting by women and men.

One example of this phenomenon bears repeating. One woman lawyer described her behavior toward clients as much more caring than that of her male associates. She claimed she listened more and was more responsive than the men. However, I also interviewed male lawyers who worked with her. They did not share her view. They thought she was aggressive, and one described her as "a barracuda." I suspected these interpretations all had a measure of truth. I followed this lawyer's career over time (an advantage of one's research projects being interconnected and lasting over a long period of time). Finding similar discrepancies in other interviews led me to consider, first, how people's multiple roles may call out different, even competing and contradictory behaviors and, second, even within one role a person may exhibit a range of behaviors, any one of which might be seen to characterize a person's entire personality.

Such observations led me to several papers on multiple roles and on the protean woman[8] in American life. I incorporated these ideas in further research on women lawyers, an associated study of flexible and part-time work in the profession. In the year following the glass ceilings study, I met with Hirsh Cohen, the vice president of the Alfred Sloan Foundation, who was beginning to focus on the loss of trained professional workers because of time pressures in their workplaces. He was thinking about investing in studies that would examine the ways in which flexible and part-time work and technology might be a response to the problem. This led me to think about how the data I had gathered for the glass ceiling study would be suitable for further study of part-time work. Carroll Seron, a colleague who had published a study of lawyers in small firms,[9] collaborated in the research that covered part-time and flexible work in the large private law firms I had investigated before, as well as in small firms, government agencies, and the legal departments of large corporations.

With a grant from the Sloan Foundation,[10] Seron and I studied the impact of rising work-time expectations on lawyers' careers. We found that many firms and organizations recently had instituted formal policies that permitted part-time work schedules, and we were to learn that less than 3% of lawyers chose to work part time. In general, lawyers who chose part-time work were seen as less committed than others, and part-timers were given less important work to do. In short, the lawyers who worked part time (often working forty or more hours a week) were stigmatized. We found further that part-time law employment was usually granted only to women with children and that the few men who took such schedules found themselves even more stigmatized than the women. The men were the butt of negative feedback not only at work but also in their communities. Some found their manhood was questioned, and some encountered hostility from other parents—for example, mothers who were suspicious of a man who opted to care for children during the "normal" workday. It was clear that norms at work and in society supported the idea that women might legitimately work less than men at the same level of a profession, but they would pay for it by being placed offtrack. And the norms specified that men were expected to conform to workplace conventions and give their profession first priority. Even when couples had careers of similar rank, we found that they agreed to a division of labor at work and in the home that favored the male career. This was usually regarded as a rational economic decision rather than any acknowledgement of inequality, but the consequences certainly placed the women in a less favored professional position.

The research I have done on gender issues in the law has led me to the question of time as a construct that embodies social meaning. My current conceptual work integrates time with other indicators of boundary distinctions and analyzes the ways it is used to maintain gender and other role and status distinctions. This work sees time constructs as social control mechanisms that maintain boundaries (e.g., of the "true professional" or of work-family "conflict").[11] I am interested in time references as part of a discourse that denies agency in the process of control (e.g., employers who suggest that "in time" women will reach the same levels as men in the organizational hierarchy but do nothing to help them) and attributes agency to time (e.g., "time heals all wounds") rather than identifying the time choices made by individuals or the choices made for them. A recent paper[12] seeks to understand the social controls that prevent role transgressions—for example, individuals who assume roles not traditional for their sex, such as women who work as coal miners or men who work as telephone operators. It looks at the ways in which time ideologies (e.g., the professions as "greedy institutions"[13] and gender ideologies (e.g., the prescription of "intensive mothering"[14] restrict social change.

This work is really a continuation of the research project I began more than 30 years ago when I asked why women couldn't be lawyers (or doctors or members of Congress). Rapid social change has altered the rules by which individuals play out their lives, but my research agenda has altered to target the new conditions. My goal has remained constant, however, and it has created one lifelong project—documenting and analyzing the structural, cultural, and personal forms of distinction and exclusion.

NOTES

1. Alan Blum and Peter McHugh, "The Social Ascription of Motives," *American Sociological Review* 36 (1971): 98–129.

2. Betty Friedan, *The Feminine Mystique* (New York: Norton, 1963).

3. Who is today, of course, a justice of the Supreme Court of the United States.

4. Cynthia Fuchs Epstein, *Women's Place: Options and Limits in Professional Careers* (Berkeley: University of California Press, 1970). The book also caught the attention of some policymakers, who invited me to work on issues of women's employment as part of a White House Committee on the Economic Status of Women (headed by the chair of the Council of Economic Advisors), to testify on affirmative action at an Oval Office meeting with President Ford, and to work on the National Academy of Sciences Committee on Women's Employment and Related Social Issues.

5. Cynthia Fuchs Epstein, "Positive Effects of the Multiple Negative: Explaining the Success of Black Professional Women," *American Journal of Sociology* 78, 4 (January 1973): 912–33.

6. Cynthia Fuchs Epstein, *Women in Law* (New York: Basic Books, 1981); 2nd ed., with a new epilogue (Chicago: University of Illinois Press, 1993).

7. Cynthia Fuchs Epstein, *Deceptive Distinctions: Sex, Gender and the Social Order* (New Haven, Conn.: Yale University Press, 1988).

8. See Cynthia Fuchs Epstein, "Multiple Demands and Multiple Roles: The Conditions for Successful Management," in *Spouse, Parent, Worker*, ed. Faye Crosby (New Haven, Conn.: Yale University Press, 1987); and Cynthia Fuchs Epstein, "The Protean Woman: Anxiety and Opportunity," in *Trauma and Self*, ed. Charles Strozier and Michael Flynn (Lanham, Md., and London: Rowman and Littlefield, 1996), 159–73.

9. Carroll Seron, *The Business of Practicing Law: The Work Lives of Solo and Small-Firm Attorneys* (Philadelphia: Temple University Press, 1996).

10. Two graduate students, Robert Saute and Bonnie Oglensky, did major research on this study and became coauthors of our book *The Part-Time Paradox: Time Norms, Professional Work, Family and Gender* (New York: Routledge, 1999). Two other graduate students, Martha Gever (who had worked on the glass ceilings study) and Elizabeth Wissinger, also contributed to the work.

11. Cynthia Fuchs Epstein and Arne Kalleberg, "Time and the Sociology of Work: Issues and Implications," *Work and Occupations* 28, 1 (February 2001).

12. Cynthia Fuchs Epstein, "Border Crossings: The Constraints of Time Norms in the Transgression of Gender and Professional Roles," in *Rethinking Time and Work*, ed. Cynthia Fuchs Epstein and Arne Kalleberg (New York: Russell Sage Foundation, in press).

13. A. Coser, *Greedy Institutions: Patterns of Commitment* (New York: Free Press, 1974).

14. See Sharon Hays, *The Cultural Contradictions of Mothering* (New Haven, Conn.: Yale University Press, 1996); and Mary Blair-Loy, *Divided Loyalties* (Cambridge, Mass.: Harvard University Press, forthcoming).

DOROTHY E. SMITH

RESISTING INSTITUTIONAL

CAPTURE AS

A RESEARCH PRACTICE

Until this women's movement, I'd never noticed how deeply I was committed to an intellectual life outside myself. I became aware, along with other women of that time, that the intellectual and cultural world in which we had been active had no place for us as subjects. I had occupied a borrowed subjectivity that was essentially at odds with my existence as a woman, and my existence as a woman had no intellectual, political or institutional voice or consciousness.

It is hard to describe how deep this alienation went. I only became aware of its depth in the process of finding out how to locate myself in what was alienated and starting from there. It was not a deliberate move, although it had its discipline. The process of unraveling the intellectual nets that trapped me could not be stopped once started. At the time, I thought of it as being in labor. In childbirth, your body is taken over by a massive muscular activity, unwilled and uncontrollable; you can ride the wave, but you don't manage it. I worked with it by trying to be true to it. Above all, I had to avoid assenting to or recreating the division between intellect, on the one hand, and, on the other, my being as a woman, a sexual and motherly being, anchored in her everyday life.

One commitment I made, therefore, was to what I thought of as telling the truth. I do not mean this in any ultimate sense, nor that it was simply a matter of speaking it. What telling the truth might be was always to be discovered in wrestling with the disjunctures between the essential falsifications of institutional participation and how I thought and felt and found myself in my everyday world. This was a disciplined effort of discovering how and what to speak or write.

In those days, when women came to speak to each other as women, we found that we did not have a language (it's easy to forget this strange interlude). We started with sharing our experiences as women, necessarily situated in our bodies. What we had experienced as women had remained inchoate, uncrystallized in speech, and describable as experience only in the retrospect of feminist discourse. It was elucidated, brought out into the light, as we talked. And the experiences were given names, now so familiar that it seems they've always been there: sexual harassment, violence against women, domestic abuse, discrimination, comparable worth, silencing, and more.

We discovered that the intellectual and cultural world in which we had been active had no place for us as subjects. On our side was the work of finding out, with other women, how to speak our experiences *as* women and how to hear other women—something we weren't at all used to. On the other side was the order of the intellectual and cultural discourses positioning women where they did not belong and organizing their familiar and unseen exclusions. Sociological theory and methodological practice at that time aimed at displacing or overriding the particularities and perspectives of subjects located in our everyday with a universal subject who was secretly male (and white and Western). The struggle to find a new way of speaking meant finding ways in which experience could be spoken into sociology and spoken faithfully. I, like others, had to learn a different way of being a subject in sociology. And that could not be done without transforming the discourse (and therefore being transformed).

Universalizing the male pronoun was no minor historical move; the very dichotomy of mind and body relies on refusing to admit the implications of bodily presence into the philosophical or sociological text. Objectivity relied on the absence of women, the absence of gender. Once women enter as legitimate subjects, the separation of mind and body is put in question. Formulations of objectivity such as those characteristic of sociologies that aim at a view of the social from an Archimedian point outside it are undermined once knowers are gendered. If there are gender differences, then there are bodies. And mind *in* a body must be located in a particular place at a particular time; it must be positioned.

Returning to gender forces a return to the local particularities of bodily being. For me, in the early days of this phase of the women's movement, this meant recognizing just where I was as a woman, at that time and place, oriented toward particular others: my children, my neighbors, my children's friends, their teachers, and so on. I discovered that I was living in two modes of consciousness, one very definitely where my body was and where there was lots of work involving bodily activity to be done; and one as a sociologist, where I went to work, whether at home or at the university, inhabiting a wholly different mode of consciousness, a consciousness mediated by texts, participating in a discourse the order of which was pregiven. I described this experience in an early article as a bifurcated consciousness.[1] I became aware that the kind of consciousness—awareness, attention, thought, intentionality, or memory—that operated in me when I was at home and focused on my children and household was radically different from the consciousness that went to work at the university or when, at home, I was preparing for lectures or reading sociology for the pleasure it gave me.

I began to think about how to remake sociology. Rather than transporting the sociological subject into the transcendence of sociological theory, I would have to begin in the actualities of people's everyday lives and experience and, from that standpoint, explore the beyond-the-everyday into the social relations and organization in which the everyday is entangled.[2] This early work was the academic surface of my work as an activist in the local community in Vancouver, Canada. My attempts to connect with activism in the community were a process of mortification. Women activists were deeply distrustful of academic tendencies to assume the authority of a knowledge that from the standpoint of activism was ignorance and pretension. For I don't know how long, I did the legwork and said nothing. I learned to shut up even when I might know something that would contribute. It was instructive, if deeply frustrating.

After a while, with other women, I turned toward developing organizations that would connect university women beyond the university. With women from the community colleges, we set up an association of women in colleges and universities. We wanted to involve teachers in the public school system, but they were involved in the teachers' federation and directed their efforts to making changes there. We also created a research center for women outside the university. Our idea was to bring our research know-how to examining issues and problems from the point of view of women in the community. In the various contexts, I learned (to my discomfort) how sociology turned the world of activism upside down, turning those we were working with into the objects of study. An embarrassing meeting with a group of women trade unionists taught me how sociologists, claiming to be interested in putting sociology to work in their interests, somehow always ended up making them the object of study. I didn't think this was a problem of our intentions but simply of how sociological discourse organized consciousness. If there was to be a sociology that could be of use to activists—if they needed a sociology at all, which most would have said they did not—it had to be one that could discover and analyze the forms of power in which their work was embedded.[3]

The sociology that I, and others working with me, have constructed rejects a view of people and the social from within the discourse, organized by its concepts and theories. Its problematic is of the everyday world, reflecting the actualities of a contemporary world in which what we find in the local settings of our daily lives participates in and is shaped by relations that connect us with multiple other such settings of people's activities. The aim is to explicate for people from where they are how the everyday organization of their local activities is coordinated with and participates in the extended social relations that rule contemporary society. It started as a sociology for women and has become a sociology for people.

Those who have taken up this sociology have focused their inquiries in diverse ways. My own interests have been in finding out how to make the disjuncture between the experienced world and the world of institutions and of discourse—theory, concepts, ideology, beliefs, and knowledges—examinable as people's doings in the everyday world. More and more I've come to see texts (or documents) as the essential coordinators of institutions and large-scale organizations.

With one or two exceptions, all the research I have done since my dissertation has emerged from problems and puzzles I have experienced. My research into the workings of texts comes out of my experiences as a reader. In writing this autobiographical account, I have been recognizing a persistent theme. It is the problem of what I've called in my title "institutional capture." In all, I have published six pieces of research into textual materials.[4] There are other related researches and some unpublished, but here I shall focus only on "K Is Mentally Ill: The Anatomy of a Factual Account," "The Active Text," "Ideological Methods of Reading and Writing Texts: A Scrutiny of Quentin Bell's Account of Virginia Woolf's Suicide," and "Texts and Repression: Hazards for Feminists in the Academy." Though the first of these, "K Is Mentally Ill," began before the women's movement, it was working through the alienation that it brought so forcefully home to me that allowed me to take what I'd learned in writing it and turn it toward uncovering experiences of alienation in my reading. All of the six articles are in various ways concerned with a felt disjuncture in texts in which an institutional discourse overrides and reconstructs experiential or descriptive writing.

Investigating these texts originated in inchoate feelings of resistance. I didn't want to go along with the "ruling" text but found that it was difficult not to do so. In a strange way it grabbed and directed my reading. I could feel this happening, but I had no idea how the text went to work in me, its reader. Thus a particular text or group of texts became a problem for investigation out of experiences of disjuncture, the experience of becoming an agent of an institutional order to which I was opposed. It is the active relation between text and reader that is the focus of research. Investigation aims at explicating this relation. It aims at discovering what it is in a particular text that works in and on me, the reader, in the way in which it does. It must find its object as a property of the text. In this way texts can be explored as they are activated in particular local settings by particular people and as people's doings and the organizers of people's doings. Analysis explicates the relation between institutional text and individual subject as it becomes active in an individual's reading. It seeks not the idiosyncrasies of reading but the institutional.

In writing my quite respectable dissertation, I struggled with a strange dissatisfaction. I had proceeded formally. My argument took on Robert Michels's "iron law of oligarchy,"[5] the thesis that organizations of all kinds, even those committed to democracy, inevitably developed toward oligarchy. I argued that those old monsters, the state mental hospitals, were instances of organization where power tended to be distributed toward peripheral units (wards), and they created peculiar problems of control and surveillance so that patients were exposed to arbitrary mistreatment. I was left at the end of this effort with a feeling of dissatisfaction, not with the thesis as such but with the sociology that had been its maker. Looking back from positions gained later, I see that I had remained entirely within the discourse, subordinating everything I had learned during my fieldwork in a state mental hospital into the theoretical web I had created out of Michels and other theorists and studies. The state hospital I knew in this way became merely an expression or instance of the discourse. I started in theory, dipped down selectively into the somewhat chaotic fieldwork materials, and picked out and reconstructed the pieces that seemed to fit so that the story instructed by the theory could be told.

My experience of the research that resulted in "K Is Mentally Ill" was a radical illumination. In a course I was teaching on deviance, I asked students to help solve the mystery of how mental illness comes to be identified in people since there are no clear criteria: "Go out and ask people if they've ever known anyone who's mentally ill and get them to describe how they figured out that that was the problem," I said, or something like that, no doubt phrasing with proper formality. At a seminar, one student reported what she had learned, and I heard the story of someone becoming mentally ill. But later, when I went back to the written interview, I could see that it could be read quite differently. Behind the story of K's becoming mentally ill[6] is a shadowy alternative, an account of K as progressively ostracized among her friends. Designating her as mentally ill is a piece of the machinery of that ostracism. How had I been trapped into hearing it first as an account of someone who was becoming mentally ill? I don't know why I decided to research this. Though clearly it belonged in some way to the field of deviance, it was research quite unlike anything I'd seen before. It drew on my way-back, (before sociology), reading of the Oxford philosophers (notably Gilbert Ryle and J. L. Austin). For the first time in my sociological work, I knew I was discovering something that I hadn't known in advance. This was its radical character for me.

The research consisted of a series of highly detailed commentaries on virtually every sentence. These commentaries sought to explicate how I read the passages subject to commentary. I emphasize that I was not interested in my interpretations or subjective responses. I know, of course, that these were there, but I wanted to explicate how the text went to work in me and how I went to work in becoming, as I would now say, the text's proxy in finding in the text what I was instructed to find. Since then, to clarify the distinction between interpretation and reading, I've introduced the notion of a text-reader conversation, in which one side of the text is obstinately fixed and unresponsive to the reader's interpretations. The reader activates the text. Of course, she may activate it selectively or erroneously, but she takes up its words. They become in a sense hers as she activates their meaning. My analysis of "K Is Mentally Ill" explicates the text's part as the reader becomes its proxy.[7] Interpretation lies in the other part of the text-reader conversation, her response to what she reads.

Sometime in the early 1970s, Bill Darrough, now of the State University of California at Los Angeles, showed me two texts that he'd been working on. One was from the *Berkeley Barb*, an underground newspaper in Berkeley, and the second a public response from the mayor of Berkeley, incorporating a report from the chief of police. The text in the *Berkeley Barb* was written in the form of a letter from a professor who reports what he interpreted as an unjustified police attack on people gathered on the street. The mayor's response, incorporating a report to him from the chief of police, rejected the professor's account and insisted that the police had acted entirely properly. The contrast between the two versions fascinated me, as it had Darrough. In reading them, I had taken sides—automatically. I took the professor's part in his accusation that the police actions were an attempt to incite violence from the people gathered on the street, giving the police an excuse to take stronger action. I'd had a English friend who had been involved in a protest against the House Un-American Activities Committee (HUAC) meeting in San Francisco sometime before the Free Speech movement emerged on the Berkeley campus. She had been hurt when the police used fire hoses to wash the protestors down a marble staircase. Later she was deported. I was astonished and appalled at the police actions. My husband and I, pulling our son in a wagon, joined the picket lines the next day outside what, if I remember correctly, was the courthouse in San Francisco where the HUAC had been meeting. I was deeply influenced by the Free Speech and antiwar movements in the United States, particularly in how I learned not to assume the virtue and truthfulness of those in authority nor to give their authority more than conditional consent.

I took the side of the professor and against the police, but I could not fault the police account except in quite minor ways. I researched the two texts in much the same way in which I had researched the account of the interview that told the story of K's becoming mentally ill, but my efforts were fruitless. I even developed an elaborate formalized system of notation that I thought might enable me to refine my analysis and to contrast the two versions—a useless enterprise, the products of which were long since lost. I worked on this originally as two contradictory accounts. Bill Darrough and later Peter Eglin adopted a similar approach.[8] Bill wrote ethnographically; Peter analyzed the practical reasoning of students in discussion of the two versions. Their approaches were different from mine, even though then I didn't know what mine would be. I had promised Bill not to publish before he did, so I was in no hurry, but I did set the problem aside—easy to do if you're a housewife and mother with two small children and a full-time job. Perhaps there's a way in which a problem goes on working in you even though you're not conscious of it.

This history entered into my reading of the two texts but gave me no satisfactory analysis. But at last I found the key. It was to see the two as a kind of conversational sequence that went from reading the professor's experiential account and his challenge to the police to the response in the police version embedded in the mayor of Berkeley's letter to the public. Though the texts were now old, this sequence was preserved. I wanted to trace the reading experience (my own) of going from finding the professor's vivid account to an institutional text that overpowers it, the account of the same events provided by the chief of police. The latter did not, I came to think, provide a different version of what occurred. Rather it reconstructed the professor's experiential story by providing it with an institutional frame that transformed what had been represented as seriously improper police actions to those properly mandated. The professor was shown to be a naive witness. The explicit moral of the story for the reader was to become "sophisticated." To be sophisticated was to grasp what seems ordinarily offensive as an expression of institutional order.

My analysis focused on how the second text *went to work* on the first. I discovered a style of writing that, in redescribing the experientially told story, had the capacity to subsume it under higher order sets of terms that reinterpreted it. The original severe critique of police action is reconstructed as proper police procedure. And the reader is active and complicit in this reconstruction.

The reconstruction is achieved stylistically. The mayor's version, containing the police chief's report, is not just a rebuttal of the professor's but also a process of conversion of one kind of account into another. A special relation between the two is activated in reading the second. The institutional account redescribes the sequence of events and, in particular, the police actions as properly mandated. Most striking is the way in which the professor's experiential representation of those events is subsumed by the institutional. The latter is also a description, but it is a description at a higher level of abstraction, one that has the capacity, activated by the reader, to treat the experiential descriptions as expressions or instances of an institutional regime. Incidents that in the professor's account appear to involve the arbitrary use of force are not denied; they are simply redescribed in terms that show them to have been instances of proper police behavior.

There is a style of writing and speaking that, given a reader who knows how to read and speak it, captures her as agent of the institutional regime. In reading, I, the reader, made the words of the police chief's report my own and reread the professor's experiential account in its terms. Here was the power, as I activated it, of the police chief's report and here was the site of the unease that originally motivated my exploration.

I had, since I was in my teens, been reading and rereading Virginia Woolf's novels. I was in my early teens when the newspapers reported that she had committed suicide. When I read Quentin Bell's account of Woolf's madness, leading up to her suicide, I was affronted. I could see in it, I thought, the workings of the same conceptual practices that I'd analyzed in "K Is Mentally Ill." Examining the text, I could locate in it a textual sequence that progressively isolated her. As in my reading of K's story, Bell's account of the period leading to Woolf's suicide in terms of mental illness also had its shadowy alternative. I thought then—though I had no evidence and hence didn't put it into the paper—that Woolf's suicide might be seen as somehow coming out of a similar process of encirclement that I had seen at work in the progressively closing circle of friends that was defining K as mentally ill. In *Mrs. Dalloway*, Septimus Smith, traumatized by his experience in World War I, jumps out of a second-floor window, falls on the spiked railings below, and dies. Is it because he is mad? Not directly. He is desperate to escape the powers of the Drs. Bradshaw and Holmes, who held that people who are ill must be separated from those they are close to and must be treated with a regime of enforced rest. As Septimus waits in the upstairs living room of the apartment, he hears Dr. Holmes pushing his way, against the resistance of his wife, up the stairs. He plunges out of the window to escape.

Edwin Lemert[9] has described what he calls a "dynamic of exclusion." It is this dynamic that appears in the story of K's becoming mentally ill. The individual is enfolded in a progressively closing circle of people who may be family, friends, coworkers, or relatives, who are talking with one another behind the individual's back and coming to agree that she is mentally ill. We can see this dynamic in the story of "K Is Mentally Ill," and I thought I could see it in Bell's account of Woolf's suicide. What my analysis could show was just how Woolf's life in the months before her death was constructed as an account of her mental illness, how emotions were detached from the normalizing contexts of wartime events and constructed as nominalized states, "a mood of apprehension," for example, that lent themselves to interpretation as symptoms. Sequences of shared preoccupation and feeling between Woolf and her husband, Leonard, are subsequently told without Leonard's presence. The dynamics of exclusion are reenacted in the text. Analysis demonstrated a dual movement: selected biographical moments are abstracted to become "symptoms"; symptoms are then subsumed under the master schema of what we would now call a bipolar mental disorder.

I don't want to be misunderstood here. I am not reverting to the earlier view, associated with the work of R. D. Laing, that what we call mental illness is somehow imposed on people and takes on its reality in that imposition. Woolf leaves us in no doubt of the reality of Septimus Smith's madness. But it is not that that leads to his suicide. There is no doubt either of Woolf's madness. There may, however, be doubt about her suicide. The treatment of rest and enforced separation from friends and company had been earlier imposed on Woolf (and also, with devastating effect, on Charlotte Perkins Gilman). She had herself suffered previously the brutal rationality of the psychiatric treatment of the day. Virginia Woolf wrote vividly of Septimus Smith's experience; it's hard not to think that she drew on her own. As she went into madness, she, too, I believe, could hear the threatening footsteps of rational authority on the stairs. As Leonard Woolf and their friend the physician saw her deepening illness, they planned behind her back to get her into treatment. And so they drew the circle to its closure around her. She feared the doctors, their institutional authority, and treatment. Septimus jumps out of the window to escape; Woolf walked into a river with stones in her pockets. As the reader, the text's proxy, takes on the concept of manic-depressive psychosis as the master interpreter of events, she participates in the exclusionary loop that is organized by the concept of mental illness.

The last of the studies in this series explores a sequence of texts, beginning with an internal departmental report on the chilly climate for women in a western Canadian university's political science department. The report describes and protests against the multiple everyday affronts that make up a departmental climate chilly to women. Though not fully finalized, the report came to be circulated widely in the university, and the senior male faculty came to believe (though, according to my information, erroneously) that it had been distributed widely through Canada. They wrote a formal letter to the chair of the committee that had prepared the report, calling on her to withdraw it and implying that if she did not do so she might be subject to legal action. On the campus locally, there was an uproar.

The language of the senior male faculty's letter was juridical. It treated the original report selectively, picking out and reassembling passages to make a fit with the formalized language of offense, accusation, and charge. Establishing the category of sexual harassment early in the letter, it was then expanded so that they could describe themselves as having been accused of "grossly obscene behaviour," although nothing even remotely resembling behavior describable in that way was in the report. This was the version that came to dominate subsequent public debate. Indeed, it did more than dominate; the logic of the dialogue between the experiential, and the juridical set up the media frame that became the standard organizer of stories. From the standpoint of the juridical, the ordinary experiences told in women's stories of the chilly climate are represented as trivialities, a structure I've heard replicated in stories told as gossip.

In these researches I am discovering, I believe, some aspects of the power of institutional discourse, including sociology, to subordinate and subdue the experiential. These researches have seemed over time to have something special to say to me about the dialectic of a self that is struggling for realization and the institutional regime that had caught her up into modes of knowing and acting that came from outside herself and in which she could not, as herself, play a speaking part. In writing a sociology for people, I have wanted a sociology in which people's accounts of their own worlds could be heard without reinterpretation—but as subjects, not as objects. Exploring how the texts go to work in the reader and how the reader becomes an agent of the text she reads is not a literary endeavour. It is through and through sociological. It investigates social relations mediated by texts and explicates the way in which the text and the reader's competence as a reader construe her consciousness in a mode that she has not chosen. And in more recent work, as yet unpublished, I am examining the stylistic properties of institutional discourse that enable its capacity to subsume experientially based accounts and how institutional discourse enters into the production of local activities as expressions or instances of an institutional order.

My commitment to telling the truth as best I can has taken this path. It is not a path that simply explores my subjectivity. It takes, rather, the subjective as a point of entry into the social as it is objectified in someone's local practices. The ethnographic strategy is one of explication. The experience of alienation locates a specific disjuncture that is present in my consciousness as reader, but the discursive forms I examine as my own practices are not exclusively mine. I have not focused on the idiosyncratic but on the general characteristics of institutional forms of discourse and on the practices of readers that operate them. The studies are part of my life story, not just my curriculum vitae. They trace a course of thinking that seeks to recreate in my textual ethnographies the discursive forms that coordinate consciousnesses in institutional regimes.

NOTES

1. D. E. Smith, "Women's Perspective as a Radical Critique of Sociology," *Sociological Inquiry* 44 (1974): 3–13; published as a chapter entitled "Women's Experience as a Radical Critique of Sociology," in *The Conceptual Practices of Power: A Feminist Sociology of Knowledge*, ed. D. E. Smith (Boston: Northeastern University Press, 1990).

2. D. E. Smith, *The Everyday World as Problematic: A Feminist Sociology* (Boston: Northeastern University Press, 1987).

3. The late George Smith, gay activist and dear friend, described the intersection of institutional analysis and activism in "Political Activist as Ethnographer," *Social Problems* 37 (1990): 401–21.

4. The articles include "K Is Mentally Ill: The Anatomy of a Factual Account" (originally published in German in 1976), in *Texts, Facts and Femininity: Exploring the Relations of Ruling*, ed. D. E. Smith (London: Routledge, 1990), 12–51; "The Social Organization of Subjectivity: An Analysis of the Micro-Politics of a Meeting," in D. E. Smith, *Texts, Facts and Femininity*, 53–85; originally published as "The Intersubjective Structuring of Time," *Analytic Sociology* 11, 1 (1979); "The Active Text," in D. E. Smith, *Texts, Facts and Femininity*, 120–58; "Ideological Methods of Reading and Writing Texts: A Scrutiny of Quentin Bell's Account of Virginia Woolf's Suicide," in *Conceptual Practices* 176–96; "'Politically Correct': An Organizer of Public Discourse," in *Writing the Social: Critique, Theory, and Investigations*, ed. D. E. Smith (Toronto: University of Toronto Press, 1999), 172–94; and "Texts and Repression: Hazards for Feminists in the Academy," *Writing the Social*, 194–223.

5. Robert Michels, *Political Parties*, trans. Eden and Cedar Paul (Glencoe, Ill.: Free Press, 1949).

6. A conscious reference to Kafka's K in *The Trial*. The essay was first published in German: D. E. Smith, "K ist Geisteskrank," in *Ethnomethodologie. Beitrage auf einer Soziologie des tagslebens*, ed. E. Weingarten, F. Sack, and J. N Schenkein (Frankfurt: Suhrkamp, 1976), and in Germany the reference to Kafka was noticed. I don't think it has been elsewhere. The tendency was to treat the "K" as an initial by putting a period after it.

7. I've written more about the reader as the text's proxy in "The Social Relations of Discourse: Sociological Theory and the Dialogic of Sociology," in D. E. Smith, *Writing the Social*, 133–56.

8. William D. Darrough, "When Versions Collide: Police and the Dialectics of Accountability," *Uraban Life* 7 (1978): 379–403; Peter Eglin, "Resolving Reality Disjuncture on Telegraph Avenue: A Study of Practical Reasoning," *Canadian Journal of Sociology* 4 (1979): 359–75.

9. E. M. Lemert, "Paranoia and the Dynamics of Exclusion," *Sociometry* 25 (1962): 2–20.

BARRIE THORNE

14

THE INS AND OUTS OF OTHERING

To cut across boundaries and borderlines is to live aloud the malaise of
categories and labels; it is to resist simplistic attempts at classifying, to
resist the comfort of belonging to a classification, and of producing
classifiable works.

—Trinh Minh-Ha

Gender, race, and other lines of social difference[1] sometimes seem frozen
and fixed, like ice; they may also feel fluid in meaning and significance,
like water; and, on occasion, these lines of difference may almost seem to
evaporate. This metaphor, borrowed from Troy Duster,[2] evokes complex dynamics that have long fascinated and also disturbed me. The women's liberation movement of the late 1960s opened my eyes to the complexities of gender and, broadly, to the workings of categories, boundaries, and relations
between difference and power. In the ensuing decades, as the protagonist in
the movie *Groundhog Day* who revisits the same scene again and again, I have
obsessed about questions of difference, power, and knowledge. I am especially
fascinated and troubled by the complex dynamics of "Othering"—by the
ways in which the more powerful (men, whites, Westerners, and adults) sustain structured inequalities by defining differences between themselves and
marginalized and homogenized others (women, blacks, third-world people,

and children). The process is especially pernicious when controlling ideas of difference, projected through the anxieties and needs of dominants, shape the ways in which subordinates see themselves.[3]

THE EXPERIENCE OF BEING OTHERED

When I first encountered the ideas of women's liberation, I was drawn to concepts like sexism and sexual objectification, in part because they helped me understand moments when I had felt fixed, defined, and devalued from the outside because of my gender. In my first consciousness-raising group, comprising women who had been active in the antiwar and draft resistance movements in Boston and who, in 1968, moved together into women's liberation, we often discussed how it felt to be objectified by men. With collective and energizing anger, we began to confront men who called us "chicks," and, cringing at the ways in which we had perpetuated our own subordination, we criticized the slogan "girls who say yes to guys who say no," which had been emblazoned on a political button we had worn in the early days of the resistance.

During those years of New Left activism and changing consciousness of myself as a woman, I was a graduate student in sociology at Brandeis University.[4] I wrote my doctoral dissertation on the resistance and included an angry chapter on the subordinate position of women in the movement (this chapter was the basis of my first journal article).[5] I wrote about women in the resistance from the stance of an other who was speaking out, naming and challenging frameworks of difference that supported male privilege and erased my full personhood.

In 1971 I began my first faculty job in the Michigan State University sociology department. The position was in social psychology, but I rapidly changed my knowledge stripes, introduced a course on sex roles, and worked with a handful of feminist colleagues to create a women's studies program. My move into feminist activism was energized by the experiences of my mother, Alison Comish Thorne, who received a doctorate in economics in 1938 but was shut out of a regular academic career by the overt sexism of universities. I was angry at the injustices dealt to earlier generations of academic women, which her trajectory exemplified; I was also inspired by my mother's many decades of community activism on behalf of the poor, migrant farmers, and women in Utah.[6]

A passionate engagement with feminism has continuously informed my research, teaching, and activism. In the early 1970s, I collaborated with a feminist psycholinguist, Nancy Henley, in research that resulted in *Language and Sex: Difference and Dominance*.[7] The subtitle reflects the way in which feminists thought about gender in the early 1970s: as a socially constructed yet relatively fixed dichotomy that facilitates male privilege and domination. We sought to revalue women's experiences and to claim voice and space—to become individually and collectively self-defining—by mobilizing on the basis of gender. This entailed riding a by now familiar paradox: the very structure (gender) that we were challenging, and that some of us wanted to dismantle, was the basis of our solidarity. During the 1970s, I continued to write with the energizing anger of a member of a subordinated group, chipping at the icy blockades of institutional and everyday sexism.

AN ADULT STUDYING CHILDREN

In 1973, when I became a mother, my sociological eye began to turn toward children and their worlds. Three years later, when my partner, Peter Lyman, and I were on leave from Michigan State and visiting in California, I designed and taught a course on the sociology of childhood, which included works of fiction, autobiography, anthropology, and history. I had to scramble to find readings since children were either invisible in the field of sociology or else tucked into small pockets of knowledge within the subfields of family, education, and criminology.[8] Prior to the movement of feminist ideas into higher education, women had also lurked on the margins of knowledge. The analogy intrigued me: the dichotomies adult-child and man-woman are rooted in differences and relations of privilege and power that are reflected in the contours of knowledge. But when I analyzed the adult-child dichotomy, I was positioned on the privileged rather than the subordinated side.

During our 1976–77 sojourn in California, I began to do fieldwork on children and gender, approaching the topic not in the top-down, defining-from-the-outside mode of research on socialization and child development, which was the then prevalent approach, but with an open-ended wish to learn about children as social actors and creators of worlds of meaning. I got access to a public elementary school whose students were predominantly white and working class; about 10% were Hispanic, mostly immigrants from Mexico; and 5% were African Americans. As I tarried out on the playground, the lunchroom, hallways, a classroom, and other settings, I tried to minimize the social distance and authority built into my adult status; in my field notes, I kept track not only of children's interactions but also of my own emotions and experiences of self.

My emotional and political positioning during the course of this project felt much more contradictory and complex than when I had written about women in the draft resistance movement or about relations of difference and dominance in the patterning of language and speech. I was trying to understand *intersecting* lines of difference—primarily age and gender but also with an eye on social class, racialized ethnicity, and sexuality. My stance as an adult loomed large, quite literally; when I stood near the thick of the action on school playgrounds, I felt like Gulliver with the Lilliputians. I tried to minimize my adult power, but no one mistook me for a child, and I could easily slip in and out of the classroom or lunchroom since, unlike the students, I was not legally required to be in school. I often identified with the girls, transported back to my own fourth-grade girl self; I also resonated emotionally with the boys, who tugged at my love for my son. And I could easily feel detached, with the child-watching sensibilities of a mother, a teacher, and (struggling to let go of the managerial mode) an adult who was trying to learn from kids. I wrote about these mixed sensibilities in *Gender Play*,[9] the book that I finally completed after many years of studying, thinking, and writing about children and gender.

Being an adult who was trying to make sense of children's worlds helped me to gain analytic distance and move beyond dichotomous approaches to gender, as did developments in feminist theory, which, during the 1980s, actively deconstructed fixed, oppositional categories and highlighted the multiple and contested meanings of gender. More than a decade of feminist scholarship had produced conceptual tools for understanding the fluid, as well as the icy, dimensions of power-laden difference. Several jolting experiences also led me to examine the complexity of my own relationships to processes of Othering. In the late 1970s, I redesigned my sex roles course at Michigan State University (MSU) to include writings by African-American and Chicana women; I titled that section of the syllabus Conflicting Loyalties: Gender, Race, and Ethnicity. I invited a Chicana faculty member to talk to the class; she questioned my framing of the syllabus and asked, in effect, Who has the conflicting loyalty? What about white women's ties to and investment in white privilege? Wow. I felt embarrassed, but her criticisms unsettled my assumptions and opened new ways of seeing.

A few years later, in a similar moment of confrontation, a lesbian colleague wrote about feeling silenced by the heterosexual assumptions made by other faculty members in the MSU Women's Studies Program, both in personal interactions and in our courses. Once again I felt embarrassed and defensive but also (with gratitude that has deepened over the years) prodded toward fuller, more dialogic, and *emotional* understanding of the workings of power and privilege. Being challenged to struggle with my own anxieties about and fears of difference, as well as with the ways in which privilege shaped my consciousness, ultimately expanded my understanding of the world.

I continued to muse about issues of power and difference as I wrote about gender relations in elementary schools. Trying to do justice to the complexities I had observed, I mapped the with-then-apart dynamics of gender and social groupings and traced varied ways of being a girl and of being a boy, including the experiences of kids who crossed into activities of the other gender, like Jessie, a girl who was a skilled soccer and basketball player, and Brian, who often played jump rope and swung on the bars. (All names of research subjects have been changed.) I came to see that gender was far more salient—marked, fixed, and frozen like ice—in some situations than in others. "Cooties" rituals, for example, framed the girls and the boys as separate, antagonistic, and also asymmetric sides since girls were seen as more polluting. I eventually realized that full understanding of gender should encompass not only moments of frozen difference (in which processes of Othering thrive), but also water-and-vapor-like moments when gender is not explicitly salient and girls and boys (and men and women) interact in more relaxed and egalitarian ways.

As I wrote *Gender Play*, I tried to attend to race, ethnicity, social class, and sexuality, as well as gender and age, but it was hard to keep multiple strands of difference at the center of the story. I worried about my depiction of Jessie, the token African-American girl in the combined fourth and fifth-grade California classroom that was at the center of my narrative. She stood out in my observations and in my field notes because of her racial positioning and also because she regularly crossed gender lines, skillfully playing team sports and fighting with boys, as well as playing jump rope and claiming a "best friend" in the somewhat separate world of girls. I argued that as the only African American in a nearly all-white classroom, Jessie was ambiguously located in the kids' prevailing gender system. She maneuvered the problematic terrain of "goin' with" heterosexual teasing rituals by assuming the position of matchmaker. I concluded that line of analysis by writing that her unusual navigation of the field of gender relations "was also a navigation of race relations in a situation of tokenism; gender and race were being mutually constructed."[10] Even as I wrote that sentence, I knew I had barely begun to demonstrate its generalizing claim.

I continue to worry that I portrayed Jessie's experience too much from the perspective of a socially distanced, white adult observer. But at least I had gotten to know her. This was not the case for a mixed-age group of eight to ten nonbilingual, Spanish-speaking girls and boys who regularly played dodgeball on the playground of the California school. The group was highly visible because it was unusually mixed by age and gender and because, in a school whose students were mostly white and English-speaking, it was the largest recurring playground group of kids who spoke a different language and were racialized as other—not only by other kids and teachers, but also by me. In my analysis of kids' social groupings, I pointed out that other lines of difference—in this case, speaking only Spanish in an English-speaking environment—may mute the salience of gender, and, in this case, age as well. To sustain a lively, ongoing group game of dodgeball, the relatively few Spanish-speaking kids reached across other lines of difference. I also pointed out that the then prevailing "separate worlds" framework, which assumes that girls and boys live in sharply gender-divided worlds, obscures the presence of mixed-gender groups like this one.

My field note descriptions of the Spanish-speaking, dodgeball-playing group were a boon to think with, but my portrayal was very much from the outside. When I was doing fieldwork in the fourth and fifth-grade classroom, I had tried to interact with Alejandro and Miguel, two members of the dodgeball group, but they spoke virtually no English. I noted ways in which they were marginalized in the classroom: the teacher didn't speak Spanish and had to deal with the rest of the class, and the two boys mostly sat in disengaged silence except when a bilingual aide dropped in to work with them. In the gender-divided, U-shaped seating arrangement, other boys maneuvered Miguel and Alejandro into sitting in the contaminated space next to the girls. In my field notes I remarked at the striking transformation of these two boys—from silent and self-protective to confident and animated—when the recess bell rang and they ran to join the Spanish-speaking dodgeball group. I didn't know Spanish, and I didn't want to be too pushy and snoopy, so I watched the group only from a distance. Why, I later asked myself, didn't I get someone to translate? Or learn some Spanish and try to reach these children? Or talk to the bilingual aide about their experiences? Once again, I became alert to and then obsessively thought about the distant interpretive comfort zone and the self-deceived ignorance of the privileged—in this case, a native English-speaking, white, highly educated adult who was empowered to watch and write about the "nature" of a group subordinated by immigration status, racialized ethnicity, social class, and age, without real dialogue or efforts to learn about their experiences from the inside.

MOVING TOWARD RESEARCH ON
CHILDHOODS IN URBAN CALIFORNIA

In 1980, after four years back in Michigan, my family and I returned to northern California for a two-year visit. We enrolled our son, then in third grade, in a public school that offered him the opportunity to be in a bilingual Spanish-English classroom.[11] We liked the idea and hoped that he would learn some Spanish and become more bicultural. He indeed learned a few Spanish words, although it was not the two-way immersion program we had imagined. He danced and sang in a Cinquo de Mayo performance and came home with news of what appeared to be a racialized playground conflict between two groups of older boys, "the *cholos*" and "the surfers." One day, well into the school year, I asked our son if he would draw me a map of his class and where different kids sat. Being in a generous mood (imagine growing up with a mother who studies children), he drew four round tables, two quite large, with individual names of the kids, all English-speaking, who sat around them, and then two quite small tables at one side, which he simply labeled "Spanish kids." This map of a classroom, as my verbal representations of the school playground I had observed several years before, framed Spanish-speaking kids as different, distant, and homogeneous—as others. The resonance haunted me, and I renewed my efforts to help our kids (by then we had two) understand and challenge racism.

I realized I had a long way to go myself in struggling with issues of difference, power, and Othering. During those two years in California and after we returned to Michigan, I kept reading and teaching about these issues, extending my knowledge of the political economy of class, race, and gender; the history and culture of varied ethnic groups and of lesbians and gay men; the politics of representation; and the psychodynamics of Othering.

In 1987, Peter and I accepted jobs at the University of Southern California (USC), and our family once again headed west. We bought a home in South Pasadena, where our children entered ethnically diverse public schools (one starting high school; the other, fifth grade). For reasons I'm still trying to sort out, their subsequent experiences with difference were much more constructive and less racist than in our son's third-grade year. By then, accelerated rates of immigration (California has received more immigrants than any other state since the immigration laws changed in 1965) had dramatically altered the racial-ethnic and cultural landscape of urban areas. Driving along Western Avenue in Los Angeles, one could see commercial signs in many different languages and even scripts (Chinese, Korean, Japanese, Vietnamese, Thai, Arabic, and Hebrew), with striking juxtapositions of culture.

The cultural variety of contemporary California was, and is, thrilling; it's an incredible place to experience and think about, personally and sociologically. But the last three decades of immigration have also been accompanied by widening income gaps (25% of children in California now live in poverty; the state also has an unusually high proportion of families with incomes over $200,000 a year, while the middle class is pinched and shrinking). The juxtaposition of groups with different languages and national origins in urban areas and in public schools is sometimes a story of cooperation and mutual learning but often one of social distance, mistrust, friction, and open conflict, as in the 1992 racialized, violent "disturbances" in Los Angeles. Many of the more affluent, disproportionately white families have pulled out of urban public schools, in effect leaving the democratic challenge of working with diversity to those who are less class-privileged. During the 1990s, California elections became the site of xenophobic backlash targeted at immigrant families and children with the passage of Proposition 187 (later declared unconstitutional), which would have eliminated social services, including public schooling, for undocumented immigrants; Proposition 209, which eliminated affirmative action in admission to public colleges and universities; and Proposition 227, which sharply curtailed bilingual programs in public schools.

Fascinated by the changing social and economic landscape in California and wanting to know more about the ways in which immigrants and nonimmigrants experience this shifting cultural and economic mosaic, I began to conceptualize a new research project focused on childhoods in urban California. I am interested in economic restructuring, globalization, and declines in state provisioning for families and children as they are organized and experienced on the ground, in particular urban areas. How do families who are differently positioned by social class, immigration status, and racial ethnicity organize their daily lives? How are different worlds of childhood constructed and interrelated? How do children and their parents encounter, make sense of, and rework social divisions and power-laden categories of identity?

With these overarching questions in mind and with funding from the MacArthur Foundation Research Network on Successful Pathways Through Middle Childhood, I enlisted the collaboration of a colleague, Marjorie Faulstich Orellana, who organized and did most of the fieldwork and interviewing in our first research site, an enclave of low-income, mostly undocumented immigrants from Mexico and Central America in the Pico Union area of Los Angeles.

I took responsibility for organizing and doing much of the fieldwork in a second site in northern California, which I located in 1996 after Peter and I moved to jobs at the University of California, Berkeley. This site is the intake area of a mixed-income, ethnically diverse public elementary school in Oakland, whose students (according to official records for the 1996–97 school year) were almost 50% African American, 17% Asian (the children of immigrants from Hong Kong, China, the Philippines, Vietnam, Laos, and Cambodia), 14% Hispanic (the children of immigrants from Mexico and Central America), 13% white, and 6% other (with parents from places as diverse as Yemen, Eritrea, Egypt, and Denmark).

These official categories gloss enormous cultural and ethnic variations, and unpacking them to find out how kids, teachers, and parents understand and negotiate ethnic and racialized categories and meanings, as well as other lines of marked difference, is a central strand of the research project. Three years of collaborative fieldwork, both in and outside of the Oakland school, and over 160 interviews with kids and parents from a range of social-class and ethnic backgrounds have resulted in a daunting pile of data. My old obsessive themes—the dynamics of difference, power, and Othering—are at the core of the ethnography that my collaborators and I are developing. I'm intent on moving from the outside into the mutually recognizing inside of groups like the Spanish-speaking dodgeball players on that school playground in 1976–77. Detached perspectives can be useful, even essential, but getting inside worlds of meaning, more fully recognizing rather than simply classifying and fixing particular configurations of experience, is crucial not only to good ethnography but also, I believe, to working for social justice. It's a continual challenge since the dynamics of Othering are deep, complex, and recurring.

To bridge gaps of language and culture and to promote shared adventures in learning and teaching, I recruited coresearchers from backgrounds that parallel some of the diversity of contemporary California. Marjorie Orellana is fully bilingual in Spanish and English and taught for 10 years in a Pico Union elementary school before entering graduate school and completing a doctorate at USC. Anna Chee, a USC doctoral student who migrated to California with her parents when she was in junior high, interviewed Korean immigrant kids and parents in Pico Union. I involved University of California Berkeley, graduate and undergraduate students, from varied backgrounds in team fieldwork and interviewing in Oakland. Eva Lam is an immigrant from Hong Kong; Hung Thai is from Vietnam; Erèndira Rueda, Ana Gonzalez, and Gladys Ocampo all speak Spanish and have parents who migrated to California from Mexico; Nadine Chabrier's parents are African American and Puerto Rican; Allison Pugh and Eileen Mears, like me, come from white, more class privileged, U.S.-rooted families.

This listing doesn't begin to convey the complexities of working together and of our various adventures in the field and with one another. Each person's past experiences and cultural and language skills shaped, in part, what they noticed and (especially for non-English-speaking "subjects") what they could learn but not with clear one-to-one matching. Hung Thai turned out to be a skilled and empathetic interviewer not only of Southeast Asians but also of African-American mothers. I got to know and to some degree moved inside the experiences of an extended family of Yemeni immigrants. Nadine Chabrier's observations of African-American, Chinese immigrant, and white kids are illuminating. Identities and angles of vision proliferate. We shared information and insights, and disagreed with and sometimes challenged one another. Piecing together the data and making sense of them is a huge challenge.[12]

Once again I have experienced startling, often unanticipated moments of coming face to face with my projections onto imagined, different others. During my fourth month of fieldwork in the Oakland school, I had my first extended conversation with Lorna, an African-American fifth-grader who spent part of each day in a separate program for visually impaired students. As we sat side by side on a playground bench, she told me, in a voice of happy anticipation, that her best friend, Sokley, would be coming back the next week from a month-long family trip to Cambodia. Lorna explained that Sokley's family came here from Cambodia "because of a war," and they had gone back for the first time since they left Cambodia in order to see their relatives. Sokley was keeping a journal and taking pictures during her trip, and she was going to report on it to the class. Lorna went on to talk about the fun that she and Sokley had had together, such as going on a VIP (Visually Impaired Program) field trip and inventing a way to write Braille on paper with Magic Markers. Lorna said that in class they had talked about the special foods families eat at holiday time. She pointed to an African-American girl who was playing jump rope nearby: "Her mother bakes special cornbread only for Christmas, and Sokley's family eats rice with every meal." Lorna said that Sokley was teaching her to say words in Cambodian. My difference-and-immigration-obsessed ears perked up at the talk of rice and speaking Cambodian, and I said, "It must be neat to be friends with someone from another culture, who speaks another language." Lorna looked puzzled, and then, in a gently correcting voice, replied, "She's just normal." Lorna took my fixed marking of difference and melted it back into human, normalized form.

The jolts of consciousness that I have described in this chapter are at once personal, political, intellectual, and emotional. As a target of Othering, I have felt diminished and self-doubting; I have also experienced the energizing anger of collective challenges to subordination. As I have gotten older, I have gained more power and authority, thanks in part to the gains of feminism, as well as my age, social class, and racial positioning. I have found that consciousness raising when one is in a privileged position is often set in motion by challenges to the complacent not-noticing that sustains the status quo; it moves through the squirmy, defensive terrain of guilt and embarrassed discomfort and then—an outcome I've learned to crave and to struggle toward—to greater empathy and broadened understanding. Struggles for justice are also struggles with the self.

NOTES

1. Minh-ha Trinh, *Woman, Native, Other* (Bloomington: Indiana University Press, 1989), 107–8.

2. Troy Duster, "The 'Morphing' Properties of Whiteness," in *The Making and Unmaking of Whiteness*, ed. Brigit Brander Rasmuseen, Eric Klinenberg, Irene J. Nexica, and Matt Wrey (Durham, N.C.: Duke University Press, 2001), 113–37.

3. Stuart Hall provides an excellent review of theories of Othering: "The Spectacle of 'Other,'" in *Representation: Cultural Representation and Signifying Practices*, ed. Stuart Hall (Thousand Oaks, California: Sage, 1997), 223–90. I often make this a theme in my teaching, drawing upon works by Simone de Beauvoir, *The Second Sex*, trans. H. M. Parshley (New York: Knopf, 1951); Frantz Fanon, *Black Skin, White Masks* (London: Pluto Press, 1986); Edward Said, *Orientalism* (New York: Penguin, 1978); Patricia Hill Collins, *Black Feminist Thought* (New York: Routledge, 1990); Jessica Benjamin, *The Bonds of Love* (New York: Pantheon, 1988); Marilyn Frye "The Arrogant Eye," in her *The Politics of Reality* (Trumansburg, N.Y.: Crossing Press, 1983); and Maria Lugones, "Playfulness, 'World'-Travelling, and Loving Perception," *Hypatia* 2 (1987): 3–19.

4. Barrie Thorne, "Brandeis as a Generative Institution: Critical Perspectives, Marginality, and Feminism," in *Feminist Sociology: Life Histories of a Movement*, ed. Barbara Laslett and Barrie Thorne (New Brunswick, N.J.: Rutgers University Press, 1997), 103–25.

5. Barrie Thorne, "Women in the Draft Resistance Movement: A Case Study of Sex Roles and Social Movements," *Sex Roles* 1, 2 (1975): 179–95.

6. See A. C. Thorne, *Leave the Dishes in the Sink: Adventures of an Activist in Conservative Utah* (Logan: Utah State University Press, 2002).

7. Barrie Thorne and Nancy Henley, eds., *Language and Sex: Difference and Dominance* (Rowley, Mass.: Newbury House, 1975).

8. Barrie Thorne, "Re-Visioning Women and Social Change: Where Are the Children?" *Gender & Society* 1, 1 (1987): 85–109.

9. Barrie Thorne, *Gender Play: Girls and Boys in School* (New Brunswick, N.J.: Rutgers University Press, 1993).

10. Ibid., 128.

11. In retrospect, I can see how the landscape of my family's experiences in California changed as a result of rapidly changing demographics. Since the 1965 changes in U.S. immigration laws, California has received more immigrants than any other state. Between our California sojourns in 1976 and 1980, the number of immigrants from Mexico and Central America increased, as did the number of bilingual public school classrooms.

12. Three recently published essays from the California Childhoods Project (which was funded by the MacArthur Foundation Research Network on Successful Pathways Through Middle Childhood and by the Sloan Foundation through the UC Berkeley Center for Working Families) include Marjorie Faulstich Orellana, "The Work Kids Do: Mexican and Central American Immigrant Children's Contributions to Households and Schools in California," *Harvard Educational Review* 71 (2001): 366–89; Marjorie Faulstich Orellana, Barrie Thorne, Anna Chee, and Wan Shun Eva Lam, "Transnational Childhoods: The Participation of Children in Processes of Family Migration," *Social Problems* 48 (2001): 572–91; Barrie Thorne, "Pick-up Time at Oakdale Elementary School: Work and Family from the Vantage Point of Children," in *Working Families*, ed. Rosanna Hertz and Nancy Marshall (Berkeley: University of California Press, 2001).

EVOLVING IDENTITIES

Part III

JOSHUA GAMSON | WILLIAM H. FRIEDLAN

SHULAMIT REINHARZ

VERTA TAYLOR

ROBERT R. ALFORD

15

MUSICIAN, SOCIOLOGIST,

AND HEARING PERSON

A CRISIS OF IDENTITIES

started taking piano lessons from my mother at the age of five and have been a serious amateur pianist all my life, mostly of chamber music. I have played most of the trios and quartets in the concert repertoire: Mozart, Beethoven, Schubert, Brahms, as well as Faure, Poulenc, and Copland. The high point of my pianistic career was playing—with considerable power and authority—Beethoven's Second Piano Concerto with a Santa Cruz orchestra in 1988.

Forty years ago I received my doctorate in sociology from the University of California at Berkeley. I taught first at the University of Wisconsin at Madison, then went to the University of California at Santa Cruz, and finally, in 1988, to the Graduate Center of the City University of New York. Research and teaching have been central in my life.

Twenty-two years ago I discovered a new way of playing the piano that transformed my playing. I began to take lessons and attend a summer piano institute in Amherst, Massachusetts, devoted to the work of Dorothy Taubman, a Brooklyn piano teacher.

Twenty-one years ago I began wearing hearing aids, as a result of hereditary nerve deterioration. My father was almost completely deaf by the time he died at the age of 90, seventeen years ago.

Fifteen years ago I realized that my discovery of a new way of teaching and playing the piano could become a sociological question about the conditions and consequences of cultural innovation and public knowledge. Up to that moment, my musical and sociological identities had never connected.

I began doing research at the Taubman Institute. I have tapes from master classes and lectures, interviews with about forty pianists and teachers, and field notes from a number of workshops, lectures, and conferences. I have also collected most of the monographs in English on piano technique. In 1990, I sent a questionnaire to 1500 pianists and teachers who had attended the Amherst Institute or who are members of the New York State Music Teachers Association, asking about their professional and musical backgrounds, their knowledge of the basic concepts of piano technique, their teaching experience and philosophy, and whether they were in physical pain when playing. I intended to conduct interviews with neurophysiologists and cognitive psychologists, as well as physicians in the new specialty, performance medicine. I wanted to conduct interviews with leading piano virtuosi, such as Leon Fleisher, about their experiences with physical pain.

Ten years ago I lost the ability to hear music. I stopped taking lessons, playing, performing, and going to concerts. At this moment, I can still teach small classes and can converse one on one in a quiet environment, but I do not attend meetings, colloquia, noisy parties, the theater, or loud restaurants. I have a profound hearing loss, according to the clinical categories. I may soon be a candidate for a cochlear implant.

Five years ago I published (with Andras Szanto) an article in *Theory and Society* on the piano project.[1] By the time the article was published, I was already losing my motivation to work on the project, undoubtedly in part because of the loss of music. I have not done any serious work on it since, although I have a wealth of data and lots of ideas. I can still play the piano with some facility, and listeners tell me that the sounds are musical, but I hear only noise. I am coping with a "disabled" identity.

This brief narrative summarizes a crisis of three identities: musical, sociological, and most recent, a disabled identity. If I can find a way of accepting that identity, I may be able to release the emotional and intellectual energies that will enable me to return to this project. Or I may decide that I am facing new and different challenges in life and work.

Even beginning this chapter has posed issues for me. Which aspect of myself, which identity, am I presenting to you? These few introductory para‧ graphs are written from the standpoint of what might be called the metaself, the aspect of myself that is momentarily overseeing, monitoring, and report‧ ing on the subselves, although not now absorbed and defined by any one of them. I am caught among identities, unwillingly relinquishing my musical identity, resisting my disabled identity, and paralyzed in my sociological iden‧ tity (at least for this research project). Because of these dilemmas, I cannot write a paper in orthodox linear form. Instead, I am going to present three discontinuous sections of it, one in the voice of a sociologist, a second in the voice of a musician who is grappling with the loss of music, and a third by a person who is confronting the dilemmas of personal transformation.

CULTURAL INNOVATION:
THE CASE OF PIANO TECHNIQUE

[This section, slightly revised, was delivered at the National Conference of the Arts, in Jacksonville, Florida, in 1991. The presentation is explicitly within a sociological identity, applying sociological concepts to a problem that derived from my musical identity. No mention is made of my growing hearing loss, only a year later resulting in the loss of music.]

I am both a sociologist and a pianist, and this project combines those inter‧ ests. About a decade ago, I discovered the work of Dorothy Taubman, a Brooklyn piano teacher who has synthesized a way of teaching piano tech‧ nique that is apparently quite new and has a growing number of adherents. Its practitioners claim that application of her principles enables performers not only to play with power, accuracy, and musicality but also to avoid the pain that has recently been acknowledged by many pianists.

I am thus studying an educational innovation in cultural knowledge in vivo, at a stage when the outcome is quite uncertain. Her work may become institutionalized as the right (even "scientific") way to play the piano (public knowledge), or it may remain the private lore of a small group of initiates.[2] The cognitive metaphors about skilled body movements that constitute this claim to new cultural knowledge are found piecemeal in the literature on piano technique but have nowhere been synthesized in this way. One prob‧ lem is that there seems to be a tremendous discrepancy between the practices of piano teaching and those of performing artists. Gaps also seem to exist among how people teach, how they play, and the principles advocated in the pedagogical literature. In fact, there seems to be little relationship among the theoretical knowledge of such pedagogues as Tobias Matthay, the clinical knowledge conveyed by the manuals written by such virtuosi as Gyorgy Sandor, and the actual practical knowledge conveyed by rank-and-file piano teachers. The fascination of both musicians and audiences with the image of the musical genius and a belief that virtuosi are born, not made, helps maintain these cultural discontinuities.

The skills conveyed by conservatory teachers—individual master craftsmen—are mostly private lore about repertoire, interpretation, and career management. Because of the absence of public knowledge, the disciple can never be quite sure whether or not he or she has mastered the knowledge since it is not based on analytic concepts formally organized into theoretical knowledge that is the common property of the profession and defined as the legitimate basis of training.

Worse, many of the ways in which the piano has been traditionally taught may produce pain. Strengthening the fingers by exercises, stretching into hand positions, isolating the fingers from the hand and arm, all reduce the coordination of the whole body and create potentially destructive tensions. Because there is considerable disagreement about whether or not knowledge of the physiology of movement in relation to the mechanics of the piano exists and because there are no strong incentives to develop that knowledge, existing modes of teaching piano technique persist, almost unchallenged.

The implications of this rather strange situation can be put in the form of several paradoxical hypotheses: the great pianists do not play the way in which they were taught, although they teach that way. Conservatory teachers do not teach technique; they expect students to come to them with polished techniques for coaching. The less a young prodigy obeys her teacher, the less likely she is to suffer from pain and injury.

One consequence of the highly competitive market for virtuosi may be jealous guarding of the tricks of the trade, the knacks, among the disciples and, presumably, the masters. The skills may be mystified; they become identified with a particular individual rather than being the public property of the entire musical community. Because of the identification by students of their learning of skilled body movements with the unique personality and charisma of an individual virtuoso, it is difficult to redefine the knowledge as potentially universal, as contributing to general human capacities, and thereby to convert it into potentially public knowledge about how human bodies can most efficiently control the piano. (I use the mechanical metaphor quite consciously to offset the aura of artistic uniqueness.)

Conservatory students—the potential artist performers—have the worst of both worlds. They are commodities in a cultural market but have no firm basis of knowledge that allows them to guarantee performance. Because the occupation is organized as a profession, the master teachers and artists control access; but because the knowledge is not formalized and public, they have an additional source of power over their students. They not only have professional power but also guild and craft power—the power of the master over the apprentice, as well as the power of the established professional over the student.

Some of the dilemmas involved in the potential transition from private lore to public knowledge in the case of piano technique are illustrated by the method developed by Dorothy Taubman, a Brooklyn piano teacher for forty years. Her method is based on a critique of the previous work of Tobias Matthay, Otto Ortmann, and Jacob Helmann, synthesizing some of their concepts and adding new elements. Taubman claims to have formulated a physiologically appropriate way of coordinating the fingers, hand, and arm that will ensure consciously controlled and comfortable movements, that is, never painful or tension-producing playing.

The Taubman method exhibits, in embryo, all of the characteristics that might lead to institutionalization of new public knowledge of piano technique, that is, a new paradigm. There is a body of analytic concepts—the walking arm, shaping, in and out, rotation, and so on—that are tools to analyze the physical and musical requirements of particular passages. Exemplars are drawn from analyses of musical passages, showing how they can be played efficiently, accurately, and comfortably by using the concepts to plan the movements of fingers, hand, and arm appropriate for a particular passage. In addition, there are documented cases of pianists who have been cured of pain by using the Taubman principles.

A summer institute at Amherst College has been established to teach the Taubman method. The concepts are becoming formalized: Taubman is writing a book that presents the details of the method, applied to examples, that the reader can test at the piano. The lectures at the Taubman Institute of Piano present the analytic concepts and demonstrate their applicability to the classic repertoire (and are available on video). There is a growing body of practitioners at different levels of training: the Amherst faculty (students of Taubman and students of their students) and a growing number of community and professional teachers around the country who apply the concepts in their own playing and teaching. Also, faculty members of the institute have showed videotapes and have lectured at meetings of various state music teachers' associations, spreading the word about the pedagogical usefulness of the method.

In all of these various ways, the Taubman method is fulfilling the requirements for institutionalization of public knowledge, with one key exception. Her work still remains an approach associated with one person and is not yet recognized as legitimate by the relevant elite musical institutions and pianistic constituencies.

My entry point into these issues is the effort by a cadre of teachers and pianists to institutionalize Taubman's work. The efforts of the Taubman Institute of Piano to create a Taubman "credential" is a strategy of professionalization. Taubman's book in progress on piano technique is an investment in the potential legitimacy of "scientific" concepts and method. The Taubman school is ambivalent on the issue of artistic education. On the one hand, to make inroads into conservatory education, it must claim artistic validity and the highest level of musicianship and esthetic interpretation of the piano literature. On the other hand, to try to reach the widest audience of music and piano teachers in other schools or community teachers, it must appeal to them on the classic grounds that a new body of coherent and systematic knowledge will give them a much more secure claim to be fully trained professionals.

Legitimazation and institutionalization of the principles underlying Taubman's work requires that she be able to prescribe routine diagnoses and treatments. A certain position of the hands and fingers must definitively indicate twisting, stretching, or pulling and have a certain treatment (i.e., straightening the hand or moving the fourth finger in) that can be objectively observed and prescribed. If there is no regular correlation between specific body positions or movements and specific consequences (whether pain and inaccuracy or power and speed), then training of teachers in Taubman principles will be very difficult, and the claim to scientific or even clinical knowledge will be hard to establish.

Will there be a Taubman method like the Matthay, Ortmann, or Leschetizky methods? Will her work become a recognized approach, standing alongside the many others? Will Taubman remain one of the many piano teachers who have trained some students and some concert artists and have formulated a pedagogical method that has become part of the multiple heritages of the field, available to those who happen to come into contact with one of her subsequent generations of student teachers? Or will her method become the dominant mode of piano teaching, recognized as establishing the truly scientific basis for understanding the skilled body movements required to play the piano? These questions are still open. The answers may not depend upon the validity of her method, that is, that her concepts are neurophysiologically and mechanically the best way to control skilled body movements. A variety of institutional circumstances, some already alluded to, will also affect the historical fate of her method.

Since the above was written, I have lost touch with my former coparticipants in the Taubman Institute of Piano, have stopped taking piano lessons, and have stopped listening to music. I still read the reviews of piano concerts in the New York Times, with painful nostalgia. The institute continues, although it moved recently to Bennington College. More and more "Taubman teachers" are working within academic institutions, as well as functioning as private teachers. The issue of how cultural innovations originate and become diffused into established practices and behaviors remains an important topic for sociological theory and research. But the personal dilemmas for me remain intact.

CRISIS OF MUSICAL AND SOCIOLOGICAL IDENTITIES

Below, in chronological order, are excerpts from letters and research memoranda written between 1991, when I realized that my hearing loss was threatening my ability to hear music, and 1995, when I was on the verge of stopping work on the music project. First is a letter written to my "Taubman teacher," Edna Golandsky, from whom I took lessons for about 10 years, from 1980 to 1991. Edna is Taubman's heiress apparent. She gives lectures and master classes based on Taubman's work.

September 16, 1991

Dear Edna:

I want to give you the reasons for my decision not to take piano lessons this year, and probably not any more. My goal of improving my musicianship and technical ability assumes a simple capacity to hear what I am playing. I started losing the ability to hear music, ironically, soon after I moved to New York in 1988, with high hopes of finally mastering the Taubman method. The few lessons from you that I had last year were difficult for me, as you undoubtedly realized.

I am feeling a lot of pain about my hearing loss, and its consequences for my ability to enjoy my own playing and that of others. I went to a concert of a pianist last year at Carnegie Hall, and could not even recognize a piece that he was playing that I knew very well. This summer at our family ranch in California, my son Jonathan played the first Chopin Ballade that I have worked on with you. I did not know what it was.

The problem is not only volume but that the sounds are distorted. Even when they are loud enough I cannot distinguish one note from another. The same thing occurs with consonants in speech; they are simply a blur because my brain cannot distinguish among them. According to my audiologist, I only comprehend 20% of the meaningful sounds that I hear (i.e., spoken words). A minimum of 60% is needed for full comprehension.

I still get some pleasure out of playing chamber music, although I have to adjust my hearing aids frequently, particularly when, in a rehearsal, we stop and talk about a passage. I intend to keep doing that as long as I am able.

I have not given up my commitment to learn what I can about Mrs. Taubman's work, and how best it can be transmitted to more and more people. Nor do I want to lose touch with the friends whom I have made at Amherst. Thus, I intend to come to your workshop on October 6th, and to the potluck afterwards, to say hello, and to continue learning about Mrs. Taubman's work.

May 21, 1992: A letter to Nancy Garniez, director of the Alaria Chamber Players in New York, based at the Mannes College of Music. I was coached by Nancy from 1988 to 1992. Alaria was and is committed to helping dedicated amateur musicians perform at the highest level of their ability.

Dear Nancy:

I am looking into new hearing aids; high technology may yet restore my ability to hear music. I have been finding it increasingly difficult to discern pitch differences. You may recall that measure in the Beethoven Trio where I was playing a B flat instead of an A flat. I literally couldn't hear the difference. I am "hearing" with my brain instead of my ears.

I mention this partly because I will have the difficult decision to make in the fall whether or not to return to the Alaria nest, and the only reason I would not is because of my hearing. I will call you in early September.

[Following are excerpts from my research notes, taken during the last time I attended the Taubman Institute of Piano in Amherst, in July of 1992. Edna Golandsky gives the morning lectures on Taubman concepts and principles.]

Edna started the first lecture by citing a study that claimed that 75–80% of musicians suffer some degree of pain. She mentioned, disapprovingly, the "no pain, no gain" philosophy of practicing. She emphasized that the muscle tensions and motions responsible for injury are so small, so subtle, that they are invisible, and cited the remarkable number of occupations and activities causing hand and arm injuries: computer operations, meat cutting, writing, housework, etc. But even the articles reporting these figures repeat the same error of ascribing the injuries to "overuse," rather than "misuse." Some of them even recommend the exercises and movements that reinforce pain.

[Comment: Amherst is, like many other occasional social worlds, a convergence of persons at moments of personal transformation. Many of them are in crises of identity or transition, from one career to another. The Amherst experience becomes significant for many people because of this: Henry Micklem of the University of Edinburgh is resigning his position as professor of biology (in his late fifties), two years after his wife died, to become a piano teacher. He may move to California or New York, to study with Nina Scolnik or Edna. Cindy Rose, whom I interviewed yesterday, quit a fifteen-year career as a nurse two years ago to become a piano teacher, and she is here for all three of the main motives: playing, teaching, and pain. The school resolutely avoids any references to anything about these personal crises except in the letter to faculty that reminds them that "it is essential that everyone working with injured pianists be sensitive to their physical and emotional pain."]

[Comment: Many faculty members were at the first lecture today, to be reminded of the first principles of the Taubman theory. This is probably part of the dense network of supervision (Foucault might call it "surveillance") of Taubman teachers or would-be teachers. I am inclined to look at it positively or, perhaps better, tolerantly, as part of the necessary attempt to ensure some conformity to the basic concepts. Foucault emphasizes the negative aspects of surveillance because of his focus upon mental hospitals, prisons, the army, and bureaucracies. But, little social worlds where skills are being taught to voluntary, nay, eager and willing, participants—cultural knowledge of folk dances, tennis, guitar playing, and the Go game—need expert teachers and willing novices for the knowledge to be propagated and perpetuated. In this case, where the knowledge is still esoteric (it has not yet become the common cultural property of the society), it may be even more necessary for new recruits to be supervised carefully, particularly if, as the theory holds, a misapplication will lead to a worsening of the problem, that is, continued pain.]

Edna then demonstrated the different ways of holding the hand that immediately communicate the difference between a "normal" way of holding and moving and a distorted, potentially painful way of moving. She said to hold our right hands in a clawlike position, as if we were clutching a ball in our palm. One orthodox school of piano playing actually recommends that hand posture. She asked us to move our wrist back and forth with our hand in the claw position. One can move, but only slowly and with effort. Then we were asked to let go of the claw position and to move the wrist back and forth. One can move rapidly and easily.

Edna said, Don't "tilt," "twist," or "drop" the wrist. These are common causes of injuries, particularly carpal tunnel syndrome. And don't "individualize" the fingers; never move the fingers independently of the wrist and forearm. This is a cardinal Taubman principle, she said, but also violates some ancient piano orthodoxies. "Every finger feels individualized when it is working together."

The lecture ended at 11:00 A.M., and a few minutes later Edna began a "diagnostic clinic," in which several injured musicians had twenty minutes or so with her. They sat at the piano and demonstrated how they played, while she watched their hands and gave to them as well as to the audience of about fifty people, her analysis of what was wrong. Their teacher, or "practice associate," stood nearby, watching Edna and the student.

After lunch, went to the master class with Mrs. Taubman. I could hardly distinguish one pitch from another in the Schubert A Major Sonata and a Scriabin sonata. My brain supplied the Schubert melody since I had heard it before, but the Scriabin was just a jumble of sound.

I could hear some of Mrs. Taubman's comments, but not all. I am wondering if it is worthwhile for me to attend the master classes (or the lectures, for that matter). I need to spend time finding more people to interview, perhaps writing them up while everyone is otherwise occupied with lessons and concerts.

I am feeling doubly isolated here, and it is very painful. For one thing, for the first time, I am not a participant. I am not taking lessons, not going to diagnostic clinics with technical problems, not practicing. This new situation brings home to me the brutal fact that I am no longer a functioning pianist and musician, and it is difficult to accept. I feel—this may or may not be true—that people are already treating me differently because I am not involved in the same personal goal of trying to improve my playing, as they are.

We are simply not sharing the same experiences. We are not occupying the same social space.

The other, and of course related, reason is that I am here as a researcher, taking notes, observing, interviewing. This is an awkward position to be in, particularly because it is a shift in social relationships. Always before, even when engaged in my piano project, I was also a musician and functioning pianist. I am worried that my loss of ability to hear the music will reduce my commitment to the project. It may reinforce it, as a kind of sublimation, an intellectual involvement in the world of the piano that replaces my musical involvement. Or, it may simply be too painful to work on if it brings me in continued contact with musicians and performers. Is this a momentary mood at Amherst, where the contrast between my former role as active participant and present one as passive observer is bitterly real?

I went for a walk instead of going to Robert Shannon's Schubert concert, and was feeling deeply the loss of music. I went into the woods alone, just before nightfall, and the forest was beautiful. There has been rain the last few days, and everything was fresh. The paths were covered with pine needles, with low flowers coming up through them. Just before dusk, the fireflies came out, and at one point, there were dozens, flickering on and off. Later on, when Susan Day came back after the concert for the continuation of our interview, she said that the Moments Musicaux were "magical."

The last master class: while Frank Levy was playing, I looked around the room and saw about twenty faces of people I had interviewed in some depth during the last two weeks. I knew a lot about them—their family situation; whether they were injured or not; their qualms or faith in the Taubman program; their aspirations, ambitions, and fears about playing and teaching the piano. Most of them had expressed ambivalences and anxieties that I had promised to keep in confidence.

I had talked to Frank Levy the day before about his experiences with renowned concert pianists Leon Fleisher and Emanuel Ax. Both had encouraged him to come to Amherst and work with Mrs. Taubman. He spoke eloquently, in a soft French accent, about his desires to become a teacher. [July 1992: Excerpt from a interview with an experienced piano teacher, new at the Amherst institute. She had been unable to play for several years because of physical pain.]

R.A.: But you wouldn't have also been in such emotional pain if you didn't see the promise of Mrs. Taubman's work, right? If you had just said to yourself: there is nothing I can do. I can't deal with this.

M.R.: Oh, right. I was also just in a rage at my teachers, for not having known what to do. And it wasn't even their fault. There's still a little tinge of that anger. I am grieving for what I might have done. I have to say, though, for the tools I had, and the teaching I had, I did really well. How did I stay with it so long? As you were saying, people cling to their music, because they love it so much. You hear music and you just want to play. It's a joy.

When I watched the videotape of her student playing the Rachmaninoff Third, I just cried because I know he is so free technically.

[January 31, 1993: Excerpt from another letter to Nancy Garniez of the Alaria Chamber Players in New York City.]

Dear Nancy:

I have not attended any Alaria concerts because of my hearing. I can no longer distinguish harmonies or even dissonances and can't tell Mozart from Schoenberg. The last semester I participated in Alaria I was actually "hearing" very little "music." Chords were (and remain) a jumble of noise. So, I no longer attend concerts of any kind, have not played the piano since I left Alaria, and don't listen to anything on the stereo. Essentially, I have lost music.

As you can imagine, this is a very painful situation since music was a central part of my life. I am throwing myself into my work—teaching, reading, writing—as some compensation (or sublimation, as the case may be).

Thanks very much, and good luck with your concerts, recitals and teaching this year.

[January 30, 1993: A letter to my stepdaughter, Katrina Walker.]

Dear Katie:

As you know, I am not playing the piano any more because I can't hear harmony or pitch. Chords are a big blur, and I can't distinguish major from minor, so there is no point. It is interesting how important the brain is. I can play a piece that I know well for someone, and they will enjoy it. I know that I am playing it musically because my brain knows how to move the fingers and how much pressure to apply to achieve a singing melodic line. But I am not hearing it as music, only as a jumble of sound. I can write about this loss "objectively" and mostly don't feel too bad—one can't go on brooding forever—but sometimes an incredible wave of sadness sweeps over me. It happens at night, when I wake up playing the Brahms B Major Trio with my fingers and "hearing" it sharply and vividly.

[January 30, 1993: Self-explanatory letter to the Amateur Chamber Music Players Society (ACMP) of America.]

Amateur Chamber Music Players, Inc.

Dear Fellow Chamber Music Lovers and Players:

I enclose the membership form for updating, indicating that my entry should be deleted completely. I feel very bad about this and wanted to explain briefly.

My hearing has been deteriorating for some years and has finally reached the point where I can no longer distinguish harmony; I can't tell a major from a minor chord. No one told me that this would happen as a result of nerve damage, and it came as an absolutely shocking and horrifying development a year or two ago to realize that I was no longer hearing music. I can actually play quite well—because I can still hear sounds—but my brain supplies the music, not my ears.

I am writing not just to tell you my sad personal story but also partly to see if anyone else in the ACMP has had this experience and has found any medical or other help for an analogous loss. I have obviously been to the best specialists (none of whom have been musicians, however) and have been told that nothing can be done. My condition is hereditary (my father was completely deaf by the time he died) and degenerative. But just in case. . . .

Also, I thought that before I lose connection with the ACMP that I would let you know that, like many of your correspondents, I also have had wonderful experiences with a wide variety of musicians over the years. One of the most memorable was meeting Dutch musicians during a fellowship year at the Netherlands Institute for Advanced Study in the Humanities and Social Sciences (I am a sociologist by trade) in 1981–82. Before I left California, I wrote a letter to a number of Dutch musicians. Several answered, and the result was a number of wonderful sessions: an afternoon of Mozart piano music with the retired ambassador to Indonesia and his charming German wife, at their home in The Hague; an evening of Brahms quartets with a family—the violist was a well-known astronomer, the cellist a cello teacher, the violinist daughter was a member of the Netherlands Philharmonic—on the bank of the Rhine River in Leiden; and there were others.

The ACMP is a wonderful institution; it has become an adjunct of my musical life that I will miss very much. Thank you.

[March 14, 1995: An excerpt from an e-mail to Lynn Chancer, a sociologist now at Fordham University. Lynn is an accomplished pianist.]

Dear Lynn,

As a pianist, as well as a friend, you are one of the few people I can share this with. I am reading Frank Conroy's *Body and Soul*, about a young pianist, that has a lot of intimate details about how to learn to play the piano, different teacher's styles, and—the point here—the joy of making music. One scene I read last night was his first performance of a Mozart Concerto with orchestra. It movingly described his musical phrasing, his sense of his body, his hands, the connections among the phrases, his answering of the phrases in the orchestra and the other piano, his total immersion in conveying the rise and fall of the melodic line, and his visceral response to the harmonic changes. The account evoked deep feelings in me, both the memory of the joy in music, but also the pain of its loss. . . . I wept.

I don't often remember particular musical moments now, but at times like these some come back to me . . . the opening of the Faure Piano Quartet . . . the andante of the Brahms Piano Quintet . . . the slow movement of the Schubert B Flat trio—all pieces I know by heart and cherish. "By heart" is a wonderful metaphor, I just realized.

[This is a brief autobiographical sketch that I wrote for an early draft of my last book, The Craft of Inquiry.*]*[3]

About the time that *Powers of Theory*,[4] was published, I became interested in the sociology of music, although I did not dignify it by that name. It is only after one has finished a study or has to describe it to outsiders that one legitimizes it by means of an established subdivision of academic discourse. The origins are always more humble. A pianist all my life, I had been attending a piano institute at Amherst College in Massachusetts since the summer of 1982, just after returning from a year at the Netherlands Institute for Advanced Study in Wassenaar, Holland.

The "macro-micro" argument at this point is that the political economy of the international concert market for pianists creates enormous competitive pressures upon an ever increasing number of concert pianists, producing emotional and physical stresses that neither individuals nor institutions are prepared to cope with. Recent discovery that a remarkable number of pianists suffer acute physical pain is responded to differently by the virtuoso, pedagogical, and medical worlds of the piano. Deep emotional bonds among mother, teacher, and child prodigy lead to denial of pain until—all too often—it is too late. The potential virtuoso can no longer play professionally and becomes a teacher, reproducing pain in the next generation of pianists by teaching the way in which one was taught.

That book has been put aside to finish this one.[5]

[The "music book" is still put aside, for reasons that may now be clear. I have not wanted to (or been able to) return to it.]

METASELF OR PERSONAL TRANSFORMATION?

My brother David, a philosopher of the humanities and a fierce critic, read the above and questioned my fundamental distinctions. He argues that the "self" of the second section may actually be replacing the professional, scholarly, sociological self of the first section. He argues, as a possibility, that my core identity is really changing. This chapter, therefore, rather than "manifesting what you say it does (the multiplicity of identities) is actually the anatomy of an evolution." He thinks that it "may now be a time for me to 'emulate' colleagues who have left professional sociology to become journalists, poets, novelists." He says that he uses "the word 'emulate' deliberately because there is no 'scientific' or 'professional' model for such a transition." If this is true, David believes, this chapter is "not the 'autobiography of a discontinuous human being' but is the 'autobiography of a budding artist.'"

For a person who adopted a scholarly and professional identity forty years ago, this is a difficult message to hear. I am not sure it is true. Certainly, I am continuing to work on research projects in political sociology and methodology, without fundamental skepticism about the intellectual enterprise. Perhaps I can find a way to combine a personal narrative with an exploration of the sociological issues I summarize in the first section.

I should end with a report of a decision about the sociological project and/or some conclusions about myself, in effect a "happy ending." Perhaps I should discuss the implications for "theories of identity and the self." No such punchlines will be offered. The chapter will remain only a narrative of reflections on my present state of mind, being, and self.

A *haiku* summarizes my present moment. My parting thoughts and feelings, via a three-stanza haiku:

> Echoing in my head.
> Melodies and harmonies
> Never to be heard.
>
> Outside that prison,
> Life, love, even work, go on.
> Daffodils will grow.
>
> The earth turns, immune
> To the petty dilemmas
> Of my many selves.

NOTES

1. Robert R. Alford and Andras Szanto, "Orpheus Wounded: The Experience of Pain in the Professional Worlds of the Piano," *Theory and Society* 25 (1996): 1–44.

2. Robert R. Alford, *The Craft of Inquiry* (Oxford: Oxford University Press, 1998).

3. Ibid.

4. Robert R. Alford and Roger Friedland, *Power of Theory* (New York: Cambridge University Press, 1985).

5. Alford and Szanto, "Orpheus Wounded."

GARY L. ALBRECHT

16

SOCIAL-CLASS TENSIONS

AND VALUE CONFLICTS IN

THE DISABILITY WORLD

TIME AND CIRCUMSTANCE

Riding the New York subway on the way to a late afternoon class one cold January day, I read a preprint version of C. Wright Mills's *The Sociological Imagination*. In the first few pages he says:

> The sociological imagination enables us to grasp history and biography and the relationship between the two within society. That is its task and its promise . . . It is by means of the sociological imagination that men now hope to grasp what is happening to themselves as minute points of the intersection of biography and history within society.[1]

As a young graduate student in the mid-1960s, I was struggling with the conflicts raging between socially engaged academics like C. Wright Mills, on the one hand, and those who opted for a Weberian-based view of sociology as a value-free science, on the other hand. Mills's quote captured me.

Being new to the city and mesmerized by the monotony of the train's stops and starts, I once missed my transfer between the A and the D trains. I looked at my new map of New York City and said to myself, "I can still make class if I get off at 125th Street and walk up to Columbia through Morningside Park." This first experience of climbing the hill from Harlem to Morningside Heights gave me an unforgettable lesson in social class by observing the street life, how people treated each other and reacted to me. The distance between the poor at the bottom of the hill and those with opportunities at the top was enormous, even though they lived in close proximity. At Columbia I was studying the structural dynamics and life consequences of social class in a doctoral seminar that was analyzing different theoretical explanations of social position and mobility. As students, we were encouraged to develop an objective eye for social patterns and to grapple with various operational measures of social position and mobility. Yet, debating theoretical positions, developing mobility tables, and learning the rudiments of structural equation modeling did little to quell my personal discomfort and rising anger with the inequities evident on the streets around me.

My growing passion about the disparity between the worlds of the poor and the privileged was reinforced on my first job as a research assistant. I responded to an ad in the sociology department and was hired as an interviewer in Harlem, the South Bronx, and Bedford Stuyvesant as part of Patricia Sexton's study of black adolescents' transitions to adulthood. The chances of African Americans getting into college and having some way to support themselves through four years of school was minimal at that time. Even if they did, they had to learn a whole new culture and class-specific set of behaviors. Finding and holding a job with any sort of future presented insurmountable challenges. Being poor and a member of a minority group enhanced one's chances of becoming dependent and disabled. The physical and social environments were stifling. Sexton's study was aimed at identifying those African-American high school students who stood the best chance of completing an university degree, if given the opportunity and support, and enrolling them in a special program at New York University designed to help them graduate in four and a half years with a college degree. The program was enriched with tutors in mathematics and English and placement in summer jobs that would socialize them into the white-collar work world.

My experiences in interviewing promising high school students at Benjamin Franklin High School in the South Bronx for the Sexton study contradicted most of the research findings that I was learning in my sociology classes about the characteristics of "successful" and upwardly mobile adolescents. Many of the brightest and most motivated students in the South Bronx did not come early or stay late after school because they did not want to be hassled by or involved with the drug dealers or gang bangers who preyed on those who hung around the school. They did not belong to clubs or play sports because they lived by themselves or in broken families. They needed to work to survive. They often had to come late or miss a few days of school to take care of sick siblings. Between work, family responsibilities, and school, they had little time for friends or a lively social life. They could not afford them. In spite of these circumstances, numerous adolescents studied hard and had a burning desire to learn and to get ahead. Those who survived had learned incredible discipline and good work habits, but they needed opportunities to break out of their oppressive and often dangerous environments. Their example quietly moved me toward activism.

This was the 1960s, when racial tensions and injustices ran strong. John F. Kennedy had just been assassinated. Malcolm X was giving fiery sermons in Harlem, preaching a form of Islam that seemed to offer more to oppressed blacks than mainstream Christianity or Judaism. He, too, was shot down. Claude Brown had just written *Manchild in the Promised Land*, portraying what it was like to grow up Hispanic and poor in New York City. Martin Luther King, Jr., eloquently led a nonviolent movement against racial discrimination until he, too, was killed. Betty Freidan and others formed and led a nascent women's movement that at first was ridiculed but quickly began to show results. The United States's involvement in Vietnam provoked heated controversies about the power of the military industrial complex and what the United States was doing in Vietnam. Whom were we helping? Whom were we killing and for what reasons?

During this period, I was shaken by an incident outside my advisor's office in the sociology department. A student in his thirties with a thick manuscript on his lap sat on the bench next to me, quietly crying. When I asked him what the matter was, he broke down sobbing and said, "Professor X has had my dissertation for three years and has not had time to read it yet. I have been living on the edge of poverty for nine years, trying to do my Ph.D., but I can't take it any more." I felt what he felt—that the powers-that-be in the department had abandoned their responsibilities to both those outside and inside the system. All of these perceived injustices and social upheavals culminated for me in a life-marking experience when student demonstrations on the steps of Low Library, against perceived abuses of power and authority on the part of the administration and faculty, closed the university for a time.

I joined the protests. The purported ideal of constructing and practicing sociology as a "value-free" science did not fit the history or experiences of New York City or the nation in the 1960s and early 1970s. I learned that much of the best sociology is rooted in biography, history, personal experience, and the foundations of American pragmatism—the desire to make a difference. Given these personal experiences, which were in marked contrast to the professional socialization we received in the mid- to late 1960s, I was deeply influenced by the arguments of C. Wright Mills. How could one live among and study inequities and not be moved to do research on these issues, hoping in some small way to make a difference?

DISABILITY AND INEQUALITY

Careers are often made from one's surroundings, not formulated through some careful strategic plan. My days in New York in the 1960s did not provide the flashing insight into what research I would do during my career, but they did focus my attention on and put fire in my belly over the social-class inequities and the abuse of power seen in everyday life. I grew up in a working-class family in Seattle, one that struggled during the end of the Depression and through World War II. Family stories told of worrying about where to get a job; of burying uncles who died in bloody invasions of Pacific islands, leaving their futures and families behind them; and of those who were seriously disabled in combat or by accidents in heavy industry during the war. In some sense, these roots, concerned with struggle, survival, and disability, unwittingly shaped my experiences as a student in New York City.

As a student, I began to notice how the inequities of social class and the experience of disability were inextricably intertwined in the lives of the poor and the vulnerable. While in graduate school, I shared an apartment with other students on the edge of Harlem. We and the African-American and Hispanic communities of Harlem shared the experience of living on little money in Manhattan. It was an experience that makes one observant and creative, yet I knew I was only here for some student years and had a future as a professor. For my neighbors, this was their life forever.

During those years, I noticed numerous people in Harlem, the South Bronx, and the subways late at night who talked to themselves, told disjointed stories to no one in particular, had visible physical disabilities, and were taking drugs to feel better or dealing to survive. Poverty, disability, and discrimination seemed to go hand in hand. The poor who lived in these dangerous neighborhoods were likely to have jobs that would disable them through accidents, work conditions, or chronic physical and emotional stress. They were also likely to be shot, stabbed, or addicted to some substance by the mere fact of living in that environment (the exceptions being the few but remarkable high school students I encountered in the Sexton study). The majority were physically or psychologically compromised. They were at further risk because they did not have adequate health insurance, job benefits, or social support. The poor became disabled, and the disabled became more isolated and vulnerable. I discovered that these people were not necessarily deviant but different; many were disabled by their experiences and the environment. They belonged to the wrong social class and race to have opportunities and hope for a future.

At the same time, I wondered how some of them could cope and make a life while others became trapped in the revolving door of crime and jail or were shunted into hospitals and state mental institutions. How could some young men and women from the same family, from the same social class, and reared in the same environment end up in prisons, physically disabled, or in mental hospitals, while others climbed the ladder into such occupations as ministers, shopkeepers, and police officers?

I carried these persistent questions about how the vulnerable deal with risk and disability in tough environments to Emory University in Atlanta, where I was looking for a dissertation topic while I was teaching and doing research. This is where I discovered the world of disabled people, which would give a focus to my sociological and activist interests.

Every day I had lunch in an Emory cafeteria in the Health Sciences Center, where I met two professors: Arthur Falek, a human geneticist who was working on birth defects, and John Basmajian, a neurophysiologist, anatomist, and physiatrist. When they asked me what I was doing for my dissertation, I told them I was interested in studying how adults defined, reacted to, and adjusted to disabling events and environments in their lives. They listened to me, paused, and said, "Why don't you study people with physical disabling conditions?" John Basmajian proffered, "Do your dissertation on traumatically injured young spinal cord patients; start when they enter the hospital and follow them for a few years to see how they adjust. I can tell you exactly where the site of the damage is to the spinal cord and how severe it is, and I can estimate with some reliability what kind of function this person will have in two years. The level of injury would be predictive of whether or not the person would ever walk again or be a wheelchair user and what kind of life the person will probably have." They both chimed in: "It could be an important study. You can address the questions you're interested in. You can follow these patients for a year and a half from entry into the hospital to discharge, rehabilitation, and return home. You can study them and their families. We'll help you." I took their advice.

I sampled 122 young, male, spinal cord patients, traumatically injured by automobile and diving accidents or by guns and knives in violent situations who were admitted to Grady Hospital in Atlanta and to the Georgia Warm Springs Foundation in Warm Springs. I followed them from the time of hospital admission to one year after discharge.

I discovered that adjustment to each person's unforeseen event was predicated on having competent medical care and rehabilitation services when they were needed, a stable environment, and a family (social support system) that struck a balance between being too pushy or too overprotective.[2] On the surface these findings were interesting but did not fully capture the social-class forces at play. How were poor African Americans and working-class whites to cope when they did not have adequate insurance, stable families, living situations, an education, or job skills and lived in an oppressive environment?

This conundrum raised larger, more structural questions about how the poor, disenfranchised, vulnerable, and disabled were treated in American society. While continuing to study on the quality of life of disabled people, I returned to the work of C. Wright Mills to think about how the larger political and economic system affected the lives of disabled people.

SOCIAL-CLASS TENSIONS IN THE POLITICAL ECONOMY

The opportunity to work on class tensions and the political economy of disability on a structural level presented itself when I moved from Emory University to a joint appointment in the Kellogg School of Management and the Department of Sociology at Northwestern University. My move offers an excellent example of how one's environment shapes one's work. I did not fully appreciate it at the time, but the Department of Sociology and the Kellogg School of Management were two different worlds, with conflicting value systems and social-class orientations that promoted very different views of disability research and the disability world.

The faculty in the Department of Sociology had been deeply affected by the conflicts of the 1960s and early 1970s and expressed an activist bent. Howard Becker, for example, taught legions of students about the importance of doing fieldwork, of understanding the worlds of those who were disenfranchised or seemingly on the margins. His work on outsiders, on labeling, and on deviance and difference influenced how we viewed the world.[3] Junior faculty and students alike became engaged in such types of research. Richard Berk was evaluating large social interventions in high-crime neighborhoods that were all a part of the Great Society movement. Allan Schnaiberg was developing a research program on how the political and economic forces in society shaped the definition of and response to environmental problems resulting from pollution, chemical spills, and nuclear waste. A recurrent theme in all of the work was its emphasis on marginal people, the disenfranchised and those without knowledge or power. Our interest was in understanding how those seemingly without power could organize to effect change social. In a bit of oversimplification, the emphasis and identification were with the have-nots, or those on the outside looking in.

The Kellogg School of Management operated in another world. Its announced goal at that time was to become one of the top-ranked business schools in the country. This meant recruiting very able students with at least two years of business experience who would pay high tuition to acquire professional training, enabling them to get high-paying, fast-track jobs at major corporations. The emphasis was on helping students land an important job with considerable opportunity for upward mobility in a prestigious firm and ensuring that they made a great deal of money. This system was contingent on inducing the best international companies to come to the Kellogg school to recruit and on establishing close relationships with top executives at major corporations. This was done through a high-profile, executive Masters in Management program. Kellogg planned to build and operate a luxurious building on Lake Michigan to train midcareer and top management in executive-training programs. If this were done well, it was a win-win situation for the school and the managers. The managers became credentialed by a highly ranked school, and the faculty who taught in these programs and did related consulting considerably enhanced their base academic salaries. At the same time there was pressure on the faculty to build strong research credentials by attracting funding and by publishing in the best journals. In a sense, this was the best of all worlds for a faculty member who wanted to be in a nationally ranked school and earn a high salary. Although not obvious at first blush, the faculty in all departments was made up primarily of economists who shared a similar set of values.

There was an uneasy tension between sociologists in the Department of Sociology and faculty in the Kellogg School of Management. The sociologists were suspicious of academics who were openly moving in the business world, training students in a value system in which success equaled money and power, and earning a higher salaries than the sociologists in the College of Arts and Sciences. The administrators and economists in the management school, for their part, looked down on the sociologists, who talked about but rarely entered or worked in the "real world." In a reductionist sense, for one group business, money and power were to be held in suspicion. For the other group, research that was engaged with people at the margins of society or that was not centered in the major institutions of business and government that made the world go around was not particularly interesting or important. The problem was one of social-class orientation and of values.

THE RESOLUTION OF SOCIAL-CLASS TENSIONS, VALUE CONFLICTS, AND DIFFERENT ACADEMIC PERSPECTIVES

From my point of view, there was something to be learned from both camps. To understand the experiences and lives of disabled people, I needed to be a sociologist who was engaged in that world. I needed to understand the relationship of disability to social class. On the other hand, to understand the structural barriers faced by disabled people, by the outsiders, I needed to understand and analyze the American political and economic system and discern the forces and values at work. I learned that to do this in a credible way I would have to enter and observe the worlds of government and business that shaped the lives and opportunities of disabled people and their families. This eight-year effort resulted in *The Disability Business: Rehabilitation in America*.[4] In this book, I argued that disability is a socially constructed problem, and rehabilitation goods and services are commodities for sale in a marketplace. The interplay of the political and economic forces in this marketplace determine what happens to disabled people and their issues. In retrospect, my joint appointment in sociology and the school of management enabled me to keep the theoretical grounding and value orientation of a sociologist with an activist orientation while at the same time exposing me to the interior worlds of government and business, where I was able to see how the forces were aligned and how decisions were made that affected disabled people and the disenfranchised.

This position in two worlds made for better research and analysis. It was, however, ultimately untenable in terms of personal values. I found myself devoting all my energies to teaching very bright and experienced students the technical skills and strategic abilities that would help them make a great deal of money from other people's illnesses and disabilities.

At this time, I moved to a school of public health, where I was able to continue my research on the quality of life of disabled people and the political economy of disability. There I trained students to use their skills to improve the public health of the nation and address the social-class inequities that characterize the health care and social welfare systems. In this sense, the study of disability became an opportunity to employ a sociological perspective to study one type of social-class inequity. This work satisfied my desire to be an academic and to try to make a difference in people's lives.

In reflecting back on my career, I deeply appreciate the advice of C. Wright Mills—to recognize the insights that can be gained from integrating one's biography and historical circumstances into one's academic work. The best and most satisfying work seems to be that which builds on personal experiences and values as they play out in a historical context. A sociological training provides the theoretical and conceptual tools to ask important questions and design studies to test propositions, helping us to better understand what we see and experience. This biographic grounding, historical contextualization, and academic preparation give focus to our lives and careers.

NOTES

1. C. Wright Mills, *The Sociological Imagination* (New York: Oxford University Press, 1967), 8.

2. Gary L. Albrecht, "Socialization Experiences in the Rehabilitation Process," *Health Services Research* 14 (1973): 67–72; and Gary L. Albrecht and Paul C. Higgins, "Rehabilitation Success: The Interrelationships of Multiple Criteria," *Journal of Health and Social Behavior* 18 (1977): 114–29.

3. Howard S. Becker, *Outsiders: Studies in the Sociology of Deviance* (New York: Free Press, 1963); and Howard S. Becker, ed., *The Other Side: Perspectives on Deviance* (New York: Free Press, 1964).

4. Gary L. Albrecht, *The Disability Business: Rehabilitation in America* (Newbury Park, Calif.: Sage, 1992).

CHRISTOPHER WINSHIP

17

IN DEFENSE OF FOXES

There is a line among the fragments of the Greek poet Archilochus which says, "The fox knows many things, but the hedgehog knows one big thing." . . . Taken figuratively, the words can be made to yield a sense in which they mark one of the deepest differences which divide writer and thinkers, and it may be, human beings in general. For there exists a great chasm between those, on one side, who relate everything to a single central vision, one system, less or more coherent or articulate, in terms of which they understand, think and feel—a single, universal, organising principle in terms of which alone all they are and say has significance—and on the other side, those who pursue many ends, often unrelated and even contradictory, connected, if at all, only in some *de facto* way, for some psychological or physiological cause, related by no moral or aesthetic principle.

—Isaiah Berlin, *The Hedgehog and the Fox*

At the disciplinary level, sociology is, itself, foxlike, containing individuals with multiple theoretical perspectives and methodological approaches. It also considers any aspect of social behavior as within the legitimate domain of its analysis. Of course, these multiplicities are something for which sociology is often criticized. It is a field that lacks a single coherence.

Sociology's lack of coherence means that it is a discipline, unlike, say, economics, in which foxes can thrive. Because of the multiplicity of its perspectives, it is able to tolerate individuals who singly reveal multiple commitments that is foxes, although within sociology there are always questions of where their loyalties, if any, truly lie.

In his book *The Hedgehog and the Fox*, the English political theorist Isaiah Berlin examines whether Tolstoy was a fox or a hedgehog.[1] He argues that although Tolstoy was deeply and genetically a fox, he thought one should be a hedgehog. Berlin suggests that the key issue for Tolstoy in *War and Peace* (as well as in his other work) was the role of free will and determinism in history: "he is above all obsessed by his thesis—the contrast between universal and all-important but delusive experience of free will, the feeling of responsibility, the values of private life generally, on the one hand; and on the other the reality of inexorable historical determinism."[2]

In this chapter, I reflect, in part, on my self-understanding as a fox. I built my reputation as a high-tech, quantitative type. Within the quantitative world, there are two quite distinct perspectives, that of a statistician and that of the econometrician, both fields I identify with. The statistician believes in the primary reality of the data themselves and wants to understand their structure, whereas the econometrician more typically sees data as being more epiphenomenal in character, having been generated by underlying behavioral structures that he seeks to uncover. Talk about two radically different views of the world. Thus, even a quantitative type can be a fox.

My goal for this chapter is to argue for the methodological and scholarly virtues of the fox. Before engaging in that argument, however, I examine two basic questions. First, how and/or why does one become a fox? Second, what does it take to succeed as a fox? These two questions are essential since it makes little sense to talk about the virtues of foxes if we don't first understand why some individuals are foxes and others hedgehogs and, second, if we don't understand what it takes to be a fox. I discuss these issues primarily in the context of my life and professional career. I do so not out of any great sense of self-importance but because it is in terms of my own life that I have, in part, come to find answers to these two questions.

THE GENESIS OF ONE FOX

Berlin makes it clear that Tolstoy would prefer to be a hedgehog but that he has no choice—he is a fox. This seems correct. We cannot choose to see the world in one or in multiple ways. We may, of course, deny that we see things from a certain perspective, but this is denial. The question is not what we acknowledge seeing but what we actually see. Why, then, do some individuals see like foxes and others like hedgehogs?

Few of my academic colleagues are aware that I grew up in a family of therapists, though colleagues occasionally have told me that I am one of the most touchy-feely quantitative social scientists that they have ever met. My father and stepfather are both psychiatrists, and my mother and two of my three sisters are psychiatric social workers. As I was growing up, dinner conversations were always focused on some individual, perhaps an anonymous patient or someone known to the family in the community. The question was to understand why they had so many problems and to discover a way in which they might resolve them.

I loved these conversations. If my parents did not offer up some poor soul for analytic sacrifice, I was ready to suggest a friend or classmate. One of the things that made these conversations fascinating was the socially and economically diverse set of patients my parents saw. We lived in New Britain, an old Connecticut factory town that was as economically, socially, and ethnically diverse as America itself. Although I grew up in the wealthy West End, I went to grade school with a full span of children, including those from the local orphanage. New Britain was a most fruitful initial field site for studying processes of social stratification.

For many years, I also wanted to be a therapist, and I believe I would have been a good one. I enjoyed thinking about people and what made them act as they did. Moreover, the deluge of presents received by my family each Christmas by grateful patients provided some evidence that through therapy it might be possible to actually help people. My parents had devised a life in which they had somehow created that magical combination—they were quite well off financially and yet were also contributing significantly to the social good.[3]

I often jokingly tell people that having grown up in a family of therapists, my adolescent rebellion was to become a quantitatively oriented sociologist. Actually, there is much truth in this quip, though I was certainly rebellious in many ways as an adolescent during the late 1960s. The transformation, however, was not sudden. Although I had decided by the eleventh grade to become a sociologist, had taken a sociology course that summer at the local community college, and in my senior year had carried out a lengthy survey of my entire boarding school (Hotchkiss), I planned to become both a psychiatrist and sociologist. I somewhat naively saw nothing problematic with a career in which one was equally committed to two quite different intellectual and professional perspectives. I went to Dartmouth as a freshman with shoulder-length hair and a full beard; a box of IBM punch cards, containing the data from the survey I had done; and the full intention of doing both premed and sociology.

Although I still find the psychological-therapeutic perspective compelling, as a college student I became disillusioned with it for several reasons. Certainly, first and foremost, I was frustrated with the idea that persons should always be understood at the individual level. When my family and I talked about individual problems, more often than not they concerned relationships. Yet, the diagnoses were always in terms of the individual.[4]

Second, the idea that there was a deep intentionality in all behavior seemed wrong. Whether in trying to analyze the behavior of someone at the dinner table or explaining why a member of the family had done something, my family always assumed that there was some deep, hidden motivation. There were never any unintended consequences.

But why choose to be a quantitative- or mathematically oriented sociologist? I had always been extremely good in math but quite weak in languages. In fact, I am moderately dyslexic, something that wasn't fully diagnosed until I was in graduate school; it was simply an unknown problem when I was growing up. For most of my youth, I was considered to be lazy when writing and spelling. In fact, Harrison White, my graduate advisor, accused me of this fault.

Math was a language with which I felt comfortable. It was easy to see when one made mistakes. Also, when I went to Dartmouth in 1968, math modeling had become a hot area in the social sciences and in sociology in particular. Unbeknown to me, I had come to a university with a number of the leaders in this new area of research. At Dartmouth were James Davis, Robert Norman, John Kemeny, Laurie Snell, and later Joel Levine.

I did a double major in sociology and mathematics. My thesis provided a solution to a long-standing problem in balance theory: how to extend Heider's theory (a friend of a friend is a friend; my enemies' friends are my enemies) to the situation in which there were degrees of enmity and friendship. I later published the thesis in the *Journal of Mathematical Sociology*.[5] As a piece of mathematics, the paper is elegant. As a piece of writing, it is horrid.

The point of this personal story is that I had no choice but to be a fox. My family literally, though not unhappily, forced me to see the world from a therapeutic perspective. Unless I had been born with different genes or simply was never given the opportunity to learn any math, I was also going to understand the world in mathematical terms. There was never any possibility that I would see things from only one perspective.

In *The Hedgehog and the Fox*, Berlin describes the host of negative reviews that *War and Peace* received when it was published. Tolstoy was accused of charlatanism and intellectual feebleness. His philosophy of history and his philosophical musings were generally considered superficial. He was attacked for his lack of facticity with respect to the historical record. Unsurprisingly, Berlin goes on to defend Tolstoy as being grossly misunderstood. He argues that the core problem is that Tolstoy's critics fail to appreciate that he is attempting to understand the same phenomena from multiple perspectives.

I went through graduate school rapidly, perhaps too rapidly—three and one-half years. Instead of writing a dissertation, I submitted three published articles as a thesis. I learned some sociology, though not enough. I did take quite a number of courses in statistics and economics. The primary article in my thesis was "The Allocation of Time Among Individuals,"[6] which took a formal model of an economy from General Equilibrium Theory in economics and showed how, when it was assumed that prices were fixed, it could be used to model the way in which people allocate time with each other. "Prices" were fixed to "one" since the amount of time I spent with you by necessity was equivalent to the time you spent with me.

My experience in the job market was a disaster. I was interviewed by twelve departments but received no offers—surprising, perhaps, in that I am now a full professor at Harvard. Everywhere I went a few mathematical economists loved my paper on time. The few sociologists who were supportive of a math-modeling approach also liked it. The vast majority of sociologists, however, had little idea of what I was doing and most certainly believed it irrelevant to sociology. No offers were forthcoming. I retrenched and was offered (by an economist) a one-year postdoctorate at the Institute for Research on Poverty at the University of Wisconsin, which was then followed by a postdoctorate for two years at the National Opinion Research Center (NORC) at the University of Chicago. I went to the Midwest to receive the training in sociology that I had failed to obtain at Harvard. Although I knew quite a bit of sociology, statistics, and economics, I hadn't learned how to speak coherently to each group individually, much less how to speak across groups. Most important, I had no ability to show sociologists how the perspective of another group, in this case, economics, might provide useful insights.

During my second year at NORC, I received a phone call from Ackie Feldman, then chair of sociology at Northwestern. He wanted to know whether I would consider a position in sociology there. At the time, sociology as a discipline was very much in the middle of the methods wars. Departments were divided internally and externally by whether they believed that a qualitative, ethnographic approach or a quantitative, statistical approach was the correct way to proceed. Northwestern had the reputation of being radically qualitative. Howie Becker and Arlene Daniels were there. John Kitsuse had been there in the past. Dick Berk had left a few years earlier on less-than-good terms with the department. Although Northwestern was a mere fifteen miles away, it took Ackie Feldman three telephone calls to convince me to visit. The visit went extraordinarily well. Howie Becker and I sat and talked about the virtues of Kemeny and Snell's *Finite Mathematics*.[7] I gave a reasonable talk about the problem of measuring inequality based on recent work in economics.

The position at Northwestern was joint with the undergraduate program in Mathematical Methods in the Social Sciences. My dual interests in sociology and math modeling were suddenly an asset. I went to Northwestern, was promoted with tenure three years later, and promoted to full professor four years after that. By the time I left for Harvard in 1992 (having previously turned it down in 1986), I had chaired the program in Mathematical Methods in the Social Sciences, as well as the sociology department. I had helped start the statistics department, held a courtesy appointment in economics, and had been a long-term member of the Center for Policy Research (now the Institute for Policy Research). Northwestern was a place where a strategy of multiple academic selves was not only possible but also a recipe for success. I had also learned how to be multilingual. Even though the multiple disciplines I was in couldn't be integrated into a single coherent theoretical approach, I at least had learned how speak within the perspective of each.

THE VIRTUES OF THE FOX

We may admire real foxes for their cleverness and perhaps their sense of roguishness. The idea, however, that they are virtuous seems peculiar. Similarly, academic foxes may be admirable, but they hardly seem virtuous. They lack a coherent perspective or commitment to any intellectual perspective. And then there is the question of loyalty.

I want to argue for the virtues of the fox in the scientific enterprise. Obviously this is, in part, self-serving. I do, however, think that foxes make an essential contribution, and thus their behavior should be tolerated, if not rewarded. My argument has four parts. First, I contend that an important source of new insights is the migration of ideas from other disciplines. Second, I argue that different types of research problems require different methodological approaches. Third, I suggest that the ability to hold multiple perspectives provides a powerful means for self-criticism. Finally, I argue that the ability to maintain multiple perspectives provides at least a partial means of dealing with the problem of objectivity.

BORROWING IDEAS

In her book *How Institutions Think*, Mary Douglas[8] argues that no one really has a new idea. Rather, academic research proceeds when individuals first recognize the importance of undervalued ideas and then promote them by showing how they can contribute to solving outstanding intellectual problems. But where do undervalued ideas come from? One possibility is from earlier work in the field. Many researchers have been successful by mining the works of earlier scholars. Douglas herself relies extensively on Durkheim in her own scholarship.

To look only to one's own field for undervalued ideas, however, is highly restrictive. It amounts to returning to old mines to see if any gold or silver has been left behind. The other possibility is to explore new fields, that is, other disciplines, for ideas. Of course, searching here may be quite unrewarding since the intellectual agendas of other disciplines are often quite different than those of sociology. At times, however, one can find gold. Let me give an example from my own experience.

When I was a postdoctoral student at NORC, I spent a lot of time working with and studying the works of Jim Heckman. At this time there was considerable interest in sociology, particularly in structural equation models and path analysis. One of the outstanding problems at the time was how to do path models when one had discrete variables. In fact, some scholars claimed that it wasn't possible to do a true path analysis in that case. My frequent collaborator, Rob Mare, who was then at the University of Wisconsin, Madison, and I were working through Heckman's 1978 article on dummy endogenous variables.[9] Heckman was interested in estimating the effect of a treatment when assignment to treatment was endogenous. Over the years this developed into an extensive line of research for which, in 2001, he received the Nobel Prize in Economics. There are significant rewards for being a hedgehog.

In reading Heckman's article, it was clear to us that there were two different ways to think about discrete variables. In one case, a discrete variable was simply a crude measure of an underlying continuous variable. In the other case, it was truly discrete, which implied that it had to be handled as a nonlinear variable. Doing path models in the first case was absolutely straightforward and simply involved estimating the coefficients for the underlying continuous variables. In the second case, one needed to recognize that the standard formula in path analysis was simply a special case of the chain rule in calculus, a formula I had learned in my second math course at Dartmouth. Having been a math major paid off. The insight that the chain rule could be used to carry out a path analysis when someone had nonlinear equations was something Kate Stolzenberg[10] had just finished an article on. Given the insights of Heckman and Stolzenberg, the solution to path analysis with discrete variables seemed so obvious that it almost was not worth writing up. We did so, however, and much to our surprise it was considered a path-breaking piece of work.

USING THE RIGHT TOOL

One of the dumbest fights that has ever occurred in sociology has been the debate over whether quantitative or qualitative methods are the "true" method for this discipline. In terms of intellectual politics, the fight is quite understandable. Starting in the late 1960s, quantitative methodology began to dominate sociology, and qualitative-oriented sociologists—for both intellectual and personal reasons—were concerned that their type of sociology was being pushed to the sidelines. As a result, they fought back, and departments became deeply divided. Certainly, one of my vulnerabilities when I was first in the job market was that I was seen as someone who only knew math; that is, I was an extreme quantitative type.

Unfortunately, the methods battle was defined as which method was the "true way" of doing sociology. Somehow the idea that different methods provided different ways of understanding a phenomenon was not considered. Yet, this should be a key methodological doctrine for sociologists.

I see this in the work I am currently doing on Boston's efforts during the 1990s to deal with the problem of youth violence. During this decade, homicide rates fell by 80% in Boston. Both the local press and the national press have attributed this drop to work done jointly by a group of black ministers known as the Ten Point Coalition and by the Boston Police Department. The ethnographic evidence also seems to support this belief. A close examination reveals that the police and ministers were dealing with critical gang issues together. There is one problem with this argument. Homicide rates dropped precipitously in a number of large cities during the 1990s without any such partnerships. The quantitative data challenge the qualitative data in critical ways.

If, however, we simply examine the quantitative data, key insights are also missed. As in many evaluation problems, the important effects of a program are often different from those it was designed to have from or what people think it does. What I have shown in my research on the Ten Point Coalition is that the involvement of ministers has been instrumental in two ways: (1) creating legitimacy for the police when they do act in ways that are in the best interests of the community and (2) improving community-police relations. New York City's homicide rates also fell dramatically during the 1990s. However, in Boston, community-police relations are now the best they have been in decades, whereas in New York they have probably never been worse than during this period.[11]

What this example illustrates is that quantitative and qualitative methods can help us discover different types of truths. In doing so, they may force us to consider how the findings obtained through each method can be rectified. I hope that the result is a more holistic and accurate understanding of the phenomena we are investigating. Each is an imperfect tool in discerning the truth. By using methods in complementary ways, we can achieve a better, though almost certainly still quite imperfect understanding of the topic we are studying.

SELF-CRITICISM

Allowing one's research to be criticized is key to high-quality research. The criticism can come from others or from oneself. One of my current areas of research is counterfactual models of causality, which has two parts. First, there has been a set of papers and now a book in progress with my former student, Steve Morgan, aimed at explicating recent research in statistics and econometrics on counterfactual causal models.[12] Second, I have written a series of articles with my colleague Marty Rein at MIT on the policy misuses of causal reasoning in the social sciences.[13] The initial impetus for the work was the extensive and often poorly argued criticisms of *The Bell Curve*.[14] Ultimately, it resulted in a broad criticism of the use of causal reasoning by social scientists titled, "The Dangers of Strong Causal Reasoning."[15] One of the most effective ways of criticizing is by being fully cognizant of both sides of an argument.

THE ELUSIVENESS OF OBJECTIVITY

I have just argued that as sociologists we need to study problems by multiple methods. Implicit in my argument has been the position that we need to be willing to see phenomena from different perspectives. How, then, are we to get at the objective truth? Such a question assumes that there is a position from "nowhere," or a "God's-eye" view that can be used to determine what in fact constitutes the objective truth. I don't see how any social scientist today can believe that such a position is tenable. Is objectivity, then, impossible?

I have always found the East Indian story of the elephant and the blind men to be particularly useful. The essence of the story is that each man believes the elephant to be something quite different since each has felt a different piece of the elephant's anatomy. This story provides two key insights. First, just because each individual perceives the elephant differently does not mean that every person's perceptions are equally correct. If the man holding the elephant's tail describes it as being like a tree, that is a fairly poor description. If other men feel the elephant's tail, they may well disagree with his description. The analogy may also lead to poor predictions how the elephant will behave. Second, understanding what an elephant in fact is involves "seeing" it as a whole. This might be done if the blind men discuss their perceptions and are willing to assume that no one of them actually has the "truth." The other possibility is for them to trade places and for each to feel different parts of the elephant. Neither strategy will allow one to perceive the elephant from a position of "nowhere," but both are good strategies for coming up with a reasonable holistic account of what an elephant is.

The idea that we should move around and study social life from different vantage points is, of course, the strategy of a fox. It is similar to that of a set of start-up internet companies that David Stark at Columbia and Monique Girard at Columbia have been studying in Silicon Alley in New York City.[16] What is interesting about these companies is that they are very nonhierarchical. Girard and Stark describe their structure as a hetrarchy. In addition, these companies do not have a long-term business plan, nor do they have well-defined products. Rather, they are set up around work teams that sometime overlap. The job of a work team is to explore some portion of the Internet business environment in an attempt to discover what might be potentially lucrative business niches. Essentially these are businesses that are set up to succeed in an information-poor environment, where no one really knows what will succeed.

It impresses me that if social science is to thrive, it needs at least in part to act like these companies. Science, by its nature, involves exploring problems where we don't know the answers.[17] Of course, there are dangers. It may be difficult to explain or justify to the world what one is doing, and of course, one may come up empty-handed.

STRENGTH IN DIVERSITY

When I had my disastrous first experiences in the job market, I often thought about changing fields and becoming an economist. Economics was and is a field where mathematical ability is highly valued. However, every time I started to seriously consider this alternative, I was repelled by the intellectual narrowness of economic thought. Economics is not narrow in that it only studies how an economy works. Far from it. Economists have been willing to study anything that sociologists do, from the family to religion. Rather, it is that economists typically attempt to understand all social phenomena in the same way—as the choices made by utility-maximizing individuals. For me, becoming an economist was a recipe for intellectual claustrophobia.

Sociology's intellectual diversity is one of its greatest strengths. Unfortunately, it, too, often becomes something that divides us, as scholars become committed to one or the other approach as the "right" way to do research. What the elephant anecdote shows is that we can only get at the truth by "seeing" things from multiple perspectives. This methodological philosophy suggests that objectivity is not obtained by taking a neutral stance. Rather, objectivity is an ideal that is striven for by attempting to understand a phenomenon from many different perspectives. This is something that we should pursue both as individuals and as a community of scholars.

How, then, does one see from different perspectives? To truly see well, we need to be willing to commit ourselves at least temporarily to different perspectives. One needs to fully emphasize, if not identify with, different positions. There is no more effective way of doing this than by allowing oneself to have multiple academic selves, that is, to be willing to be a fox. The hedgehogs, of course, will always complain that they are doing the real work. Their contributions may appear to be more substantial and they may reap more rewards, but, oh, what fun it is to be a fox.

NOTES

1. Marty Rein introduced me to Isaiah Berlin's wonderful little book *The Hedgehog and the Fox: An Essay on Tolstoy's View of History* (Chicago: Ivan R. Dee, 1978), 3.
2. Ibid., 30.
3. In his fifty years of practice, my father essentially built the mental health structure of central Connecticut, that is, the area between Hartford and New Haven. He established a psychiatric floor in New Britain's General Hospital and created more than a half-dozen public psychiatric outpatient clinics in surrounding towns, as well as

equal number of mental health programs in local public schools. He is still practicing at eighty-three.

4. In the late 1960s, the idea that mental illness involved family and group dynamics was just starting to come into vogue in the works of Gregory Bateson, R. D. Laing, and Murray Bohen, among others.

5. Christopher Winship, "A Distance Model for Sociometric Structure," *Journal of Mathematical Sociology* 5 (1977): 21–39.

6. Christopher Winship, "The Allocation of Time among Individuals," in *Sociological Methodology 1978*, ed. Karl Schuessler (San Francisco: Jossey-Bass), 75–100.

7. John G. Kemeny, Hazlehon Mirkil, J. Laurie Snell, and Gerald L. Thompson, *Finite Mathematical Structures* (Englewood Cliffs, N.J.: Prentice-Hall), 1958.

8. Mary Douglas, *How Institutions Think* (Syracuse, N.Y.: Syracuse University Press, 1987).

9. James J. Heckman, "Dummy Endogenous Variables in a Simultaneous Equation System," *Econometrica* 46 (1978): 931–61.

10. Ross Stolzenberg, "The Measurement and Decomposition of Causal Effects in Nonlinear and Nonadditive Models," in *Sociological Methodology 1980*, ed. Karl Schuessler (San Francisco: Jossey-Bass, 1979), 4549–88.

11. Christopher Winship and Orlando Patterson, "Boston's Police Solution" (editorial), *New York Times*, March 3, 1999. In the work I have been doing in Boston's inner city over the last seven years as part of my research on the Ten Point Coalition, I have been struck by the similarities between the families I encounter and those my parents spent their professional lives dealing with in the various public mental health clinics where they worked. Boston does not have any truly "bombed-out" areas, such as those found in the South Bronx or West and South Sides of Chicago. For several decades, with some short exceptions, it has also enjoyed a low unemployment rate. Yet Boston certainly has its ghettos, where poor and often highly dysfunctional families live. To my surprise, I find myself seeing much of what I observe in these communities through my parents' eyes.

12. Christopher Winship and Stephen L. Morgan, "The Estimation of Causal Effects from Observational Data," *Annual Review of Sociology* 25 (1999): 659–707.

13. Martin and Rein and Christopher Winship, "The Dangers of Causal Reasoning in Social Policy," *Society* 25 (1999): 657–707; Winship and Rein, "Policy Entrepreneurs and the Academic Establishment: The Bell Curve Controversy," in *Intelligence, Political Inequality, and Public Policy*, ed. Elliot White (Westport, Conn.: Praeger, 1997), 17–49; Winship and Rein, "The Dangers of 'Strong' Causal Reasoning in Social Policy," *Society* 36 (July/August 1999): 38–46.

14. Richard J. Hernstein and Charles Murray, *The Bell Curve* (New York: Free Press, 1994).

15. Christopher Winship, "The Dangers of 'Strong' Causal Reasoning: Root Causes, Social Science, and Poverty Policy," in *Experiencing Poverty*, ed. Jonathan Bradshaw and Roy Sainsbury (Burlington: Ashgate, 2000) 26–54.

16. Monique Girard and David Stark, "Distributing Intelligence and Organizing Diversity in New Media Projects," *Environment and Planning* 34 (2002): 1927–29.

17. When I was in college, I was a serious rock climber. I had two very different kinds of climbing experiences. When I was following a route that had already been set by someone else, the logic was always one of "working it out." However, establishing new routes often involved intensive exploration since one literally didn't know where one was going. Not too surprisingly, putting in new routes was considerably more psychologically taxing than simply following an established one.

SHERRYL KLEINMAN

18

FEMINIST FIELDWORKER

CONNECTING RESEARCH,

TEACHING, AND MEMOIR

Fieldwork is about paying attention. We don't primarily attend to what outsiders might consider the attention-grabbing moments—a fistfight, or an outburst of tears—but to mundane, systematic patterns. Yet, knowing that one is meant to notice patterns hardly tells us where to look or what to focus on.

As a symbolic interactionist, I was trained to notice patterns of speech, interaction, identity, meanings, and so on. I learned to cultivate the double vision of the qualitative symbolic interactionist: individuals are products of social-historical circumstances *and* act with or upon them. Actions are broadly defined and can include anything from resistance to resignation.

But which patterns of speech, interaction, identity, and meanings will I pay attention to and what story will I tell? These questions can't be answered without understanding who we are and what we believe—our identities and ideologies—as we do the work. Such self-knowledge is not meant to move us past our biases so that we can arrive at an "objective" understanding of those we've studied. Rather, we can use knowledge of our identities and ideologies to recognize and take responsibility for what we see, how we put our story together, and the stance we take.[1]

Over the years, as I became a *feminist* fieldworker, I learned to pay attention to different things. My stories did not leave interactionist matters behind but instead linked such concepts as identity, emotion work, and interaction to the reproduction of inequality.[2] I learned to listen to what Alison Jaggar refers to as "outlaw emotions"—"our 'gut-level' awareness that we are in a situation of coercion, cruelty, injustice or danger."[3] Such feelings, which I have called my "twingeometer,"[4] are sources of data, not analysis. They provide hypotheses that we then must scrutinize.

In this chapter I look at how becoming a feminist fieldworker shaped my analysis of a holistic health center, informed my unofficial study of undergraduate students' resistance to feminism, and inspired my turn to sociological memoir writing. As a feminist fieldworker—whether working on a project, teaching, or going about my daily life—I try to pay attention to the smallest acts (including my own) to understand how they reinforce or challenge inequalities. This approach affords me an unceasing job and an integrated life.

WRITING *OPPOSING AMBITIONS*

I collected data on a holistic health center from 1980 to 1985, shortly after taking to my first academic job. I applied the skills I had acquired as a fieldworker in graduate school to the setting, taking copious notes on members' meetings and taping in-depth interviews. At the time I was still finishing my first book, but when I completed *Equals Before God*,[5] I decided to turn my attention to analyzing the health center, which I later called Renewal.

What ensued were years of picking up the manuscript, working half-heartedly on it, and then putting it away, sometimes for one to two years at a time. This is not necessarily a bad thing. In the interim I wrote other work, particularly in the sociology of emotions. But I knew that the study of Renewal pained me in a way I had not experienced in previous projects. In 1990 I seriously considered dropping the project. I started to think that if I had left Renewal behind years ago and had started a new field study, I'd probably have turned the second (albeit imaginary) project into a book by then. "Cut your losses" resounded in my head.

What was the problem? *Growing pains*. I was changing—slowly—my understanding of the world, sociology, and myself. Every time I picked up the pages of analysis I had written earlier, I felt uncomfortable, though it wasn't clear to me how I might change the story or, more accurately, what a legitimate story might be. It was as if a different figure-ground combination occurred every time I reread thought pieces and drafts. To bolster my confidence I walked around my apartment, pretending to give a lecture on my (latest) version of the story. As I spoke into my microphone (a black pen), I tried to become committed to my words. Then I'd put down the pen and move to the keyboard, getting down the words I had just delivered to the couch and coffee table.

It took me a long time to recognize that my identity as a feminist was evolving; the kind of feminist I became when I finally committed to working on the book was not the person who had collected the data. This also gave me pause. Might I have ignored important data because I had seen Renewal through a different lens?

Let me give you some details about Renewal, a holistic health center. The structure of the center mirrored members' dual concerns with being both a conventional and alternative organization. One part of Renewal was constituted by six private practitioners (four men, two women) who were paid directly by individual clients and then gave a portion of their earnings (determined by the board) to the organization. This payment was sometimes referred to as rent. The other, "educational" part of Renewal was nonprofit and was run by three or four staff members (all women) and several volunteers (almost all women). Low-cost classes and workshops were offered to the public through this part of the organization. Staff did the office work for Renewal—including taking phone calls for the practitioners—ran the physical plant, and put together the membership bulletin. They also helped produce the newsletter that announced classes. Practitioners received about $30 an hour for their services as psychotherapists, nutrition therapists, massage practitioners, and stress managers. Since Renewal was often in the red, staff members were often unpaid and received $4 an hour when they did get paid. Overlap existed between the two parts: practitioners did some volunteer work, often headed major committees, and sometimes taught workshops. Staff, volunteers, and practitioners were represented on the board.

My problems with the organization were many.[6] I had expected it to be less hierarchical; I increasingly became disillusioned with the staff, who struck me as wimpy; I found the key characters too conventional in some ways (meetings often centered on the budget rather than on holistic healing) and too hippyish in other ways (they spoke in a language that psychologized and essentialized interaction, especially conflict).

In hindsight, it is clear that members of Renewal were contradicting their own ideals. They had a largely individualistic notion of equality—every person is equally valuable regardless of status. Yet, by their own standards, they did not treat each other equally. The male practitioners—especially the two male founding members, Jack and Ron—received the most money, affection, and respect in the organization and had the most influence over Renewal's policies and practices. Jack was chair of the Board of Directors and sometimes facilitated retreats where members were meant to discuss problems at Renewal. (Was this not a conflict of interest?) As a therapist, he was adept at using psychological and emotional language to direct meetings and retreats. Ron headed the committee that determined classes and workshops. Since the board made most decisions, from hiring and firing to approving committee work, having influence on the board was no small matter.

I had trouble recognizing the rather obvious contradictions because I was too busy worrying that I was not living out the empathetic role of the field-worker.[7] Although my observations might have pushed me to blame the men for their actions, I reserved my growing lack of empathy for the underpaid women. Like housewives, the staff women at Renewal took care of the male practitioners (their "husbands") and the center (the "family"). I kept asking myself why they would do this, but my question was rhetorical and accusatory, not sociologically genuine.

As a liberal feminist at the time, I wanted to believe that women could be successful if we just tried hard enough. This was something I needed to believe as a twenty-seven-year-old female assistant professor—one of two women, both of us without tenure—in a highly ranked sociology department. I was also the sole qualitative researcher in a quantitative department. Although I wasn't crazy about the male practitioners at Renewal and distrusted some of their psychologizing, I was preoccupied with the idea that the women were, by the standards of status, money, and influence, failures. I disidentified from them, probably because I needed to believe that I, unlike these women, could achieve the status of the successful men.

I eventually did interviews with the staff women and learned to understand and even appreciate how they had come to their subordinate position. At the time, I was reading cultural feminism, including Carol Gilligan's work on (alleged) differences in moral reasoning between women and men[8] and Jean Baker Miller's work on the "new" psychology of women.[9] Both books validated what Gilligan called an "ethic of care." Miller argued that although caring for others was largely devalued by men (and some women) as "unmasculine," it was central work for humankind. These works helped me appreciate the caring work and sacrifices made by the women of Renewal, which I had earlier dismissed because of their association with devalued femininity.

The women had come to Renewal at a time of vulnerability: one had just gone through a divorce; another had just emerged from being at home alone with a baby; still others had just moved alone to the area. They were looking for two things: connection with like-minded people and a sense of competence. The women were willing to work for Renewal for next to nothing because they believed in the cause of holistic health, they were more interested in personal growth than in a paycheck, and they prided themselves on their emotional labor and the sacrifices they made for the center. In fact, not receiving much money reinforced their belief in themselves as authentically alternative. Interviewing the staff women increased my respect for them. In a short time they moved from weakling to saints in my eyes.

My growing regard for the staff women did not lead me to question the core men's motives. Rather, I decided to understand their point of view just as I had understood the women's. In talking to the male practitioners, I learned that they were from middle-class backgrounds and had decided to become alternative healers rather than conventional health workers (or something else). They wanted to work in a place that offered more than office space. They sought, and indeed had put together, a center in an old house where they could feel comfortable and talk to like-minded people between clients. They wanted to build a center that offered services (such as classes) to the wider community, not only individual services. It was also clear that they worked hard as board members and practitioners.

So, if the staff women wanted feelings of connection and competence from Renewal, and got them, and the men wanted an unstuffy place to ply their trade, and did so, then who was I to say that there was a problem? I began to question, once again, whether I could really speak of inequalities at Renewal.

This equal-but-different story made me feel better for a while. It allowed me to believe that, like a good fieldworker, I was taking on the perspective of those I had studied. But my nagging feelings about inequalities remained. My twingeometer went off every time I tried to convince myself that I should favor the participants' accounts over my observations. I could not dismiss my growing sense that gender inequalities were central to the story.

As I read works by other feminist authors (e.g., bell hooks, Alison Jaggar, Sandra Bartky, and Marilyn Frye), I became more convinced that my twinges were leading me to a better story. The problem with accepting the practitioners' and staff members' accounts as equal stories masked the fact that the practitioners, especially the male practitioners, gained advantages (material, symbolic, and emotional) at the expense of the staff. That the women *liked* (for a long time) their nurturing work, especially vis-à-vis the male practitioners, did not negate the existence of inequality. Sandra Bartky's analysis of women's nurturing of men (more general) as a false kind of power fit well with my emerging analysis of the staff women at Renewal:

> The *feeling* of out-flowing personal power so characteristic of the caregiving woman is quite different from the *having* of any actual power in the world. There is no doubt that this sense of personal efficacy provides some compensation for the extra-domestic power women are typically denied: If one cannot be king oneself, being a confidante of kings may be the next best thing. But just as we make a bad bargain in accepting an occasional Valentine [in heterosexual relationships] in lieu of the sustained attention we deserve, we are ill-advised to settle for a mere feeling of power, however heady and intoxicating it may be, in place of the effective power we have every right to exercise in the world.[10]

That the women found it acceptable to receive no money at all while the practitioners received their pay regularly from clients did not render it fair. That the men benefited much more from the arrangements at Renewal—materially, symbolically, and emotionally—than the women held true whether participants acknowledged it or not.

Once I accepted this judgment—that systematic inequalities existed and should constitute my analysis—I was freed to write a story that fit the feminist I had become. Or perhaps I should say that this analysis made me into a more systematic feminist. Members of Renewal became interesting to me as a group of people who had *good intentions* with regard to equality but who failed to see even the blatant ways in which they contradicted their ideals. Much of the story I wrote[11] examined how members reproduced gendered inequalities at Renewal while still maintaining their belief in themselves as good people, committed to an "alternative" way of life. I ended the book by generalizing members' blindnesses to *all* of us who are so invested in our "alternative" identities that we cannot bear the idea of noticing our contradictions: "When we take on the identity of feminist, leftist or antiracist we can do one of two things: don the identity and feel good about ourselves for having it, or see it as a symbol of a lifetime commitment to critical self-reflection and radical action."[12]

TEACHING ISSUES

My commitment to radical action partly emerged from and changed my teaching. In the 1980s, while I was having trouble understanding the story of Renewal, I taught mostly courses in social psychology, sociology of work, and socialization. In 1989, the chair of women's studies asked me to develop an undergraduate course on race, class, and gender. I did so reluctantly. Although I had read some work in feminist theory, along with a smattering of empirical studies on gender, race, and class in order to help me analyze my data on Renewal, I did not think I knew enough to teach an upper-level course. Little did I know that learning the material would be the easy part; figuring out how to handle students' resistance to what we read would be the challenge.

Although I didn't initially think of myself as a fieldworker in the classroom, I used my observations and conversations with students to come up with a format that would best fit the material, as well as handle students' resistance. In my previous classes, I had mostly lectured and done occasional small-group work. Although students rarely challenge the lecture format if they think of the material as objective (though they may find the format boring), they are much more resistant to sitting through lectures on feminist material. Students are apt to define lectures on gender inequality as a way for a teacher to shove her own agenda down their throats. The lecture format also makes it easier for students to distance themselves from the material and keeps them from discovering the conclusions for themselves.

Quite quickly I came up with a format I have kept for many years. Each day two students cofacilitate the class with me. I meet with them for two or more hours the week before, and we plan the day. This allows me to spend informal time with students, gives them opportunities to talk with me about the course, and makes them "own" the material. It also deflects from me as the center: the Teacher with a Feminist Agenda. Not that I hide my goals; the syllabus makes clear that we will analyze inequalities, especially as they relate to our lives. And two of the books I use have "feminist" in the title. Although students know that I play a large part in what we do in class (and I am the one who chose the readings), having cofacilitators and student discussion de-centers authority and gives students more room to handle the material. Over the years, I have come increasingly to direct the show. When we meet, I offer the facilitators questions, exercises, video clips, and so on that have worked well before. In the classroom, the cofacilitators ask questions, tell us what to do next, and occasionally comment, but I remain the anchor (and students, by and large, are grateful for this). I jump in whenever I wish and handle the difficult comments or confusions. This sometimes means that I give what one student called "lecturettes."

There is always small-group work in class, often a lot of it, as well as discussion in the large group (of about forty students). Students also have to write a reflection paper about the readings each day, so that discussions are informed by the readings and students' thoughts about them. As I see it, I've become a guide, helping students recognize, first, that systematic inequalities exist and, second, that they, too, have some choice over whether they will reinforce those inequalities in their daily lives or challenge or interrupt them. Much like members of Renewal—and most of us—the undergraduates (mostly white, middle-class, straight women) want to believe that their situation is now acceptable. After all, the women are students at a good state university in which they now constitute a majority (60%). Most are from middle-to upper-middle-class backgrounds; some are athletes; many have traveled abroad. Like members of Renewal, students want to believe that they are good people, and they do not want to hear that anything they think, say, or do might reinforce the disadvantages of others, including other women. The men don't want to believe that they have privileges as men that come at the expense of women. White students don't want to believe that they have advantages over people of color. Women don't want to believe that anything they do or say—for the most part, unintentionally—might reinforce their own disadvantages. (For example, we discuss women's use of sexist language, trashing other women, or going along with or telling sexist jokes.)

At first, students' reactions to the material surprised me. In my naiveté, I had believed that students, particularly the women, would say, "Wow, I hadn't thought about things that way before. Thank you!" That's how I had felt when I first read the same materials. As a fieldworker-teacher, I knew that this surprising finding meant that I needed to study the students as a group with beliefs and behaviors that I wanted to understand, including differences among them (in race, class, gender, and sexuality, as well as in previous exposure to women's studies classes).

I came to understand students' initial belief in the near equality of gender as analogous to the feelings I had when I took my first academic job. I, too, needed to believe that things would be fine if I just worked hard enough. Most of my students are seniors; they will be looking for jobs in a few months or a year. They don't want to believe any bad news.

Students' resistance to the bad news also made me aware of my goals as a teacher. I don't want them to learn the material and forget it after the final exam. Perhaps every teacher feels this way. But when I taught courses in social psychology, I was not as invested in students' retention of the lessons learned. With courses in inequality, I want students to think about how they could lessen the inequalities, even in small ways. I want them to take what they had learned and apply the material to their lives and, immodest as it sounds, to have them do this for life. My goal is to get them to take steps, even baby steps, to live a sociologically mindful life.[13] In so doing, they will recognize that each of their actions is part of a larger whole and that everything they do has consequences for others, as well as themselves. After years of figuring out students' resistance and finding ways to deal with it, I can say that most students do say thank you for "lifting the veils" (as one student put it)— by the *end* of the course.

How do I structure the course to make it possible for students to become feminist observers? I begin by having them read Marilyn Frye's foundational article on what she calls "the oppression of women."[14] Frye uses the metaphor of a birdcage to represent the systematic wires that keep women oppressed, even as some of us have privileges of race, class, sexuality, and so on:

> Consider a birdcage. If you look very closely at just one wire in a birdcage, you cannot see the other wires. If your conception of what is before you is determined by this myopic focus, you could look at that one wire, up and down the length of it, and be unable to see why a bird would not just fly around the wire any time it wanted to go somewhere. Furthermore, even if, one day at a time, you myopically inspected each wire, you still could not see why a bird would have trouble going past the wires to get anywhere. There is no physical property of any one wire, *nothing* that the closest scrutiny could discover, that will reveal how a bird could be inhibited or harmed by it except in the most accidental way. It is only when you step back, stop looking at the wires one by one, microscopically, and take a macroscopic view of the whole cage, that you can see why the bird does not go anywhere; and then you see it in a moment. It is perfectly *obvious* that the bird is surrounded by a network of systematically related barriers, no one of which would be the least hindrance to its flight, but which, by their relations to each other, are as confining as the solid walls of a dungeon.[15]

Frye's piece provides a frame and a hypothesis for the course. She's a feminist philosopher, not a sociologist, so she gives little empirical proof. The sociological work on inequality we read for the rest of the course fills in the rest. Each day we examine a different "wire" (e.g., sexist language, the second shift, the wage gap, sexualizing of women in the media, and rape). But pointing out the wires is not enough. If Frye's argument is to be supported, then all the wires should be related to one another. As I see it, this is a fieldwork puzzle: relate the pieces (individual wires of inequality) to each other and see if they come out in an integrated whole (birdcage of oppression). After a couple of weeks, I push students to link the different wires through discussion questions and exercises. By the end of the course, students show (through exams and exercises) how, for example, the second shift can reinforce the wage gap or how sexist language reinforces a rape culture.

The students' ability to make links grows through the course. But let me return to the day, early in the course, when we read Frye's article. On that day I show the students a video of a 1997 "Prime Time" TV segment ("The Fairer Sex?") that I use to cut through some of their denial about gender inequality. Through hidden cameras, the video compares the experiences of a white, middle-class woman and a white, middle-class man as they buy cars, take clothes to the dry cleaner, apply for jobs, or try to get a tee time on the golf course. I ask the students to list the wires as they watch the video. This gives them the chance to see that even within a fifteen-minute video of one woman's life, there are many wires to list.

Most of the female students believe that gender discrimination is a thing of the past, perhaps something their mothers or grandmothers might have experienced, or that it exists only in subtle forms. And most of the students believe that they have never been discriminated against on the basis of their gender. I point out that we, as women, can't really know about all the discrimination that might have happened to us because we don't have crews from TV networks who are paid to monitor us on a daily basis. In addition, the video shows the rather blatant behavior on the part of the men who work at the employment agency or sell cars. Even when Diane Sawyer confronts them, they say such things as "Women just don't make good territory managers." The students learn that whereas gender discrimination may be hidden, it is not necessarily subtle.

I also introduce on this day the concept of false power. This is the idea that members of an oppressed group can learn to feel flattered by some actions on the part of the dominant group that actually reinforce oppression. It can also include oppressed group members' actions, adornments, and so on, which they have come to like but which also reinforce their position of subordination. Sandra Bartky refers to the latter as "repressive satisfactions"[16] she includes women's use of makeup, weight-loss rituals, and shaving as examples. "False power," or the idea that one can feel empowered by behaviors, words, or objects that can be disempowering for the oppressed group, complicates the notion of pattern. Students at first want to consider the rituals they enjoy as an exception to the pattern of oppression rather than as a part of it.

Marilyn Frye's analysis of the male door-opening ritual exemplifies the idea that what appear as advantages to the oppressed actually reinforce oppression. She focuses on the fact that men disproportionately open doors for women (rather than the reverse) and that even when a man has packages, he might run up and open the door for a woman whose hands are free. Her analysis, as I imagine it, began with a puzzle: why, in a society in which women are enclosed by numerous wires, does such a generous-seeming ritual exist? Even students who find Frye's argument about the birdcage convincing balk at this part of her article. More accurately, many become angry—both women and men. This strong reaction to Frye's critique of the door-opening ritual is not only common in the South (where I teach); feminist professors in the Midwest and the West Coast have also asked me, "How do you respond to the door-opening ritual? My students refuse to accept that it has any meaning other than politeness."

One day in class, after having taught the article for several semesters, I asked, "How would you explain this behavior to a Martian?" I wasn't sure where I'd go from there, but I attribute my thinking of the Martian to my fieldwork training: make the strange familiar and the familiar strange.

One student, a man (but in other semesters a woman has offered it) said, "Well, it's polite. That's why a man does it. It's a way for men to show politeness to a woman."

I responded, "So you're saying that men do this to treat women as special?"

"Yes."

I donned a Martian voice spontaneously (humor helps) and said, "Well, I see. So in your society, women—since they are special—earn more than men do. Is this correct?"

They shook their heads.

"In your society, since women are special, they walk the streets freely without fear of violation, correct?"

Once again, no.

"Since women are so special that men open doors for them, then this must mean that women do less of the housework and stay away from dirty diapers. Correct?"

"Women, since they are special, are considered beautiful at all body sizes because their bodies are manifestations of special beings, correct?"

Once again, the heads said no.

"So, why do men open doors for women?"

One woman said, "Because that's all we get!"

Her comment got a bigger laugh than my Martian imitation.

From there I talked about how Frye was looking at a puzzle rather than trying to rob them of a cultural practice. And I introduce there the idea that what can make women (or any group) *feel* good does not necessarily make it innocent from the point of view of reinforcing a pattern of systematically related wires of inequality.

After class, I wrote a handout that described the Martian exercise and explained how one might sociologically examine the door-opening ritual. (Now I give this out at the end of class, after doing the Martian routine.) In my handout, I say that men's opening doors for women, like other rituals we'll examine later, can give people in the oppressed group a false sense of power. We may *feel* powerful (as Sandra Bartky wrote about women's asymmetric nurturing of men) but not *be* powerful. I add that such gestures may provide meager compensation for inequalities (thus placating women), may mask inequalities ("things are fine—men even open doors for us!"), or may deflect from the inequalities. And as Marilyn Frye puts it, the offer of help, since it's not needed, reinforces the idea that women are helpless and need help even with such easy matters. I also use Frye's example to show the differences between intentions and consequences.[17] I point out that sexism (and racism and heterosexism) are often unconscious. The door-opening ritual is a gilded wire in the birdcage, but even a well-furnished birdcage is still a cage.

Would I have thought of using the Martian if I had not been a fieldworker? I don't know. Would I have been as motivated to find a way for my students to get this particular point if I didn't think that such seemingly benign practices are harmful to women? I doubt it. As a feminist fieldworker-teacher, I want students to apply what they learn to their own lives, trying out a feminist lens. Once they understand the wires of inequality and the relations between them, they might care enough to try to make things better for women as a group (and generalize the lessons to the birdcages of racism, heterosexism, class inequality, etc.).

MOVING TO MEMOIR

Frye's metaphor of the birdcage is compelling. But students must be convinced that it's the appropriate one for describing oppression. Over the years I have learned that sociologically informed personal stories[18] are what make the patterns of sexism (the wires) real to students. For example, students read about a black undergraduate's experiences at a predominantly white university and learn about subtle to blatant racism among white students who see themselves as liberal.[19] Or they read one reporter's account of a lesbian's long struggle with doctors, lawyers, and families to gain legal guardianship of her recently disabled partner and learn to see connections among heterosexism, sexism, and ableism.[20] Such articles also have a humanizing effect on students. Even the student who thinks that "homosexuality is unnatural" recognizes that the lesbian partner of the hurt woman is (literally) saving her life, whereas others—especially the woman's homophobic father—are obstructing the woman's care.

Perhaps I should not have been surprised that stories work in teaching. Storytelling, whether in fiction or nonfiction, is a time-tested way to get readers to care. Writings that "show" more than "tell" a story of interaction, inequality, and power get students to listen and then to understand that life is more than a drama of personalities. Reading these articles also taught me that one can write an accessible, engaging story that communicates sociological analysis. As a feminist, I want to raise awareness and hope that a new consciousness will motivate students—beyond the course—to work for social change. If one writes in an inaccessible language, one is lessening the chances of being understood and thus one's chances of inspiring anyone to make change.

I did not "decide" to write the first in a series of what I have called "sociologically informed personal essays." I was taking a two-day workshop with ten faculty members, who were interested in integrating cultural diversity into their courses, along with fifteen minority students, mostly African-American women. At one point, the cofacilitators divided us into small groups. The workshop leader for our group asked us to sit in a circle, close our eyes, and think back to the first time we had met a person of a different race, ethnic group, or religion. It wasn't difficult to figure out where this exercise was going—we were to think of an early encounter with "difference," perhaps seeing our prejudices or our privileges. Here's what happened to me:

> An image of my family appears—mother, father, brother, sister. What
> are *they* doing here? I'm supposed to be thinking about *others*. I close
> my eyes tighter, but they won't go. They are looking at my nose. I hear
> what they are thinking: Sherryl is ugly and it's because of her big nose.[21]

This reverie took me back to age thirteen, when my mother told me that somehow she and my father would find the money to give me a nose job.

"Is it that bad?" I ask. My eyes are stinging and I'm sure my nose is turning red and puffy, growing as wide as it is long, right before my mother's eyes.

"No, no. It's not terrible," she says. "Let me show you."

Show me? "Just two things to fix. We take just a little off that," she says, lightly sweeping my bump with her index finger. Then she moves her finger to the tip of my nose and pushes it up, gently. "And just a little lift here, not much at all. A small job."

I refused the nose job, but as I wrote later, "For years I wondered, did I chicken out or did I have principles?"

I told my story to the group at the workshop after Tracy, an African-American student, talked about touching her white teacher's hair and thinking how much nicer it felt than her own. Monica, another African-American student, told us about having a crush on a white boy when she was six and hearing him say, "Why do you have such fat lips?" She showed us how she bit her lips for hours over several days to try to make them thinner.

Tracy's and Monica's stories spoke of internalized sexism and racism— they both felt they had to live up to beauty standards for women, and those that fit white models. My story was about gender oppression, as well as internalized anti-Semitism. As I wrote, "It was bad to have a Jewish nose even if you were a man because, after all, it was a Jewish nose, not just a big nose. But the real tragedy was when a girl had that nose." In my story, I also distinguished Tracy's and Monica's stories from my own: "I can pass as non-Jewish and have most of the privileges of white people." Otherwise, I would have made a false parallel[22] between my experience and theirs.

The day after I left the workshop, I wrote about what had happened. (Since I write in a notebook every day as a warmup before going to the computer, this wasn't unusual.) But after reading it to my weekly writing group, they encouraged me to revise it and send it out for publication. Although I was unsure where to send it, a graduate student suggested *On the Issues: The Progressive Woman's Quarterly*. The magazine mostly had news stories, but a section near the front was called "Talking Feminist," and some of the pieces were memoirs or essays. Eventually the piece was published there.[23]

What makes that memoir a piece of feminist fieldwork? Writing it took the same kind of attention as fieldwork, noticing the words, actions, meanings, and interactions among family members. Although the offer of the nose job was experienced by the thirteen-year-old as dramatic, from the mother's point of view it was merely an extension of her mother role. I also had to understand the meaning of the act to the mother. In writing a memoir, if one blames the mother ("What terrible mother would offer to have her daughter's nose broken in order to 'fix' it?") all one does is put the reader on one's side. This is akin to fieldwork, where we need to understand the perspective of the other. For example, recall that in my interviews with the staff women at Renewal I learned how they had come to participate there, what they wanted to get out of it, and their understandings of the male practitioners. Only when I learned about their vulnerabilities as they started working at Renewal, the connections they developed, and the sense of competence they derived from putting together the membership bulletin and so on did I see how they came *not* to notice inequalities for quite some time. (*Opposing Ambitions* also shows their growing disillusionment with the key male practitioners and with Renewal.[24])

Similarly, I came to understand that my mother was given the invisible work of sexism. It was her job to fashion me into a marriageable woman. As I wrote, "Only later did I grasp her intent. She was trying to help me get a good Jewish husband, a 'professional man,' by making me look less Jewish."

After writing "The Nose Job" I wanted to learn more about writing for wider audiences. I was lucky enough to be trained by sociologists who took writing seriously. They made me investigate ideas that lurked behind my convoluted sentences and uncover the actors who hid behind the passive voice. One of my teachers, Howard Becker, pushed all of us to say what we meant, use jargon only when necessary, and sweep away clutter. But I've learned through writing workshops that the writer—even the sociological analyst—can make room for ambiguity: if you don't know the answer, you can raise questions. Saying what you mean is key, but you might say it best through an image, metaphor, or scene.

My hope is that my sociologically informed essays will demonstrate that sociology can be evocative and analytical at the same time. I offer one example. During the one-on-one consultation with my teacher at the Paris Writers' Workshop, he suggested that I add a reverie or fantasy in one section of "The Nose Job." I later wrote:

> Where did I read about nose jobs? In *Life* magazine? *The Montreal Star*? I bet it was *Life* because I know I've seen the pictures.
>
> She has dark hair like mine. I bet her eyes are dark like mine, but I can't tell because there's a thick black line across them, protecting her from us. Could she be Marsha from down the block? That wave in her hair, just like Marsha's. But no, that's just the Jewish wave, it could be any girl. Did Marsha have a nose job? I've heard our mothers whisper "nose job" during canasta games, but no one tells.
>
> The girl's eyes follow me in shadows inside my head. Are her eyes looking down, away from the camera, matching the dragging corners of her mouth? Or does she know they'll blindfold her for the public, so she lets her eyes do what they wish.
>
> In the before, slightly after, and after pictures, I imagine her changing her gaze, changing her mind. The second picture shows the bruises from the break, the bandages so thick that she doesn't appear to have a nose at all.

In the third picture she wears a weak smile. I can almost hear her mother say, "Look happy for the camera, dear." Her eyes don't twinkle behind the blindfold, they narrow.

Her new nose cannot stand proud. It is too small for that now. It can only curtsy.

One participant in the workshop said, "You can write 'gender this' or 'gender that' in a sociological essay, but 'It can only curtsy' tells it all. It does a much better job of capturing the idea that girls are pushed to be pretty, sometimes at a terrible cost." Although I don't think that fragment tells it *all*, the comment does say what I'd like to show: images, metaphors, fantasies, compelling dialogue, and evocative scenes can convey sociological messages. If we use these techniques, we might find an audience who will want to read our work and find it useful for understanding themselves and the world.

Being a fieldworker in my everyday life means that I attend to the social patterns around me, analyze my own actions, and piece together the observations I make and the words I hear. Being a *feminist* fieldworker means that I attend to the subtleties of inequalities (in race, class, gender, sexual orientation, ability, age, etc.), including the ways in which I act as allies for those with disadvantages I lack and the ways in which I live out sexist programming.

I turned to writing sociologically informed personal essays because I came to see, through students' reactions to stories, that such writing could make sociological lessons stick. Such stories convince students that there are existing inequalities that systematically hurt people, which other articles did not. The challenge is to communicate sociological lessons in ways that get and keep readers' attention.

I have said that such writing is especially useful in teaching. I want to add that sociological memoirs—especially those based on the feminist-fieldworker approach—are just as important for sociologists to read. In my observations over the years, sociologists are no more aware of their blind spots—including how we reinforce inequality in our interactions with students, colleagues, secretaries, housekeepers at the university, friends, and family—than other people. If as fieldworkers we can piece together the wires of inequality as we study others, we could become equally adept at recognizing similar processes in our own lives. This does not necessarily lead to a life of interactional comfort and takes on the feel of a never-ending job. Yet this approach also gives me an examined life, one that integrates my writing, teaching, and, in a word, living.

NOTES

1. Sherryl Kleinman and Martha A. Copp, *Emotions and Fieldwork* (Newbury Park, Calif.: Sage, 1993).

2. Michael Schwalbe, Sandra Godwin, Daphne Holden, Douglas Schrock, Shealy Thompson, and Michelle Wolkomir, "Generic Processes in the Reproduction of Inequality: An Interactionist Analysis," *Social Forces* 79 (2000): 419–52. See also Jim Thomas, *Doing Critical Ethnography* (Newbury Park, Calif.: Sage, 1993).

3. Alison M. Jaggar, "Love and Knowledge: Emotion in Feminist Epistemology," in *Gender/Body/Knowledge: Feminist Reconstructions of Being and Knowing*, ed. Alison M. Jaggar and Susan R. Bordo (New Brunswick, N.J.: Rutgers University Press, 1989).

4. Sherryl Kleinman, "What Sociology Teaches Me," *Sociological Analysis* 1 (1998): 119–24.

5. Sherryl Kleinman, *Equals Before God: Seminarians as Humanistic Professionals* (Champaign-Urbana, Ill.: University of Chicago Press, 1984).

6. For a fuller account, see Sherryl Kleinman, "Emotions, Fieldwork and Professional Lives," in *Qualitative Research in Action*, ed. Tim May (London: Sage, 2002).

7. See Kleinman and Copp, *Emotions and Fieldwork*.

8. Carol Gilligan, *In a Different Voice: Psychological Theory and Moral Development* (Cambridge, Mass.: Harvard University Press, 1982).

9. Jean Baker Miller, *Toward a New Psychology of Women* (Boston: Beacon Press, 1976).

10. Sandra Bartky, *Femininity and Domination: Studies in the Phenomenology of Oppression* (New York: Routledge, 1990), 116.

11. Sherryl Kleinman, *Opposing Ambitions: Gender and Identity in an Alternative Organization* (Chicago: University of Chicago Press, 1996).

12. Ibid., 140.

13. Michael Schwalbe, *The Sociologically Examined Life* (New York: McGraw-Hill, 2001).

14. Marilyn Frye, *The Politics of Reality: Essays in Feminist Theory* (Freedom, Calif.: Crossing Press, 1983).

15. Ibid., 4.

16. Bartky, *Femininity and Domination*, 42.

17. Schwalbe, *Sociologically Examined Life*, 4.

18. Sherryl Kleinman, "Essaying the Personal: Making Sociological Stories Stick," *Qualitative Sociology* 20 (1997): 553–64.

19. C. R. Simmons, "The Silent Scream," in *Race, Class, and Gender in the United States*, ed. Paula Rothenberg (New York: St. Martin's, 1995).

20. Joan L. Griscom, "The Case of Sharon Kowalski and Karen Thompson: Ableism, Heterosexism, and Sexism," in *Race, Class, and Gender in the United States*, ed. Paula Rothenberg (New York: St. Martin's, 1995).

21. Sherryl Kleinman, "The Nose Job," *The Progressive Woman's Quarterly* (summer 1998), 10–11.

22. Schwalbe, *Sociologically Examined Life*.

23. Kleinman, "Nose Job."

24. Kleinman, *Opposing Ambitions*.

JODY MILLER

FEMINISM IN THE FIELD

19

A long-standing tension in ethnographic research revolves around issues of immersion—how much distance to maintain from research participants or sites, that is, how "native" to go and what level of membership (if any) to strive for in negotiating field roles.[1] Ethnographers who follow the traditional Chicago model opt for maintaining greater distance and detachment, even as participant-observers, because the potential for overidentification, or going native, is viewed as a threat to validity and objectivity. On the other hand, some contemporary ethnographers have pushed these boundaries—from peripheral and active membership roles to complete membership, whether by going native in a research setting or studying one's own community.[2]

This pushing of ethnographic boundaries emanates from at least two streams—from existential and ethnomethodological developments in sociology[3] and from challenges posed by feminist researchers to blur the boundaries between researcher and researched.[4] Among field researchers, there remains a general assumption that these issues are primarily faced by "real" ethnographers—those who are involved in participant observational work and who spend extensive periods of time in the field—rather than qualitative researchers like myself whose primary data-gathering technique is in-depth interviewing. Drawing from my personal biography and from the various ways in which my research has been intertwined with my personal life, I hope to challenge that assumption and in doing so highlight the fluidity of roles and tensions that can emerge in negotiating proximity and distance in all forms of qualitative research.

Among traditional ethnographers, the compartmentalization of "research" and "personal biography" is sometimes taken for granted, so that even the decision-making process of choosing or negotiating field roles—let alone choosing or negotiating what is to be researched—is sometimes assumed to exist in some ways outside of one's personal life. My own experiences are an illustration of how personal biography guides a research trajectory and how, even without doing field-based ethnography, tensions between identification and detachment remain. To disentangle and explore the overlap of my research and personal life, I'll begin with the story of how all of this was shaped by my particular path into academic life in the first place.

THE ROAD TO ACADEMIA

I am a Reagan-era feminist. Coming of age in the 1980s was quite a different experience from the romantic image I have of 1960s and 1970s second-wave feminism. I imagine the second wave of feminism as a time of hope, optimism about the potential for social change, and collectivist action. On the other hand, developing a feminist consciousness in the midst of ongoing social and political conservatism had made my outlook rather more cynical and pessimistic. Compared to the ideal of activist research, my own work has remained more individualistic and academic. This is in part a product of my era, as well as my personal roots.

I was fourteen when Reagan took office, though I recall having no political awareness at the time. My parents were part of the white flight of the 1970s, escaping desegregation and safely tucking their children into the epitome of small-town, midwestern America. My childhood was in many ways a prototype of "American family values": my mother was a stay-at-home mom, and my father was the poster boy for the American dream. From a working-class home, he started, when I was a toddler, as a truck driver at a company that just this year made him a very wealthy man when he—as CEO and co-owner—sold the business and retired. In my extended family of seventeen cousins, I am one of four college graduates, the only one with a graduate degree and the only self-identified feminist. So I'm both a family anomaly (considered a slacker by my extended family until I finished my doctorate and got a "real" job) and part of a larger sociohistorical trend as one of the middle-class children of upwardly mobile working-class families in the mid-twentieth century.

In my home community, which continues to reproduce so-called mid-western family values, I was not provided with much of the cultural capital necessary to become an independent "career woman," let alone an academic. My high school was small, and though my classmates and I shared a vague notion of the importance of college, we received little by way of actual career guidance. Many of them are now raising families in the same community in which we grew up, which should have been my life: I was a cheerleader, a local beauty queen, and while dating the high school football captain one of my goals was to live in a farmhouse with a wraparound porch and raise three children—a boy followed by two girls. How I went from that to my current life as an academic feminist remains in many ways a mysterious gift, though some of the key turning points are traceable.

My feminist enlightenment was hard fought. I have a hazy recollection of stumbling into an introductory women's studies course as a college sophomore and no clear recollection of why. But obviously it resonated because I decided to pursue a certificate and immediately embraced the label *feminist*. My mother recalls those days as a time when I was unbearable, coming home on weekends and fighting with anyone (which is to say, almost everyone I knew) unwilling to espouse my newly discovered political ideals.

This awakening was preceded by a clearer comprehension of my family roots. I went to a midsized state university reputed to be a public "Ivy" and attended by children of privilege unable to make the cut in the university big leagues. I was confronted with young people from wealthy regional suburbs who seemed to ooze the cultural capital that up until then I hadn't realized I'd been missing. This recognition, though emotionally difficult and a challenge to my self-esteem—having been such a big fish in such a little pond—was also one of the first crystallized sociological insights I had about the world. The kernel of knowledge remained even if my stint at this university did not. I was increasingly drawn to photography and transferred to another state university with a well-known photojournalism program.

As an undergraduate I never considered, much less understood, the idea of graduate school. The photojournalism program, though rigorous, was much more hands-on than traditionally academic. But as a senior I enrolled in a sociology seminar on violence against women that counted for my women's studies certificate. That class and the professor who taught it changed the course of my life; they were responsible for the start of my academic career, and they laid the foundations for what has become my sustained research agenda on issues of gender, crime, and victimization. There were many more students like me at this university than at the former one. My professor knew this, and he knew that he had to teach me about graduate school in order to recruit and encourage me to attend. I was able to make the connections among photography, my concern with women's issues, and my budding interest in the sociology of crime and deviance, and working with him, I gradually became more broadly politically and sociologically aware.

With the assistance of this professor, for two summers I volunteered at a residential facility for delinquent girls, where I obtained donations to start a photography class (and where, six years later, I would collect data for my dissertation). Working with these young women in constructing photographic portraits of their lives solidified my concern with the experiences of and challenges facing adolescent girls involved in delinquency. It is probably worth noting that, given my rather cloistered upbringing and the segregated nature of American college life, my work with the girls at this facility provided my first intimate contact with African Americans. It would be a year later before I had an African-American mentor in academia, and—though by that time I was well read in feminist and sociological literature on race and racism—it was not until I entered my doctoral program that there were African Americans and foreign nationals I could count among my friends and colleagues. Working at the facility, I also found myself much more comfortable with not being behind a camera. Given the nature of qualitative research, it is perhaps a great irony that I could never shake my acute discomfort with the obtrusiveness and voyeuristic feel of practicing photojournalism. But social research became and has remained my passion.

PATHWAYS INTO RESEARCH

Just like my entry into academia in the first place, nearly all of my research projects, though they share a common thread, have come about through some amount of serendipity. Early in my graduate career I attended a National Women's Studies Association annual meeting that happened to be in a nearby town. I was especially compelled by a speaker from the Los Angeles–based Black Coalition Fighting Back Serial Murders, who described systematic police callousness in investigating a string of prostitute murders in South Central Los Angeles. I decided to investigate for myself the significance of violence against street-level sex workers, and I conducted in-depth interviews with women incarcerated on prostitution-related charges at the local county jail.[5] The project had a profound and traumatizing impact on me, but it also sharpened some critical thinking skills and raised issues about women's agency and the importance of understanding the stories, definitions, and interpretations they provide, which remain a focus of my research to this day.

Though my research was not field-based, I nonetheless was deeply affected by the brutal violence recounted to me by these women. At the time I was collecting data, I routinely interviewed several women back to back in a single day. In my field notes at the time I wrote the following:

> After these experiences I really need a break. A little time away from the research. Although that doesn't stop me from thinking about their experiences 24 hours a day, or 24/7 as they would say. I lay in bed at night for what seems like hours trying to fall asleep but with images of these women's stories keeping me awake. On Friday I was really jumpy around the house in the morning. It really does make me more aware of my own vulnerability.

Reflecting on this first research experience some time later, I recognized that my internalization of the trauma of what I was told involved both naiveté and privilege.[6] What my visceral reactions were unable to capture was that the structures of my daily life safeguarded me from such violence, whereas the structures of street-level sex workers' daily lives and the oppressive contexts in which they worked all but ensured it.

On only two occasions since then—once when a gang girl described participating in the vicious beating and gang rape of a rival gang girl, and again when a Sri Lankan soldier described his routine brutality toward women on the war front—have I felt such a profound sense of anguish and helplessness. But in both instances, in relatively short order the researcher in me soon took over and I dealt with the events by focusing on the sociological insights to be gained. Sometimes now, however, I'm haunted more than anything by the simple fact that I am no longer haunted so deeply by much of what I study, that a composed analysis has become my coping mechanism when faced with harrowing stories of oppression and violence. This is reflected even in more recent field notes. Compare the preceding passage, for instance, with what I wrote upon hearing about the gang rape five years later:

> The one thing I want to get on paper now, even though I plan on asking her about it [in more detail] tomorrow, is a gang rape that members of her set participated in that she witnessed. She said a girl in the

Bloods set one of her boys up and he ended up getting jumped and beaten up real bad, put in the hospital. A few weeks later, members of her gang saw the girl walking down the street and they "snatched her" in their car and brought her to the home of one of the members, for the girls to beat her up. So she said that she and the other two or three girls there beat the girl up, and she said then the boys jumped in and beat her some, then one of the boys started ripping her clothes off, she said he just went crazy, and once he started, the other boys joined in. She said they raped her anally, vaginally, orally, and "tore her up" pretty good, she was very bloody, they spit on her and called her names. There were four of them that participated. She felt ambivalent about it, but didn't do anything to stop it. She said part of her felt like she should because this was another female, but her boy was in the hospital because of what she did. She said she watched it and was thinking thank God it wasn't her, she felt sorry for her, but didn't intervene. She said her mom yelled at her for not doing anything to stop it, that because it was another female she should have intervened. I think she looks back on it and feels pretty ambivalent about it, also about what she witnessed—obviously at least part of her identified that it could be her, and part of her was horrified at the level of brutality her fellow gang members were willing to levy at the girl—in a specifically gendered way. I plan to talk with her about it more tomorrow. She said they put the girl in the trunk of the car when they were finished with her, and dumped her out of the way by the . . . river, she said the girl was extremely weak at that point. She said she knew the girl was hoping for help, but she couldn't or didn't do it.

There's no description of my emotional reaction to the events, though I recall being quite disturbed upon hearing about the incident. By the time I wrote my field notes that day, my focus was on documenting as many of the details of the incident as I could recall, as well as adding some preliminary analyses about the tensions of being both female and a gang member. I did reinterview this young woman about the event, and it ultimately became a central focal point in my analysis of girls' gender strategies in youth gangs.[7] But this brutal gang rape all too quickly became data to me, and I continue to feel troubled occasionally at what I perhaps harshly self-define as both dispassion and misdirected intellectual passion. It's clearly a coping mechanism, but is it an appropriate mechanism for a "good" feminist? Let me explain some of how it came about.

A year into my doctoral program, I began working with a professor who is a world-renowned expert on street gangs. This also happened to be the time—the early 1990s—when research on gangs made a major comeback, in part because of the growth of gangs throughout the United States during this period.[8] Criminology in general, and gang research in particular, has traditionally been a masculine enterprise. I found the perfect niche to make a timely scholarly contribution by studying young women's involvement in these groups. As a scholar, this project was in many ways my awakening. I encountered a complex world both in the research and in my personal life that shattered whatever remaining naive ideals I held and left me with a deepened sense of pessimism. Ironically, though my experiences reoriented my commitments in the ways I've just described, at the same time they allowed me to gain a somewhat deeper empathic understanding of the worlds of the girls I studied.

If the mantra of the second wave of feminism was "the personal is political," reflecting on my own experiences and my research as my body politic, this has tended at times to become inverted. For me, the political has often come home to roost in the personal. Perhaps this is the result of being feminist in a postfeminist, individualistic rather than collectivist era. For better or worse, I've had a tendency through the years to go a little native in my commitments—not with research participants themselves but in my attachment to the broader worlds under investigation. This is not to say that as a graduate student I joined a street gang. But while conducting my research on girls in gangs, I became romantically involved with a man who was quite familiar with the lives and experiences of the youths I was studying. He was a fellow student at the time but also a self-defined recovering crack addict.

My attraction to this relationship was in many ways intellectual, grounded in the passion I felt for my research and studies. We read books in common and spent countless hours talking about my previous and current projects and about racism and urban America. Because of the time he'd spent in an urban crack market, he offered insights about and confirmation of my analyses of women's experiences in this scene.[9] Moreover, many of the young women I was interviewing for the gang project described feeling a deep sense of abandonment and betrayal because of a parent's heavy drug use. They often described gangs and street life as their alternatives to troubled home lives. All of this resonated with my then partner, who was himself struggling to rebuild a relationship with the daughter he had excised from his life during his years as a heavy drug user. Our conversations deeply enriched my research. But more than that, I realize that I felt somehow legitimized as a white scholar who was studying primarily young women of color; because my partner was himself African American, I could believe myself to be truly antiracist, willing to challenge racial segregation and oppression not (just) through research but also through my individual choice and its consequences.

Ultimately, though, the relationship itself deeply enriched the research in unanticipated ways. My visceral understanding of girls' deep sense of abandonment and betrayal became much more authentic when I found myself in a similar situation: well into the relationship but shortly after we began living together my partner slowly moved away from his "recovery" and began using crack again. My experience of his activities mirrored those described by the girls I had been interviewing. He stole from me repeatedly, and we restructured our lives to protect him from "temptation." I was isolated from family and friends but was determined not to allow him to slip back into the dangerous, brutal world he had fought so hard to leave behind. Our intellectually stimulating relationship had devolved into a one-woman rescue mission that in the end failed miserably.

As privilege would have it, I ultimately emerged relatively unscathed. Still, I occasionally look back amazed that during that period I was able to get a job in a leading criminology program, complete my dissertation, and reconstruct my life. Privilege or no, it is perhaps my greatest personal accomplishment, although one that fused with my research in a reciprocal way, deepening my sense of empathic understanding but also creating a deep scar of pessimism that remained. I became, theoretically, a Left realist.[10] Moreover, the healing process came in part with a deepening intellectual and less emotional attachment to my research, as reflected in my earlier illustration, which had occurred at the tail end of this relationship.

LIFE AND RESEARCH
AFTER GRADUATE SCHOOL

My new status as a professor also afforded me the ability to detach emotionally from my research. I was able to hire research assistants to complete the majority of interviews of a comparative sample of gang girls.[11] After that work was finished, a colleague and I received funding to conduct a related study. Given the significance of gender victimization uncovered in my gang research, we developed a broader study of violence against adolescent girls in urban African-American communities. As with my previous projects, this study has utilized in-depth interviewing techniques. But research assistants have conducted the interviews rather than me. Such an approach inevitably distances me from the field and from viscerally experiencing the project. Reading accounts on paper cannot have the same impact as hearing and being told face to face. Now it's my research assistant herself struggling with many of these issues, and they are especially salient for her as a young African-American woman who grew up in the same community as the girls she interviewed.[12]

At the same time, my impulse for going native has remained. Simultaneous with our funding for this project, I also received a Fulbright to study the commercial sex industry in Sri Lanka. I was in graduate school when my budding commitment to Sri Lanka began. Through a series of twists of fate, I developed a close friendship with the lone Sri Lankan student in our graduate program, and visited her and her family the semester before I took my comprehensive exams. Though it took six more years to come to fruition, my aspiration from that initial visit was to develop a sustained connection to the country. Research was the opportunity that enabled it to happen, though my commitment has now gone well beyond the research. My husband, his family, and a number of my closest friends are Sri Lankan, and I now spend at least four months a year in residence.

Because of my relationship with the friend from graduate school, I had ready-made social and professional networks upon my arrival in Sri Lanka. I stayed initially with my friend and her family, then shared a flat with her ex-husband, another friend, and his then fiancée, who also (my good fortune) happens to be an anthropologist. They were part of a larger network of friends who socialized together routinely, and this was how I first met my husband. In addition, by this time my graduate school friend was an assistant director at a prominent research organization in Sri Lanka, and she helped me locate research assistants for the project.

Like my previous work, my research on the commercial sex industry primarily involved in-depth interviews. Most of these were completed by members of my research team, but in this case by necessity since I was only beginning to learn the language and my initial funding period was just nine months. However, because I was also a newcomer in an unfamiliar culture, my work more broadly involved participant observation, as well as information gleaned from countless informal conversations and personal experiences.[13]

Without clear planning, my friends and acquaintances became part of my research observations, as did a wide range of experiences more or less tangential to the project itself. For example, whenever talk of my research emerged—at informal and formal gatherings or with my friends in restaurants or bars—the topic routinely drew a raucous response, along with proffered opinions, stories, and anecdotes. Many of them ended up in my field notes. I also spent many hours discussing the project with my flatmate and friend (the anthropologist), and her insights and commentaries made their way into my field notes as well. Countless other experiences provided me with important insights about the cultural contexts, class divisions, and sex and gender politics that ultimately shape the operation of commercial sex in Sri Lanka.[14]

In this way, my research was "real" ethnography to a much greater extent than my previous projects. And again, through my attachments in Sri Lanka, I went—and remain—a little native. My marriage solidified this, but it is also wider reaching than our partnership. The relationships I developed and sustained in Sri Lanka are with individuals I consider among my closest friends. Needless to say, documenting our conversations and my personal experiences left me feeling ill at ease, as though I covertly betrayed my friends by writing about them, even if the stories only remain in my field notes as contextual information. Though I've described the earlier intersections of my research and biography, my work in Sri Lanka brought me closer to the role conflicts and struggles faced by researchers in the field.

On the other hand, there are also many times when I have found the researcher role therapeutic, as a cap I could wear when I need a means of coping with the new, unfamiliar, and threatening. For instance, some time before we were married I spent a summer with my yet-to-be husband on his family estate. He comes from a prominent political family with aristocratic roots. Because Sri Lanka is a more communal culture than the United States, we spend a fair amount of time with his family when I'm in the country. Initially, and especially during that first summer, I found the family's elitism and requisite class hierarchies very difficult to deal with. Although part of this comes from my political beliefs, in large part it was also embedded in my own class background and family roots. Withdrawing into my sociological role, I could step back and analyze the nature of class divisions and upper-class entitlements to cope with my own insecurities. It became an important tool that facilitated the detachment I sometimes needed to keep myself grounded.

One of the concerns traditional ethnographers have with the process of going native is the perceived loss of one's analytic perspective. Another is the possibility that the researcher, having gone native, will fail to return from the field.[15] Although more contemporary ethnography sometimes challenges these premises, my own experiences in Sri Lanka over time offer credence to them, at least for me. Gradually I have assumed much more of a natural attitude toward the culture, with relatively little distance or detachment. It has become familiar enough that most of the time I now take it for granted in my day-to-day life. I find this somewhat problematic because I'm concerned about the impact it will have on my writing and analysis: my ability to experience the culture as fresh and new now emanates from the strength and vividness of my earlier field notes alone.

PARTING THOUGHTS

It's clear from these varied stories that my research has had a tremendous, if reciprocal, effect on my everyday life. Even those of us who typically don't immerse ourselves in the field for long periods of time nonetheless experience many of the same struggles and tensions as we move between identification and detachment. The lines between my research and personal biography have been thoroughly blurred, as my personal and intimate relationships have been intertwined, though in diverse ways, with my research. These interactions have varied from project to project and have shifted with my position and maturation. At the same time that I have tended to immerse myself personally in the milieu I investigate, I have also found at times that getting close can be problematic. Whether it's from feeling agony and helplessness in the face of oppressive circumstances or from my need to address my own insecurities or issues, I have used my research as a coping mechanism. When I need to, it allows me to put up my guard and hide behind the veneer of sociological analysis.

In sum, whereas I can't speak for all of my generation, we have been given a tall order to fill, that is, how to negotiate and make sense of our personal and research commitments within our projects. The point of my chapter has been to point up some of my own struggles with these issues, to illustrate how we, as researchers, try to make sense of the people we study, the nature of research, and our changing selves in the process.

NOTES

1. For an overview, see Patricia A. Adler and Peter Adler, *Membership Roles in Field Research* (Thousand Oaks, Calif.: Sage, 1987).

2. See Conley Dalton, *Honky* (Berkeley: University of California Press, 2000); Susan Krieger, *The Mirror Dance: Identity in a Women's Community* (Philadelphia: Temple University Press, 1983); Carol Rambo Ronai, "The Reflexive Self Through Narrative: A Night in the Life of an Exotic Dancer/Researcher," in *Investigating Subjectivity: Research on Lived Experience*, ed. Carolyn Ellis and Michael G. Flaherty

(Newbury Park, Calif.: Sage, 1992), 100–24. Carol Rambo Ronai, "On Loving and Hating My Mentally Retarded Mother," *Mental Retardation* 35 (1997): 417–32.

3. Adler and Adler, *Membership Roles.*

4. Sandra Harding, ed., *Feminism and Methodology* (Bloomington: Indiana University Press, 1987); Shulamit Reinharz, *Feminist Methods in Social Research* (New York: Oxford University Press, 1992).

5. See Jody Miller, "Gender and Power on the Streets: Street Prostitution in the Era of Crack Cocaine," *Journal of Contemporary Ethnography* 23, 4 (1995): 427–52; and Jody Miller and Martin D. Schwartz, "Rape Myths and Violence Against Street Prostitutes," *Deviant Behavior* 16, 1 (1995): 1–23.

6. Jody Miller, "Researching Violence Against Street Prostitutes: Issues of Epistemology, Methodology and Ethics," in *Researching Sexual Violence Against Women: Methodological and Personal Perspectives*, ed. Martin D. Schwartz (Thousand Oaks, Calif.: Sage, 1997), 144–56.

7. Jody Miller, *One of the Guys: Girls, Gangs and Gender* (New York: Oxford University Press, 2001).

8. See Malcolm W. Klein, *The American Street Gang: Its Nature, Prevalence and Control* (New York: Oxford University Press, 1995).

9. Miller, "Gender and Power," 427–52.

10. See John Lowman and Brian D. MacLean, eds., *Realist Criminology: Crime Control and Policing in the 1990s* (Toronto: University of Toronto Press, 1992).

11. Miller, *One of the Guys*; Jody Miller and Rod K. Brunson, "Gender Dynamics in Youth Gangs: A Comparison of Male and Female Accounts," *Justice Quarterly* 17 (2000): 801–30.

12. Toya Z. Like, Jody Miller, and Norman A. White, "Violence Against Urban African-American Girls" (paper presented at the annual meeting of the American Society of Criminology, San Francisco, Calif., November 2000).

13. See Jody Miller, "The Protection of 'Human Subjects' in Street Ethnography: Ethical and Practical Considerations from a Field Study in Sri Lanka," *Focal* 36 (2000): 53–68 (Special Issue on Contemporary Street Ethnography).

14. Jody Miller, "Violence and Coercion in Sri Lanka's Commercial Sex Industry: Intersections of Gender, Sexuality, Culture, and the Law," *Violence Against Women* 8 (2002): 1045–74.

15. Adler and Adler, *Membership Roles.*

JOSHUA GAMSON

20

PROFESSIONAL REBELLIONS AND

PERSONAL RESEARCHES, OR HOW

I BECAME BORED WITH MYSELF

was never much of a rebel. I was a shy and sometimes angry child, but my tantrums were generally directed at myself or at inanimate objects and only occasionally landed on my parents. As a teenager, when I really ought to have been hating my parents and differentiating myself from them, I found that they did little more than get on my nerves. I would call home if I was going to be late, brush my teeth if I had smoked pot, and get their permission to have a party when they were out of town. I tended to like my room neat, and sometimes I would even tell them what was going on in my life. This was always my style: as a good kid at school and at home, I pretty much got the freedom to do as I liked. Also, my parents had given me little to rebel against. I went to a public alternative high school with my parents' full support, where kids did drugs and carved "HELP" and "FUCK" into their arms and got physical education credit for walking to school. My parents just didn't cramp my style or embarrass me regularly enough for me to disown them, as any normal kid would. And, of course, in the most poignant testimony to my undissident tendencies, I eventually went into the family business.

Still, one finds a way to cope, and I seem to have built my life as an academic on a research agenda of small, covert rebellions springing from the few pleasures frowned upon when I was growing up. Research itself became a means of differentiation—not only that, of course, but at least partly tied up with establishing my own separate identity. What I chose to investigate within sociological research was driven by a quite personal desire to be what I did not think I could be and to do what I did not think I could allow myself. It was, perhaps, a less adolescent, more kindly, and more productive rebellion than I might have had earlier, and it has stood me in good stead. But after a while, if you work at it, any personal process becomes less necessary, more integrated, and increasingly stale. As I head into my second decade as an academic, my research has begun to grow more distant from, impatient with, and uninterested in my personal identity, freeing me for other research pursuits. Not that the rebellions are over; in a sense, they have taken a somewhat different form, migrating from the type of subject matter to the manner of presentation.

As kids, my sister and I had a TV quota of one hour per day—quite liberal, I suspect, in my parents' eyes but a trial for Jenny and me, who regularly sneaked home from Burns Park Elementary to have lunch and watch a clandestine, unclocked hour of "Bewitched." Like many people—especially upper-middle-class intellectuals but also lots of others—my parents believed that television was not a healthy expenditure of time. At best, it was a waste of time that was better spent playing with other kids or being creative or active rather than a passive sponge; at worst, it corrupted and spoiled us, turning us into addicted little consumers who wanted sugar cereal and faddish plastic toys ("no TV toys" was another rule), presenting us with a world that was unsafe and acquisitive and conservative and homogeneous.

I'm quite certain they were right about all that, but still, Saturday morning television was a special, almost magical time for my sister and me, and as we got older we looked forward to the Friday night lineup; even as a teenager, when I was drawn into melodramatic friendships and an active life in a socialist, Zionist youth group, I got great pleasure from watching inferior afterschool specials or "The Mike Douglas Show." I knew it was supposed to be bad for me, and I would never let it get in the way of homework. I knew I was supposed to be playing ball or making pottery or writing stories, and sometimes I did those things, too. But there was something there, some pleasure that no one around me seemed to want to understand.

Later in life, this became a sort of research agenda. My academic research gave me permission to try to understand television and its culture and, perhaps just as important, to revel in it without guilt. From my dissertation onward, I made it my business to watch television and to study some of its inner workings. So much for the hour-a-day limit: I'm a professional now. My friends joke that I watch television for a living, and they are not entirely wrong; every video rental is a tax write-off.

But this research-as-personal-rebellion was about more than the freedom to do something I'd been denied or about getting away with something. It emerged from a genuine curiosity about a medium that was discounted and disallowed when I was growing up. My dissertation about celebrity culture, for instance, which became the book *Claims to Fame*,[1] arose from the disconcerting contrast between my life as a graduate student, studying Durkheim and feminism and metamethodology, and my life at home in Oakland, in which to relax I watched "Entertainment Tonight," stocking up on empty tidbits about stars and reveling in the depressing cheeriness of hostess Mary Hart. I was determined to bring them together, to let my personal taste for celebrity culture inform and be informed by my doctorate in sociology, however silly that might seem to others.

Years later, I came up with my next book idea while watching "The Ricki Lake Show"—intrigued and entertained by a show about people who didn't want their kids to be around gay people, when I knew that, according to most academic and intellectual culture, I ought to be disgusted or at least bored. *Freaks Talk Back*[2] was, on some level, an attempt to make sense of the pleasures—voyeurism, identification, politics, and emotions—that "trashy" television was offering and to challenge those who had been dismissing such pleasures, my pleasures. This was a research agenda that took the discomfiting cultural status of television for granted, that assumed that American popular culture was commercially driven and more often than not crass and derivative and stupid, but that refused to deny its pleasures. I wanted to study not just as a distant critic, suspicious or scolding, but also as a participant, as me. The pleasures of life in a TV-driven culture, in fact, became the big question mark in my research (not only, of course, in *my* research: this was just at the time that many other academics, especially of my generation, were vigorously treating popular culture as a legitimate academic subject).[3]

My dissertation arose from the parental voice that dominates much of media studies and intellectual culture: in the TV age, image has replaced substance, manufactured personality has replaced achievement, false idols have edged out real heroes, and those who invest in celebrities are investing in falsehoods, superficialities, and artificial personae.[4] That is the voice, annoying in its knowing tone and in its dismissive attitude toward the people who spend time and energy in engaging with celebrity culture. What it seemed to miss, and what became the driving force of the research, was the possibility that people enjoy celebrities, even *with* the knowledge that fame is in large part artificially generated, that images are manufactured, that the celebrity culture involves playing with surfaces, and so on. "The space celebrities occupy," I wrote then, "is not necessarily weighty." The challenge, I thought, "was to mine the superficialities for their depths."[5] Much of my energy was directed toward getting inside the point of view of celebrity watchers; I spent time with them, observed them, talked to them, and wrote about them, with the full knowledge that I was—at least, part of me was—one of them and that none of us would be understood by being dismissed.

Similarly, when I began my research on TV talk shows, for the book *Freaks Talk Back*, I started from the recognition that daytime TV talk shows exploit and commodify the personal troubles of their often vulnerable and marginalized guests, making money off of often horrifying disclosures.[6] But that, I argued, was the easy part.

Exploitation thus ought to be the starting point for analysis and not, as it so often is, its conclusion. The puzzling thing is not the logic of commercial television, which is well documented, well understood, and extremely powerful, but why so many people, many of them fully aware of what's expected of them on a talk show, make the deal.[7]

Although I had no interest in defending the grotesque aspects of talk shows or in exaggerating their democratic potential, neither was I interested in simply documenting how bad they are for everyone. In fact, as in my earlier work, I wanted to understand the genre not just by examining its production routines but also by talking to and observing people who enjoyed it, to get some purchase on the stirrings I felt while watching "Ricki Lake." Here again was my small rebellion: I wanted to understand, from the inside, the pleasures in a popular culture I had been reared to see as distasteful, generating pleasures in only wrong, even dangerous ways.

My sister used to dress me up in drag sometimes, and we both enjoyed it. We'd use clip-on earrings, put my longish hair in ponytails, add a little bit of lipstick, and I'd wear a pair of my mother's big shoes and use a skirt as a dress. We laughed, and thought nothing of it; it was another game, and playing was always a decent alternative to fighting. But it didn't take long for me to figure out that anything "girlish"—anything that implied that a boy could be like a girl in his demeanor, activities, and worst of all in who he might want to marry—was unacceptable, even punishable, in me or any other boy,[8] and the fun drained out of dress-up games. Unsurprisingly, my own family took on and promoted the larger society's normative vision of children's gender roles. This being the 1960s and 1970s and this being a liberal, academic family, gender equality was certainly a strong norm; this being my family, there was plenty of love coming at me. But the limits were nonetheless clear: for a boy to display any femininity was embarrassing and might lead to a later life as some sort of odd, lonely creature. I was at risk, bearing quite a few of the sissy's markings. When other boys were avoiding their cooties, I liked the company of girls. I was a terrible athlete and very "sensitive," mostly meaning that I cried easily. I thought I might want to be an actor.

Like most kids, I accepted these gender notions as the natural order and did what I could to hide any anomalies or compensate for them: my avoidance of fist fights became an ideology of "pacifism," my atypical interests were camouflaged by "open classrooms," and my weakness at sports was offset a bit by my strengths as a student. Later, as I grew into a teenager and social skills replaced athletic ones in the peer-respect department, I reveled in my normality, enjoying my crushes on girls and my tight, ribbing friendships with boys. In fact, in addition to girlfriends, I had close, almost romantic relationships with boys, but the idea of gayness seemed remote and distasteful, the worst extension of the sissyhood I'd successfully erased. It's a familiar story, if a sad one: part of being a good boy, of not rebelling and staying lovable, was being a straight one.

It is no coincidence that my becoming gay and going to graduate school were coterminous: once again, research became my means of opposing some of the messages of my childhood. I was not much of a statistician, but for my statistics class I managed to write an effective analysis of the effects of education and what I called "family embeddedness" on attitudes toward homosexuality. The next year, I used a participant-observation research class as a chance to work with and study AIDS activists in San Francisco—solidifying my personal identity by putting me into contact with unapologetic, politically committed, happy gay people and jump-starting my academic identity by giving me my first publication.[9] I used my own personal identity as a point of entry: I wrote about the tension between "queer" deconstructionism and "gay and lesbian" identity construction, and about how that same tension played out in lesbian and gay film festivals; I researched boundary disputes at a lesbian-feminist music festival and in an international gay and lesbian rights organization. So much for the boy who couldn't be gay: I'm a professional now.

My research in sexualities was partly a safe, legitimate way to test out a new identity and make new friends and partly a means of announcing my own difference under occupational cover. As I wrote at the beginning of

Freaks Talk Back, "I identify with the misfits, monsters, trash, and perverts," and I became interested in research that adopted and emerged from the perspective of the stigmatized; I was, I announced, both "scholarman" and "gayman."[10] My academic work took as its starting point exactly what was missing from my earlier life: a matter-of-fact acceptance of the existence of gay people, an interest in the politics of stigma, and a respect for the courage of sissies and tomboys.

But it was also more than that. In the work that followed—in several articles about collective identity that used lesbian and gay movements as their touchstone case—I took as my research subject the construction of the norms that created such trouble for me as a child. My research was driven by a desire not just to reject those norms but also to understand their creation and their power; how people came to be excluded and marginalized on their basis; and most of all, how people went about making resistant identities around them. I wanted to understand how individuals, and especially movements, went about challenging stigma while also making claims to membership in a human family; I wanted to analyze the conditions (organizational, political, and economic) that shaped the kinds of sexual identities available to be tried on.[11] This stream of my research circled around the tension I had always felt: between the desire to belong and to rebel, to expose and challenge the stigmatizing framework and to live comfortably within it, to pass and to rage.

After a while, I suppose, I just got bored with myself. Over the past few years, the residual questions from childhood and adolescence started to lose their power. In part, this is because I had the good fortune to come of academic age in a period when both loving popular culture and loving people of the same sex have become more acceptable, sometimes even fashionable, inside and outside of the academy. In part, it is because studying something can be a killjoy and, in part, because I have been a grownup for a while. In part, it is because, by researching areas and activities that were stigmatized, I have, at least for myself, removed their stigma; by doing research that delineated and helped me claim my own identity—as a pop culture hound and as a gay guy— I have made that identity increasingly clear and unremarkable, to myself and most likely to others. The identities have settled in partly because I have researched many of its aspects, and through research I have made room for and understood many of the pleasures once denied or disdained.

My research has therefore started to shift and meander recently, into areas only tangentially related to my own identity. Whereas I earlier considered how gay and lesbian collective identity develops in response to the scandal of homosexuality, I have more recently tried to understand the political and social significance of heterosexual sex scandals, finding in them not so much reminders of the normative sexual order and the costs of transgression but "institutional morality tales" that call attention to institutional decay.[12] Whereas earlier I researched how celebrity watchers got their pleasurable meanings from stars and how talk show watchers made sense of tabloid programming, now I am studying how ownership patterns in various minority media—gay and lesbian media among them—affect patterns of content, especially the range of voices, images, and political viewpoints available. Having solidified my identity through my research, I have now let go of myself a bit. The intellectual interests remain—sexual boundary making, cultural politics, and the impact of media—but they no longer serve as covert rebellions.

Perhaps as a result, my research seems to be getting more conventional in its focus: heterosexuality and media structures. Yet the end result of the earlier, identity-driven period of my research seems also to have been a gradual coming to voice. Despite all the personal roots of my earlier research agendas, or maybe because of those roots, I wrote myself out of much of my earlier work. I was somewhat absent in the articles, hard to hear in any way other than the conventional, institutional, distanced voice of scholarly authority; the more out-there the topic, the more in-there the expression. Much of that is simply a function of the discipline inherent in academic publishing, but much of it was also a choice: to insert my bent ideas into straight journals, to think publicly and unapologetically about TV culture and queerness and the like, and to get people who might find those topics unworthy to listen to me; a distinctive voice sometimes seems a necessary sacrifice.

Oddly, as my research is becoming less focused on me, my voice is becoming more my own, and my cautious, good-boy rebelliousness has not so much disappeared as migrated from research to writing; it is less about examining discrediting topics and more about hearing myself and making myself heard in an environment that at every turn seems to want to quiet that voice, to tame it, to discipline it. Perhaps that means that, through my work, I have learned to become a self-possessed adult. Or perhaps I have just learned to love my inner brat.

NOTES

1. Joshua Gamson, *Claims to Fame: Celebrity in Contemporary America* (Berkeley: University of California Press, 1994).

2. Joshua Gamson, *Freaks Talk Back: Tabloid Talk Shows and Sexual Nonconformity* (Chicago: University of Chicago Press, 1998).

3. Michael Schudson, "The New Validation of Popular Culture," in *Critical Perspectives on Media and Society*, ed. Robert Avery and David Eason (New York: Guilford, 1991).

4. See, for example, Daniel Boorstin, *The Image: A Guide to Pseudo-Events in America* (New York: Harper & Row, 1961); Neil Postman, *Amusing Ourselves to Death* (New York: Viking, 1986).

5. Gamson, *Claims to Fame*, 6.

6. See, for example, Jeanne Albronda Heaton and Nona Leigh Wilson, *Tuning in Trouble* (San Francisco: Jossey-Bass, 1995); and Howard Kurtz, *Hot Air: All Talk, All the Time* (New York: Times Books, 1996).

7. Gamson, *Freaks Talk Back*, 7.

8. See Matthew Rottnek, ed., *Sissies and Tomboys: Gender Nonconformity and Homosexual Childhood* (New York: New York University Press, 1999).

9. Joshua Gamson, "Silence, Death and the Invisible Enemy: AIDS Activism and Social Movement 'Newness,'" *Social Problems* 36, 4 (1989).

10. Gamson, *Freaks Talk Back*, 4, 26.

11. Joshua Gamson, "Messages of Exclusion: Gender, Movements, and Symbolic Boundaries," *Gender & Society* 11 (1997):178–99; Joshua Gamson, "The Organizational Shaping of Collective Identity: The Case of Lesbian and Gay Film Festivals in New York," *Sociological Forum* 11 (1996): 231–62; Joshua Gamson, "Must Identity Movements Self-Destruct? A Queer Dilemma," *Social Problems* 42 (1995): 390–407.

12. Joshua Gamson, "Jessica Hahn, Media Whore: Sex Scandal Icons and Female Publicity," *Critical Studies in Media Communication* 18, 2 (2001); Joshua Gamson, "Normal Sins: Sex Scandal Narratives as Institutional Morality Tales," *Social Problems* 48, 2 (2001).

SHULAMIT REINHARZ

THE BODY OF KNOWLEDGE

21

In this chapter, I focus on several slippery questions: what is knowledge? Where does it come from? How do we recognize it? I consider these questions by describing two research projects, which were unusual from the start. They happened to me; I did not choose to do them. They began fortuitously, without warning, without plan. They began deep within my psyche and body because they dealt with silence, with missing pieces, with what is not there. They proceeded by making the missing visible; they ended by breaking the silence and reshaping what we know.

MISCARRIAGE

Unexpectedly, I had a miscarriage at four months of gestation age in my first pregnancy. And similarly unexpectedly, this experience became an excellent topic through which to explore the sociology of knowledge. I underwent a miscarriage in 1973 when I was a twenty-six-year-old woman, already married for five years. My pregnancy was desired and planned. But despite the fact that I was an advanced graduate student at the time and, ostensibly, was also a generally well-informed individual, I soon discovered that I knew very little about pregnancy. It turns out that pregnancy was not something people learned about in school at the time. The only direct education I had received about pregnancy was probably in the fifth grade (in 1956) when I viewed the well-known Disney film about a large smiling egg and puppylike sperm, wagging their happy tails as they swam toward each other in an unnamed river.

I believe the actual purpose of the film was to inform young girls that they would be menstruating soon. (Perhaps the related purpose was to sell a particular feminine hygiene product.) My memory of the film is hazy, but I am certain the egg-sperm encounter did not end in a miscarriage. I would be willing to bet that it ended in a baby. The film, therefore, distorted knowledge by creating a seemingly causal link between "pregnancy" and "baby" rather than supplying the more objective information that approximately 25% of pregnancies end in miscarriage and some end in abortion. Information was being distorted through omission. (I also don't believe there was any information about how the sperm got into the river in the first place.)

Let us jump forward to graduate school in Massachusetts, where at the time (1967) only married women could obtain contraceptives, which were a controlled substance. In this context, I wondered how poor, unmarried women dealt with the problem of access. To explore this question, I located a public hospital that allowed me to conduct a small study about how women made decisions about which forms of contraceptive to use. To obtain their pills, diaphragm, or IUD (interuterine device), women were required to attend a class in which a nurse taught them about their anatomy and explained how the various types of contraceptives worked.[1]

The level of ignorance among the women in these classes—even those who were mothers—was extraordinary to me. Very few differentiated between the stomach and the uterus. Some did not know about the existence of the vagina and thought that their anatomy consisted of a rectum and urethra. Women in the classes I observed knew very little about "where babies came from." By contrast, I felt knowledgeable. Socioeconomic class seemed more significant than experience. In fact, observing these women artificially augmented my belief that I was informed.

At that time, the women's movement organized and heralded informal groups in which women encouraged one another to examine their cervix. I thought that was a silly and embarrassing enterprise, although I actually did not know what my cervix—or anyone else's for that matter—looked like. Why would anyone be interested in seeing her cervix? Because I assumed that I knew much more than I actually did, I did not join such a group. My rude awakening was yet to occur.

I knew nothing whatsoever about miscarriages and did not understand what was happening to me when, a few years later (1973), I had one. Suffering from pain, confusion, and disappointment, I wrote a lengthy, angry essay (for whom?) about the miscarriage experience in the weeks after it occurred. But when friends discouraged me from trying to publish the article because it was "too raw," I put it away in my desk drawer and forgot about it.

Unconsciously, I am sure I continued to deal with the miscarriage despite my surface forgetting. During the three following years, I did not try or want to become pregnant. Finally, in 1976, I gave birth to our first daughter; the ensuing planned gap of a few years was followed by the birth of our second daughter in 1981. Two years after my second child was born, a psychologist invited me to contribute an article to a journal she was editing, an issue devoted to "topics of special concern to women." I mentioned the invitation to my husband and told him I had to decline because I didn't have anything to offer at the time. He then reminded me about the "paper in your drawer," which had been there for ten years. Apparently, he, too, had been thinking about it (knowingly or not).

Having the peace of mind that comes from actually giving birth to children, I brought the paper back into my awareness (gave birth to it) and decided to pursue work on studies of miscarriage (as well as supervising students working on the topic). I framed my studies within sociological theory, starting with an analysis of my own experience. I determined that the most interesting element of a miscarriage from a sociological perspective is *how it is explained*. What is the definition of the situation? How is a miscarriage framed? Is it an important or unimportant phenomenon? Is it a medical or nonmedical issue? What is the woman's or doctor's role? Do various cultures have diverse miscarriage theories and rituals? Are there policy implications?

Following my own experiential analysis, I tried to understand another woman's experience deeply and thus did a social-psychological study of a published case.[2] Then I collected miscarriage information from around the world and formed a series of categories into which the different cultures fell.[3] Next I did a secondary analysis of someone else's data that she had collected for a study of infertility. This particular project involved a content analysis and contrast of the woman's and the doctor's explanations of why the miscarriage occurred.

The women's movement has probably *impeded* the study of miscarriage in two ways. First, feminist sociologists have not studied the body to a large extent, in part because we prefer the social constructionist, rather than the biological-essentialist, definition of femaleness.[4] Second, because feminists are concerned with the rights of women, we typically are adamantly pro-choice. Therefore, the study of miscarriage can create confounding problems of the definition of a fetus. What exactly is a woman mourning when she mourns her loss from a miscarriage? What status does the miscarried entity have in society? In terms of impact on sociology, it gave me pleasure when my work was highlighted in the sociology textbook edited by Beth Hess et al.[5] The growing interest in the sociology of the body is a welcome change in the field of sociology.

I have received many requests for reprints and have distributed my work to large numbers of women who have had miscarriages. My work has been condensed in textbooks. Although I doubt that I have had an impact on the field of sociology through this work, I may have helped focus attention on the body as a known or confusing part of self. My study of miscarriage was prompted by ignorance of my own bodily changes and my assumption that other women were ignorant as well. I was left with this question: what does it take to make a change in public understanding of this phenomenon? Can it be changed at all? My overall framework was that something is missing when we talk about women: sociologists are unaware of how people understand their own bodies; sociologists miss the fact that there are various outcomes to a pregnancy, and they also miss the way in which human understanding is deeply linked to bodily experiences.

FINDING HEROINES

The second set of projects deals with finding heroines. Again, these projects stemmed from and culminated in my belief that the lack of necessary information led to a great deal of ignorance and misunderstanding. What is missing is positive female role models and acknowledgment that they exist—all we have to do is find them, understand them, and integrate that knowledge into a reconceptualization of history, including the history of sociology. The same was true for miscarriages: they obviously exist; all we have to do is recognize them, name them, and integrate that knowledge into a reconceptualization of pregnancy and childbirth.

I do not remember seeking heroines when I was a child, perhaps because I had my own heroic parents to consider. Their sparse but harrowing accounts of surviving the Holocaust made them larger than life for me.[6] Beyond childhood, as a sexually maturing prefeminist, American, Jewish, suburban teenager, I found my heroes in handsome Israeli men (based on the fictional Ari Ben Canaan of Leon Uris's *Exodus*), builders of a new society infused with positive values. Growing up in a town with few Jews, I assumed that this fantasy was completely original. I also used it as a way of resisting the cultural oppression of the Ozzie and Harriet image that saturated the mass media[7] and for forging an image as an "interesting hippie."

Much to my chagrin, I have discovered lately that as teenagers many now middle-aged, American, Jewish women had a crush on Ari Ben Canaan, that is, Paul Newman, one of the few known Jewish movie stars, just as I did. I believe this can be explained in part as an escape from the mundane family image of the 1950s and 1960s, but it also represents a new image of Jewish machoism. These were the days before female heroines with actual accomplishments. The only female "heroines" of the time were advertising icons with perfect bodies.[8] My infatuation, however, encompassed more than Ari and extended to fantasized Israeli males. But even this was not original.

Recently I found a literary reference to this American, Jewish, female adolescent crush. The following paragraph jumped out of the pages of Anne Roiphe's autobiography, *1185 Park Avenue*, referring to her teenage years:

> All that spring I spend hours in the Metropolitan Museum of Art. I am not looking at the paintings, which are fine enough, but not what I am seeking. I had decided that if I were an Israeli soldier on leave I might come to New York and go to the museum and walking the halls and feeling lonely, I might be happy to meet an American girl. It occurred to me that such a soldier, a veteran of '48, a fighter pilot perhaps, might ask me to be his wife and take me to Israel with him and I would grow tomatoes in the desert and drive a tractor. I already know how to steer a speedboat. I walk the halls of the museum and sit on the benches in all the galleries but I never meet an Israeli soldier. In fact no one talks to me.[9]

Now, as a sociologist, I understand that even my fantasies were not uniquely mine but instead reflected a social pattern.

In college (1963–67) I admired a few professors, particularly the mysteriously European Mirra Komarovsky (about whom I have since written biographical pieces).[10] Her intriguing appearance and mannerisms, her control over the material, her ability to bridge both worlds, and her intelligence drew me into the field of sociology.[11] As I grew older still and became involved with the women's movement and feminism, I took a critical new look at the issue of *women's place* in the arenas about which I had fantasized—Israel, professors, sociology. Fantasies were no longer enough. Now I was able to ask hard questions. How good is sociology? What about the women in Zionist history: where are they? And for that matter, where are the women in sociology? Who gets to be a professor, and why?

It was not easy to find information about women in the history of Israel at that time and even today.[12] The positive macho image I referred to earlier I now understand differently. The valorization of the Israeli male has the negative, unintended consequence of squelching recognition of the role that women play in Zionist and Israeli history. Fortunately, in the course of my search (as a thirty-five-year-old) for an inspirational and actual Israeli woman, in contrast to my crush (as a fifteen-year-old) on a fictional Israeli man, I came across an encyclopedia article.[13] Of course, one never "comes across" anything; one finds what one is looking for. This short encyclopedia entry mentioned a woman who had a role in establishing an early kibbutz.

This extraordinary tidbit propelled me into a many-year study of the life of Manya Wilbushewitz Shohat (the woman) and a consideration of the sociological theories that her actions imply. It also led me to reevaluate standard stories. Why and how are they created and sustained? The questions about the sociology of knowledge continued to intrigue me. In this case, the standard story held that a group of men had created the first kibbutz, named Degania, in 1909.[14] Stemming from this, there were two other standard and yet conflicting stories. The popular, romanticized view was that the kibbutz promoted and realized gender equality.[15] The scholarly view was that women had a hard time being accepted in kibbutzim,[16] and even when they were accepted, they were relegated to traditional female roles.[17] The two images were of "women and men plowing the fields together" or "no woman need apply unless interested in tending babies and cooking for the men." Was the glass half full or nearly empty?

Advocates of the opposing views argued with one another, but no one thought to ask this question: was Degania actually the first kibbutz? I decided to look into this area and found that Russian-born Manya Wilbushewitz Shohat had a major role in conceptualizing the kibbutz idea. Moreover, she implemented it as a gender-balanced and gender-equitable entity and then saw it dissolve into a different kind of structure over time. Beginning with my reading of an essay she published in a collection entitled *The Plough Woman*,[18] I was determined to find out as much about her as I could.

My research into Shohat, begun in 1981, continues to this day. I have published numerous articles, magazine essays, and book chapters about her.[19] In one of the first, I claimed that there are five sociological reasons that Manya is not remembered:

1. She did not form an organization that might have devoted itself to sustaining her memory.
2. She did so many important things in her lifetime that she is difficult to characterize and is not given due credit for any one thing in particular.
3. She did not write a book about herself.
4. She was married to a man who was famous in his own right.
5. She advocated some very unpopular beliefs.

These sociological insights have enabled me to understand other women in history and have led to my research on the history of women in sociology.[20] Studying Manya became an avenue for the study of the sociology of knowledge: why are certain things, people, and ideas remembered and others not?

The strong claim I made in the first article I wrote about Shohat propelled me into discussions with historians and social scientists who believed that she should *not* be given the credit for creating the first kibbutz. This, in turn, led me to an analysis *of what constitutes a priority claim.* From a sociological perspective, my work on Shohat has enabled me to understand something about the production of fame and the definition of theory. Manya Wilbushewitz Shohat created theory in action and communicated her ideas primarily through correspondence. Her nonscholarly means (action and correspondence) stood in the way of her achieving the ends that I believe were warranted, that is, being recognized as a theorist. Finding Shohat enabled me to grasp that things are not as they seem, that history is a social construction, and that everyday theories can be entirely wrong.

A few years later my question moved from the history of the kibbutz, to, rather, the social forces at work in producing my understanding of the history of sociology. Was there another history waiting to be discovered?

In 1985, I began a series of studies into the missing women in the history of sociology, uncovering first Harriet Martineau, then Jane Addams, Fay Karpf, and many, many more. Working side by side with, although hundreds of miles away from, Mary Jo Deegan and the handful of people interested in this topic, we taught courses, engaged students, and believed we were turning sociology inside out by bringing in new voices—voices of women, racial minorities, sexual minorities, disabled people, and more. Many of these people, like Shohat, had been written out of history for the same sociological reasons that apply in her case. Not only did many articles flow from my passion for this topic, but also the ideas infused my writing about other topics, such as feminist research methods.[21] Although I have experienced a lot of pleasure in re-learning and reconstructing the history of sociology, I am also profoundly frustrated.

Feeling like Cassandra,[22] who has insights that no one recognizes, I do not believe that the work that I and others have done has changed people's understanding about sociological history—for example, the relative significance of Martineau and Comte, of Martineau and de Toqueville, of Martineau and Durkheim, of Addams and Park, of Wells, and of so many more.

CONCLUSION

Learning about women's role in history, and then trying to set the record straight, is not the end of the process but rather one step of the journey. How many other types of voices are not heard? How many other bodily experiences are not tapped for the rich insight they can provide in understanding society? A sociologist is trained to be attentive to societal patterns, and that attentiveness can start from his or her own body. Clearly, bodies are shaped by society, and they shape society as well. The societal and commercial interests in the outcomes of pregnancies can lead to distorted understanding of one's own experience, which in turn can produce serious self-abnegation. Although ignorance about my miscarriage made me feel less than fully human and female, my repeated "heroine discovery experiences," by contrast, increased my sense of efficacy and female competence. And, ultimately, my training as a sociologist enabled me to make sense of both.

NOTES

1. As a newly married woman, I'm sure I was motivated in part by my own desire for such information. *Our Bodies, Ourselves* had not yet been published, and many young women, including myself, had little information about their bodies; Boston Women's Health Book Collective, ed., *Our Bodies, Ourselves: A Book by and for Women* (New York: Simon and Schuster, 1973).

2. Shulamit Reinharz, "The Social Psychology of a Miscarriage: An Application of Symbolic Interactionist Theory and Method," in *Women and Symbolic Interaction*, ed. Mary Jo Deegan and Michael Hill (New York: Allen and Unwin, 1987), 229–50.

3. Shulamit Reinharz, "Controlling Women's Lives: A Cross-Cultural Interpretation of Miscarriage Accounts," in *Research in the Sociology of Health Care*, vol. 7, ed. Dorothy Wertz (Greenwich, Conn.: JAI Press, 1988), 2–37.

4. Shulamit Reinharz, "What's Missing in Miscarriage?" *Journal of Community Psychology* 16, 1 (1988): 84–103.

5. Shulamit Reinharz, "The Study of Miscarriage," in *Sociology*, 3rd ed., ed. Beth Hess, Elizabeth Markson, and Peter Stein (New York: Macmillan, 1992).

6. In my frequent queries of students about who their heroes and heroines are, they, too, almost invariably mention their parents.

7. Susan J. Douglas, *Where the Girls Are: Growing Up Female with the Mass Media* (New York: Random House, 1994).

8. Wini Breiners, *Young, White and Miserable: Growing Up Female in the Fifties* (Boston: Beacon Press, 1992).

9. Anne Roiphe, *1185 Park Avenue* (New York: Free Press, 1999), 179.

10. Shulamit Reinharz, "Finding Her Sociological Voice: The Work of Mirra Komarovsky," *Sociological Inquiry* 59, 4 (1989): 374–95.

11. I took courses at Columbia with Amitai Etzioni simply because he was an Israeli, and I took courses with Susan Sontag simply because she was a "cool woman."

12. In 1997, I created the Hadassah International Research Institute on Jewish Women at Brandeis University. The second conference we organized was entitled "We Were There Too—Women Who Founded the State of Israel," a conference held in Jerusalem and the first one of its kind.

13. Shulamit Reinharz, "Feminist Biography: The Pains, the Joys, the Dilemmas," in *Exploring Identity and Gender: The Narrative Study of Lives*, vol. 2, ed. Amia Lieblich and Ruthellen Josselson (Beverly Hills, Calif.: Sage, 1994), 37–82.

14. Joseph Baratz, *A Village by the Jordan: The Story of Degania* (Tel Aviv, Israel: Press Department, Ichud Habonim, 1960).

15. See such works as Darin-Drabkin, *The Other Society* (London: Gollancz, 1962), 116–17.

16. Marilyn Safir, *Calling the Equality Bluff: Women in Israel* (New York: Teachers College Press, 1993).

17. Natalie Rein, *Daughters of Rachel: Women in Israel* (New York: Penguin, 1979).

18. Manya Wilbushewitz Shohat, *The Plough Woman*, ed. Mark Raider and Miriam Raider, Hadassah International Research Institute on Jewish Women (Hanover, N.H.: University Press of New England, [1934] 2001).

19. Shulamit Reinharz and J. Reinharz, eds., *Manya Wilbushewitz Shohat: A Critical Collection of Her Writings* (Jerusalem: Yad Ben Zvi, 2003) (in Hebrew); Shulamit Reinharz, "Toward a Model of Female Political Action: The Case of Manya Shohat, Founder of the First *Kibbutz*," *Women's Studies International Forum* 7, 4 (1984): 275–87; Shulamit Reinharz, "Manya Wilbushewitz-Shohat and the Winding Road to Sejera," in *Pioneers and Homemakers in Pre-State Israel*, ed. Deborah Bernstein (Albany, State University of New York Press, 1992), 95–118; Shulamit Reinharz, "Our (Forgotten) Foremother: Manya Shohat (1880–1961)," *Lilith* (Fall 1995): 28–33; Shulamit Reinharz, "Manya Wilbushewitz Shohat," in *Lines of Fire: Women Writers of World War I*, ed. Margaret R. Higgonet (New York: Penguin, 1999).

20. Shulamit Reinharz, "Feminist Distrust: Problems of Context and Content in Sociological Work," in *Exploring Clinical Methods for Social Research*, ed. David Berg and Ken Smith (Beverly Hills, Calif.: Sage, 1985), 153–72; Shulamit Reinharz, "Patriarchal Pontifications," *Transaction/SOCIETY* 23 (September/October 1986): 23–39.

21. Shulamit Reinharz, *Feminist Methods in Social Research* (New York and London: Oxford University Press, 1992).

22. Not only is Cassandra a figure in Greek mythology, her name is also the title of a book by Florence Nightingale, one of the first social scientists to use statistics and graphs.

VERTA TAYLOR

22

MY LIFE IN SOCIAL MOVEMENTS

FROM 1960s ACTIVIST

TO LESBIAN DEN MOTHER

Some things in which I take a great deal of pride are not on my curriculum vitae: that I am the first person in my family to graduate from college, that I was almost kicked out of school for my campus activism in the 1960s, and that a lesbian colleague tells me that I am known as the "lesbian den mother of sociology" for my mentoring of lesbian students and junior scholars. What is there in black and white is that I am a scholar of social movements, especially the women's and gay/lesbian movements. As the unlisted items suggest, my participation in social movements has been both bad and good for my career in academia. But despite the occasional negative effect, what is most important is that my participation in social movements has profoundly shaped—and enriched—what I write and teach.

I grew up in Jonesboro, Arkansas, not far from Memphis—John Grisham country. My father was an elected county official when the civil rights movement was changing the face of the South. The overt racism of the American South was one of the major reasons I decided to leave home to attend college. I vividly recall one of my first introductions to social movements in high school. My boyfriend and I had driven to Memphis to see Sidney Poitier in the film *Guess Who's Coming to Dinner*. We arrived early to find several hundred hooded Klansmen, burning a cross outside the theater in protest of the fact that the movie portrayed a kiss between a black man and white woman.

Leaving home to go to college was not part of my family's pattern. Because my father had already suffered a major heart attack when I graduated from high school and because we had limited financial resources, the farthest away I could manage to get was Terre Haute, Indiana, a (long) day's drive. At Indiana State University, I quickly threw myself into student activism. In what should be, but generally is not, considered an early form of feminist protest, I led a demonstration against the differential rules for women and men in the residence halls. The campus paper and FBI (Federal Bureau of Investigation) reports featured us, in bathrobes and hair rollers, walking out of the dorms at 11:00 P.M., drawing thousands of additional protesters as we marched to the university quadrangle. But it was my involvement in the antiwar and black student movement that got me in the most trouble. My membership in Students for a Democratic Society made me the target of frequent questioning by campus authorities, and I barely managed to escape suspension because of my involvement with an organization of black students who took over the university administration building to protest racial discrimination on the campus.

That involvement also helped me win a fellowship to graduate school at Ohio State. The late Clyde Franklin, then a new, young assistant professor, assigned the task of recruiting minority students, had grown up in an all-black town—Birdsong, near Jonesboro. Between my name (Verta, my grandmother's name, is more typically African American) and my involvement with the black student protests, Clyde was sure I was black. Only after offering me the fellowship did he ask and find out that I'm not. They substituted another fellowship for which I qualified, and when we became colleagues, Clyde and I always laughed about the story.

More important, my involvement in these causes awakened my sociological interest in social movements and helped to form my conviction that individuals have the capacity to help shape their own identities and destinies and to transform society through social movements. This has been the backbone of my research and teaching on women's movements; lesbian feminism; and the gay, lesbian, bisexual, and transgender movement. To show the way that individuality is integral to social science insight,[1] I relate here the interplay between my personal experiences and the structural and political constraints and opportunities that have influenced my academic career by considering my research on several different social movement projects.

I met my life partner and frequent coauthor, historian Leila Rupp, in 1978. We were both young assistant professors associated with our developing women's studies program, and Leila was looking for a sociologist trained in qualitative interview techniques[2] to collaborate on a historical project on the women's movement. I now look back at this chance meeting not only as the most profoundly important moment in my personal life but also as a significant turning point in my professional career. Working with Leila, a women's historian, was compatible with my own preference for qualitative methods that result in the development of situated knowledge located in a particular time and space.[3] It also provided much needed support for the use of postpositivist methodologies, such as feminist research methods, making it possible for me to survive the strong pressures toward quantification and scientific precision, and thus away from contextualized knowledge and qualitative research, that began to dominate the culture of the sociology department at Ohio State University in the mid-1980s.[4]

Leila and I have written elsewhere about the experience of being lesbians and feminists and researching the women's movement, in which lesbians have long played a central but sometimes closeted role.[5] In our first joint project, we researched the women's rights movement in the United States from 1945 to the 1960s, a period we characterized in our book as "the doldrums."[6] As feminists, we suspected that women who had struggled during World War II for what they called full citizenship had not been converted or overwhelmed by the "feminine mystique" in the 1950s. Still, we did not set out to prove that a women's rights movement existed, although we found one. It was not the kind of movement that we were necessarily eager to claim. It was a small movement of elite women, primarily white, middle or upper class, well educated and professional, who had developed a commitment to feminism in the early decades of the twentieth century. They did not try to mobilize diverse groups of women, nor did they seek alliances with other movements for social change. They developed strategies and pursued goals consistent with their interests and the structure of their movement. In an article based on this research, I call this an abeyance phase and elaborated the ways in which social movements can survive in hostile environments.[7]

As feminists involved in the movement as we researched material for the book, we struggled with the question of how to characterize this phase of activism. In sympathy with the critique of the race, class, and cultural bias of a movement that defines only a limited set of goals—those that have traditionally been defined by the interests of white, middle-class, Christian women—and as appropriate for a movement focusing on gender inequality, we were reluctant to call this *the* women's movement. But rather than explore what all sorts of women were doing to improve their situations, we decided to stick to women's own self-identification in defining the boundaries of their movements and to point out the ways in which the movements' class, race, and ethnic composition shaped their definitions of interests and goals, recruitment strategies, levels of commitment, and mobilized resources.

Our research revealed that the women's rights movement was able to survive and feminists were able to sustain their commitment to feminism by building a supportive community that valued feminist analysis, required high levels of commitment, was held together by intimate personal relationships, and was based to a large extent on ties from the days of the suffrage struggle. All of these characteristics helped to create a close-knit world in which participation in the campaigns for women's rights were possible, but they also meant that women not already drawn to the feminist cause would be unlikely to be recruited to the movement. In other words, organizational maintenance worked against mass mobilization.

Women's relationships, we came to believe, played a critical role in holding the movement together, as well as in limiting recruitment to a homogeneous group of women. Women formed a variety of bonds, from friendships to mother-daughter or sororal relationships to couple relationships. In considering the last, the question of lesbianism arose. In the papers of organizations and individuals, we found evidence of women who lived together in marriage-like relationships and formed communities with similar couples. Other evidence suggested that at least some members viewed some relationships between women, not always sympathetically, as lesbian or lesbian-like.

We grappled with the question of whether or not some of these women were lesbians, and also with whether or not it mattered. None, as far as we knew, identified themselves as lesbians, and some even expressed disapproval of lesbians. So, although we suspected that some of the women we encountered through the documents or in person were in intimate relationships with other women, we never asked them explicitly about lesbianism in the movement. The women we interviewed ranged in age from their mid-60s to their early 80s, and in many cases the interview turned into a kind of social event. We thought that bringing up lesbianism—even in a general rather than personal way—would have been imposing contemporary conceptions and violating the atmosphere of the interaction.

Ultimately we relied on a woman who had become a lesbian feminist scholar and had had some contact with the women's rights movements in the

1950s for perceptions about women's relationships. Only lately did we learn that another woman, African-American civil rights and feminist activist Pauli Murray, did indeed have relationships with women.[8] Our identities as lesbians in this case probably made us more aware of women's connections to other women, but they also made us perhaps too cautious in our inquiries. During this early part of my career I was more guarded about my own sexual orientation.

When we first began to talk to our classes and to community groups about our research on postwar women's rights activists, we felt compelled to explain that feminism in the 1940s and 1950s seemed anachronistic and old-fashioned rather than cutting-edge and radical. But by about 1985, we realized that feminism as an anachronism no longer needed explaining to the student-age population: they, too, had begun to think of feminism as out of date, the province of women in their thirties or forties, if not sixties or seventies. We began to worry about the costs of survival and the dangers of insularity. At that time, our lives were centered mainly in women's studies and the local women's community in Columbus, Ohio. We began to puzzle over the fact that women's culture and intimate bonds between women have, by and large, played a benevolent role in the historiography of women's movements, yet what had come to be called "cultural feminism"[9] was increasingly blamed for the death of radical feminism. It was as a direct result of our own existence in a world of women that we decided to explore women's culture to evaluate its impact on feminist activism.

Following up on work I coauthored with my student Nancy Whittier,[10] Leila and I analyzed the lesbian feminist communities in which women's culture—by which we meant not only music, literature, and art but also alternative institutions such as publishing and recording companies, recovery and other self-help groups, spirituality groups, restaurants and coffeehouses, and other women-owned businesses—is produced.[11] In addition to written sources and interviews, we relied on participant observation in our local community and at national women's events. We identified four elements of lesbian feminist culture that we think promoted survival in a period in which new recruits were not flocking to the women's movement: female values, separatism, the primacy of women's relationships, and feminist ritual. We argued that far from leading to the demise of feminism, the culture of lesbian feminist communities both served as a base of mobilization for women involved in a wide range of protest activities and provided continuity from earlier stages of the movement.

Concerning the question of lesbianism, the standpoint we took on lesbian lives in this research was quite different from that in our earlier study of the women's rights movement. Not only were we explicitly studying lesbians but we also made many of our observations as participants in a lesbian feminist community, and we ourselves came out as lesbians in the article we wrote. To be honest, the fact that we were both by this time tenured and out in almost every aspect of our personal and professional lives had some impact on this decision. But we simply would not have been able to do this research without being involved over a long period of time in the lesbian feminist community. We had knowledge of ephemeral developments that might not appear in any written sources or oral histories and were able to interview women who were willing to speak with us because they knew that we were lesbians.

We argued in this research that what has been called cultural feminism—defined by its critics as emphasizing essential differences between women and men, advocating separatism, and retreating from politics to "lifestyle" through the creation of alternative institutions—is only one ideological strand in the complex culture of lesbian feminist communities, which are made up of women with diverse views and experiences. As in a later article we wrote on defining feminism in the international women's movement in the mid-twentieth century,[12] we argued that what is important is that the debates over goals and strategies take place *within* the feminist community. So we defined "lesbian feminists," like "international feminists," not so much through an association with an ideological position as through involvement in a community in a concrete social movement with different and competing definitions of feminism.

As is clear from this research, I was rapidly acquiring what is called a "lavender c.v.," so there really was not much choice about being out. I was certainly not unaware of the risks. My experiences in what was, in the early days of my career, a very male-dominated and conservative sociology department made me all too cognizant of the dangers. From anonymous comments on student evaluations, such as "I don't think the university should allow dykes to teach this course," to colleagues' complaints that because of me there were too many lesbian graduate students in the program to my department's discounting of my work on lesbian topics, it was hard to ignore the heteronormative political climate. Perhaps one of the things that saved me is that I learned early on from my father, who as a political liberal in a very conservative region of the South, how to offer an open, sunny demeanor while holding some of my most controversial views to myself. However, if that was sometimes the way I dealt interpersonally with my more traditional colleagues, this was not the case with my teaching, research, and scholarly writing. Increasingly, my research accentuated the connections among feminist theory, research methods, and the experiences of women and other marginalized and dominated groups.

With my graduate student Nikki Raeburn, I took on the project of replicating the 1981 study by the ASA's (American Sociology Association's) Task Group on Homosexuality, chaired by my colleague Joan Huber, on the experiences of gay and lesbian sociologists in their academic careers. This was a project very near to my heart. My friend Beth Schneider volunteered my name, and I am firmly convinced that the reason she did so is because I had once written her a letter about how much I admired her courage to do research on lesbian and gay topics and that I planned to shift my work in this direction if I managed to earn tenure. Our analysis of discrimination toward gay, lesbian, and bisexual sociologists who engage in research on gay and lesbian topics and various other forms of activism by teaching and speaking in public about gay topics, mentoring and advising gay and lesbian students, and advocating equal rights in the profession and their own campuses provided a kind of social support. We found five patterns of unequal treatment encountered by gay, lesbian, and bisexual faculty, to all of which I could relate all too well: discrimination in hiring, bias in tenure and promotion, exclusion from social and professional networks, devaluation of scholarly work on gay and lesbian topics, and harassment and intimidation.[13] This research received a great deal of publicity in the profession, as well as in the newsletters of other disciplines, and was even summarized in *The Chronicle of Higher Education*. Not a single colleague in my department ever mentioned the work to me.[14]

My next major project started by having nothing to do with social movements or my personal life, although it did not end up that way. Dagmar Celeste, an ardent feminist, then married to the governor of Ohio, had suffered postpartum psychosis after the birth of their sixth child and had become a fervent campaigner on behalf of greater understanding of this condition. As a result of her influence, the Ohio Department of Mental Health, which had funded my dissertation research on the mental health consequences of natural disasters, made available funding for a sociological study of postpartum disorders. To both Celeste and Dee Roth, the director of the Department of Mental Health, I seemed a natural choice, despite the fact that I had never borne a child. At first it seemed too far afield from my interest in feminism and women's movements, but then I realized that the condition of postpartum illness might provide an opportunity to explore the broader sociopolitical context of women's mental health, particularly the connection between women's subordinate social status and their high rates of emotional distress.

I set out to understand the connection between the cultural myths and social requirements of motherhood and women's experiences of postpartum depression. But in truth my enthusiasm for the project, which required extensive interviewing of new mothers, doctors, and mental health professionals, as well as analysis of a voluminous literature on the topic of postpartum depression, began to flag. Two things revived it and made it possible for me to complete my book, *Rock-a-by Baby: Feminism, Self-Help, and Postpartum Depression.* [15] First, I discovered a social movement connection. Women's self-help groups, made up of women like Dagmar Celeste, were springing up and contesting medical, mental health, and popular conceptions of motherhood and postpartum depression. In claiming attention to the difficulties women face with postpartum depression, members of this self-help movement were questioning orthodox conceptions of femininity and motherhood, although not always in expected ways. As it turned out, my research was strongly linked to my earlier work on women's movements, after all since the postpartum movement, although in quite different ways, formed communities of women and served as sites where women negotiated new understandings of what it means to be a woman.

The second thing that changed my relationship to the research was that, in the midst of the project, I was struck by depression myself. My dark cloud came after several months of debilitating pain that led to a total hysterectomy at the age of forty-one. Almost immediately, I began to experience hot flashes, and within a matter of weeks I became anxious, unable to concentrate, and incapable of sleep. Over the next three months I was hospitalized two more times, once for complications resulting from the surgery and once in cardiac intensive care, a result of the stress of recovery and my family history of early death from heart disease. Finally, a full-blown clinical depression set in, and I could not eat much, sleep normally, leave the house, or even read a book for nearly six months. During the same period, my stepfather was diagnosed with cancer, and he died 4 months later. Life seemed hopeless and not worth living until I finally agreed reluctantly—after three months of psychotherapy and only as a last resort before psychiatric hospitalization—to take the antidepressants my woman physician had prescribed. Within a matter of days, I was back on my feet and in six months found that I was able to stop taking the medication.

Until that time, the depression I had been studying had been more academic than real. As a feminist, I had been critical of the turn toward recovery and self-help taken by the modern women's movement. As a sociologist, I had long been skeptical that helping individuals could lead to change in the social processes and institutions I truly believe are responsible for people's suffering. I vividly remember that about a year after I recovered from my depression, I gave a talk about my research on postpartum depression at a local hospital. What I had to say must have reflected the changes taking place in my thinking, for Dagmar Celeste, who happened to be in the audience, approached me and said, "I thought you understood our problem before. Now I can see you really understand what it is like to be depressed." It was certainly an illustration of the feminist research tenet that the social location and standpoint of the author shapes one's observations and interpretations.[16]

At the same time, researching the postpartum depression movement changed my views on self-help.[17] Feminist scholars have been outspoken in arguing that contemporary women's self-help reinforces women's subordination by promoting what Wendy Kaminer[18] terms a "cult of victimhood," which undermines feminism's most fundamental goal of empowering women.[19] In contrast, I saw the contradictory impulses in this form of feminist organizing. On the one hand, the postpartum support movement erodes gender inequality by targeting the practices and logic of social institutions, such as medicine, the law, and the family, that inscribe gender difference and maintain gender stratification. Activists in the postpartum self-help movement work to define a new kind of mother, cultivate cultures of emotion that violate prevailing definitions of femininity,[20] and make caring a collective project. On the other hand, by organizing around a frame of gender difference, women's self-help reinforces the binary divide that some scholars hold to be the foundation of gender.[21] So I came to see self-help as both challenging and reinforcing the traditional gender systems.

I had always approached my research with the feminist aims of challenging gender inequality and empowering women. However, this was the first project that I designed to be consistent with the core features that scholars associate with a distinctive feminist methodology: a focus on women, reflexivity as a source of insight; an emphasis on participatory methods, and a policy or action component.[22] Although I am rewarded when, as continues to occur, women tell me that *Rock-a-by Baby* helps them to make sense of their lives, I also worry that, by trying to reach both a scholarly and popular audience, I did not quite reach either. There is a serious argument in the book about self-help movements, feminism, and the reconstruction of motherhood that perhaps distracts the women who want to understand their own experiences. At the same time, I suspect that the topic—to say nothing of the title and the pink and yellow cover, adorned with a baby bottle—has kept social movement scholars from engaging with the argument in the book about the role of gender and emotions in social protest as much as I would have liked.[23]

I suppose I should have the same worry about my forthcoming book, coauthored with Leila, *What Makes a Man a Man: Drag Queens at the 801 Cabaret*. Like *Rock-a-by Baby*, this book is aimed at two audiences. Written in an accessible style, it takes on important questions about drag as a cultural strategy of the gay and lesbian movement. Because drag shows, especially in tourist resorts such as Key West, where the 801 Cabaret is located, are one of the few venues in which straight people are exposed to gay culture, we hope to appeal to their diverse audiences, as well as social movement and gender scholars interested in such topics as the variable and interactive nature of collective action repertoires and the social construction of gender and sexuality.

Sometimes we ask ourselves, how did a social movement scholar and women's historian end up by studying a bunch of guys in dresses? The first part of the answer is stranger than the question. One summer in Key West, my Southern Baptist nephew, Jason, came to visit, bringing along Sara, what one of our straight male friends calls a "friend girl," to distinguish a friend who is a girl from a girlfriend. Sara wanted to see a drag show. We had been to drag shows in Key West before, but this time we ended up at Bourbon Street, at what we now know as the "boy bar," in contrast to the 801 Cabaret, the "girl bar." What that means is that Bourbon Street features male strippers and pornographic videos and is packed with cruising men. But at that time it offered a drag show on Sunday nights, for variety. So we first met Sushi, soon to become the House Queen at the 801 Cabaret, and took Jason and Sara to the show. Sushi asked who in the audience had been together the longest. It turned out it was us ("the two lesbians, of course"), and we got a free drink. We were taken with Sushi's political talk and style of drag: although beautiful, she never pretends to be a woman, talking in her own voice, flashing her nipples, referring to her penis, and generally mixing up dominant gender and sexual categories. Having met her, we began to talk to her when we saw her on the street, luring customers to the bar. Before long, she moved across the street to the 801 Cabaret and took charge of putting on a drag show every night of the year. We loved the show and began to take visiting friends to see it. Several of them—Myra Marx Ferree, Judy Howard, and Paula England—were feminist scholars who also found the show fascinating and urged us to write about it. That first encounter illustrates two elements that made us want to write about drag: the appeal to straight audiences and the political nature of the shows. It seemed a perfect project for us: Key West was our escape to a gay world, a place that we had begun scraping and saving to visit every year in December when we were just assistant professors in order to get away from the cold and the conservatism of Ohio. It was our haven, and when Leila inherited some money from her parents, we bought a house there. We could make use of my knowledge of social movement theory and experience with interviewing and participant observation and Leila's penchant for writing for a popular audience. The more we went to the shows, the more we began to see and hear elements from the heterosexual audience that intrigued us. For example, one night a women in the audience asked us how long we had been together; then when I answered, she explained that she and her best friend were here together because their husbands bought them a trip to Key West to work on their tans. She went on to volunteer, obviously having had a lot to drink, "If I were ever with a woman, it would be her," pointing to her friend.

Because drag has been a venue that has presented gay life to heterosexuals since the 1940s and 1950s, I had the idea not just to study what the drag queens say and do in the shows but also to find out why audience members come and what they take away. With the help of Josh Gamson, who had experience in running focus groups, we recruited people to come back the following afternoon and talk about the shows. The results were fascinating. We found that what the drag queens intend—to make their audience think in a more complex way about gender and sexuality—was just what happened. Straight women reported that they were attracted to the drag queens, "and I'm not even a lesbian." Their husbands admitted to being aroused and confused. We came to think that drag shows really do have political consequences, that they embody protest and build a complex collective identity, both a gay-lesbian-bisexual-transgender identity and a broader identity that crosses both genders and sexualities.

So it does make sense that feminist scholars like us should have immersed ourselves in the world of drag queens. Our book analyzes drag shows as contentious repertoires or interactions between gays and lesbians and heterosexuals and as sites for identity negotiation, creation, and change. We are interested in whether and to what extent drag shows performed in gay commercial spaces contest dominant heterosexual gender and sexual codes and in the construction of collective identity that takes place through the contentious interactions between the performers and the audience. We use this study to enter into the debate with social movement scholars about what makes cultural forms political and to take issue with the dominant view that the definition of contentious politics should be limited to actions that target the government.[24] In that sense, this research follows my interest in culture, from cultural feminism to the culture of self-help. But the project also opened up new and fascinating worlds to us. We learned a lot about drag queens, transgender people, and gay male sexuality. One of the things that the drag queens do is to make sexuality, which is usually so private, a very public thing by talking—very explicitly—about it, performing it, and inviting the audiences to perform it. We became accustomed to using all sorts of words in public talks that usually appear only in pornography. When I spoke about this research at Harvard—Sushi was so proud she called her mother in California to tell her that she'd been talked about at Harvard—a graduate student who had come from Berkeley commented that those hallowed halls had probably never witnessed such language. We became, as Sushi regularly introduces us at the shows, "the professors of lesbian love."

We joke that, at the end of our careers, we should leave our estates to whatever department at Ohio State will accept a "chair of lesbian love." I told this to several women colleagues and administrators when we were celebrating the lesbian commitment ceremony of one of our colleagues. If having a large number of women colleagues and three consecutive women and feminist department chairs is a sign of the significant changes that have swept over my department in the past decade, what happened when we told this story points out how far we still have to go. Some laughed, but a few others seemed horrified that we might really mean it.

Not long after this incident, Leila and I had the good fortune to be hired at the University of California-Santa Barbara where the sociology department is on the other end of the spectrum (whether conceived of as qualitative/quantitative, culture/demography, politics/science) from Ohio State. I remember once when I was disappointed to have been turned down for a senior position at another university my friend and colleague Pat Martin told me that when I finally didn't want to leave Ohio State, I would get an offer that I wouldn't be able to refuse. In paradise, and among arguably the best group of feminist scholars in a single sociology department—including Kum-Jun Bhavnani, Denise Bielby, Sarah Fenstermaker, Avery Gordon, Beth Schneider, Denise Segura, and Winddance Twine—and social movement scholars Richard Flacks and Jennifer Earl, I feel much at home. Leila and I have a favorite toast, which we appropriated from a sexist remark delivered several years ago by a gay male mortgage broker in Columbus commenting either on our good jobs or good taste: "Not bad for two girls."

My life and career illustrate, I think, a pattern typical of many activists.[25] I developed a passion for sociology because of my involvement with social movements, and that has remained, although as I have become a senior scholar in the discipline and influential in my increasingly more congenial department, my activism has moved from the community outside the university to the community inside. Another feminist sociologist has noted that combining activism with an academic career means "swimming against the mainstream."[26] This brings me to my role as lesbian den mother. Knowing the risks that lesbian students and scholars face, I have committed myself to nurturing them in every way I can. I am very proud of my many students, who have gone on to teach, write books and articles, found and run organizations, and in all sorts of ways continue the struggle, both inside and outside the university, for the kind of just and peaceful world that has long been the goal of social activism. Their presence sustained me during the years when I had few colleagues with congenial intellectual interests.

The questions I have asked in my research often began with my own experiences in social movements, and the research methods I have preferred have been participatory, which allow us to see features that remain invisible or secondary to conventional research. However, I have used my experiences in the feminist and gay and lesbian movements not just to be confessional but also to try and open up possibilities for more general and universal theoretical visions. By calling attention to the gendering of social movement processes and theory,[27] my aim has been to demonstrate the way in which movements target culture, as well as the political and economic spheres, to accentuate the emotional and the cognitive and rational dimensions of protest; to illuminate the fluid and changing forms of contention, rather than a set of standard repertoires; and to document the pervasiveness of identity politics in modern societies.

NOTES

1. Susan Krieger, *Social Science and the Self: Personal Essays on an Art Form* (New Brunswick, N.J.: Rutgers University Press, 1991).

2. Kathleen M. Blee and Verta Taylor, "Semi-Structured Interviewing in Social Movement Research," in *Methods in Social Movement Research*, ed. Bert Klandermans and Suzanne Staggenborg (Minneapolis: University of Minnesota Press, 2002), 92–117.

3. Donna Haraway, "Situated Knowledges: The Science Question in Feminism and the Privilege of Partial Perspective," *Feminist Studies* 14 (1988): 575–99.

4. Laurel Richardson, *Fields of Play: Constructing an Academic Life* (New Brunswick, N.J.: Rutgers University Press, 1997).

5. Verta Taylor and Leila J. Rupp, "Lesbian Existence and the Women's Movement: Researching the 'Lavender Herring,'" in *Feminism and Social Change: Bridging Theory and Practice*, ed. Heidi Gottfried (Champaign-Urbana: University of Illinois Press, 1995), 143–59.

6. Leila J. Rupp and Verta Taylor, *Survival in the Doldrums: The American Women's Rights Movement, 1945 to the 1960s* (New York: Oxford University Press, 1987).

7. Verta Taylor, "Social Movement Continuity: The Women's Movement in Abeyance," *American Sociological Review* 54 (1989): 761–75.

8. Leila J. Rupp and Verta Taylor, "Pauli Murray: The Unasked Question," *Journal of Women's History* 14 (2002): 79–83.

9. Alice Echols, *Daring to Be Bad: Radical Feminism in America 1967–1975* (Minneapolis: University of Minnesota Press, 1989).

10. Verta Taylor and Nancy Whittier, "Collective Identity in Social Movement Communities: Lesbian Feminist Mobilization," in *Frontiers in Social Movement Theory*, ed. Aldon D. Morris and Carol McClurg Mueller (New Haven, Conn.: Yale University Press, 1992), 104–29.

11. Verta Taylor and Leila J. Rupp, "Women's Culture and Lesbian Feminist Activism: A Reconsideration of Cultural Feminism," *Signs: Journal of Women in Culture and Society* 19 (1993): 32–61.

12. Leila J. Rupp and Verta Taylor, "Forging Feminist Identity in an International Movement: A Collective Identity Approach to Feminism," *Signs: Journal of Women in Culture and Society* 24 (1999): 363–86.

13. Verta Taylor and Nicole C. Raeburn, "Identity Politics as High-Risk Activism: Career Consequences for Lesbian, Gay, and Bisexual Sociologists," *Social Problems* 42 (1995): 252–73.

14. Mary Crystal Cage, "Diversity or Quotas? Northeastern University Will Accord Gays and Lesbians Preferential Treatment in Hiring," *The Chronicle of Higher Education* (June 8, 1994): 13–14.

15. Verta Taylor, *Rock-a-by Baby: Feminism, Self-Help, and Postpartum Depression* (New York: Routledge, 1996).

16. Nancy C. M. Harstock, "The Feminist Standpoint: Developing the Ground for a Specifically Feminist Historical Materialism," in *Discovering Reality*, ed. Sandra Harding and Merrill B. Hintikka (Dordrecht: David Reidel, 1983); Donna Haraway, "Situated Knowledges: The Science Question in Feminism and the Privilege of Partial Perspective," *Feminist Studies* 14 (1988): 575–99; Patricia Hill Collins, "Learning from the Outsider Within: The Sociological Significance of Black Feminist Thought," in *Beyond Methodology: Feminist Scholarship as Lived Research*, ed. Mary Margaret Fonow and Judith A. Cook (Bloomington: Indiana University Press, 1991), 35–59.

17. Verta Taylor, "Feminist Methodology in Social Movements Research," *Qualitative Sociology* 21 (1998): 357–79.

18. Wendy Kaminer, "Feminism's Identity Crisis," *Atlantic Monthly*, October 1993, 51–68; Wendy Kaminer, *I'm Dysfunctional, You're Dysfunctional: The Recovery Movement and Other Self-Help Fashions* (Reading, Mass.: Addison-Wesley, 1992).

19. Echols, *Daring to Be Bad*; Celia Kitzinger and Rachel Perkins, *Changing Our Minds: Lesbian Feminism and Psychology* (New York: New York University Press,

276 EVOLVING IDENTITIES

1993); Naomi Wolf, *Fire with Fire: The New Female Power and How It Will Change the 21st Century* (New York: Random House, 1994).

20. Verta Taylor, "Self-Labeling and Women's Mental Health: Postpartum Illness and the Reconstruction of Motherhood," *Sociological Focus* 28 (1995): 23–47; Verta Taylor, "Emotions and Identity in Women's Self-Help Movements," in *Self, Identity, and Social Movements*, ed. Sheldon Stryker, Timothy J. Owens, and Robert W. White (Minneapolis: University of Minnesota Press, 2000), 271–99.

21. Judith Butler, *Gender Trouble: Feminism and the Subversion of Identity* (New York: Routledge, 1990); Arlene Stein and Ken Plummer, "'I Can't Even Think Straight': 'Queer' Theory and the Missing Sexual Revolution in Sociology," *Sociological Theory* 12 (1994): 178–87.

22. Sandra Harding, *The Science Question in Feminism* (Ithaca, N.Y.: Cornell University Press, 1986); Mary Margaret Fonow and Judith A. Cook, "Back to the Future: A Look at the Second Wave of Feminist Epistemology and Methodology," in *Beyond Methodology: Feminist Scholarship as Lived Research*, ed. Mary Margaret Fonow and Judith A. Cook (Bloomington: Indiana University Press, 1991), 1–15; Francesca M. Cancian, "Feminist Science: Methodologies That Challenge Inequality," *Gender & Society* 6 (1992): 623–42; Shulamit Reinharz with Lynn Davidman, *Feminist Methods in Social Research* (New York: Oxford University Press, 1992); Heidi Gottfried, "Engaging Women's Communities: Dilemmas and Contradictions in Feminist Research," in *Feminism and Social Change*, ed. Heidi Gottfried (Champaign-Urbana: University of Illinois Press, 1996), 1–20; Verta Taylor, "Feminist Methodology in Social Movements Research," Special Issue: Qualitative Methods and Social Movements Research, *Qualitative Sociology* 21 (1998): 357–79.

23. Taylor, "Emotions and Identity."

24. Doug McAdam, Sidney Tarrow, and Charles Tilly, *Dynamics of Contention* (New York: Cambridge University Press, 2001).

25. Barrie Thorne, "Political Activist as Participant Observer: Conflicts of Commitment in a Study of the Draft Resistance Movement of the 1960s," *Symbolic Interaction*, 2 (1978): 73–88; Nancy Whittier, *Feminist Generations: The Persistence of the Radical Women's Movement* (Philadelphia: Temple University Press, 1995); Sarah Fenstermaker, "Telling Tales Out of School: Three Short Stories of a Feminist Sociologist," in *Feminist Sociology: Life Histories of a Movement*, ed. Barbara Laslett and Barrie Thorne (New Brunswick, N.J.: Rutgers University Press, 1997), 209–28; Taylor, "Emotions and Identity."

26. Mark A. Chesler, "Participatory Action Research with Self-Help Groups: An Alternative Paradigm for Inquiry and Action," *American Journal of Community Psychology* 19 (1991): 757–68.

27. Myra Marx Ferree, "The Political Context of Rationality: Rational Choice Theory and Resource Mobilization," in *Frontiers in Social Movement Theory*, ed. Aldon D. Morris and Carol McClurg Mueller (New Haven, Conn.: Yale University Press, 1992), 29–52; Nancy Whittier, *Feminist Generations: The Persistence of the Radical*

Women's Movement (Philadelphia: Temple University Press, 1995); Joshua Gamson, "Messages of Exclusion: Gender, Movements, and Symbolic Boundaries," *Gender & Society* 11 (1997): 178–99; Belinda Robnett, *How Long? How Long? African-American Women in the Struggle for Civil Rights* (New York: Oxford University Press, 1997); Suzanne Staggenborg, "Social Movement Communities and Cycles of Protest: The Emergence and Maintenance of a Local Women's Movement," *Social Problems* 45 (1998): 180–204; Taylor, "Feminist Methodology," 357–79.